Born in London in September 1934, the author started school during the week that WW2 was declared. With her mother and siblings, she was evacuated to Bournemouth in 1942. They were re-united with their father on their return to Surrey in 1946. When leaving Nonsuch school, she was employed at the head office of Thos. Cook & Son in Berkeley Street, London. With an eagerness to travel and a basic knowledge of German, she was sent to Switzerland as one of their representatives. It was there that she met her future husband, a Bavarian. A further two years followed in Austria before they returned to the UK for their wedding and where they managed their own hotel till retirement.

Dedication

To my beloved husband, without whom this story would never
have been told.

Jill L. M. Birk

GASTHOF ENGEL

To Gwyneth & Bob

With very best wishes

Jill

and Rudi

AUSTIN MACAULEY PUBLISHERS™

LONDON • CAMBRIDGE • NEW YORK • SHARJAH

A CIP catalogue record for this title is available from the British Library.

ISBN 9781788780988 (Paperback)
ISBN 9781788780971 (Hardback)
ISBN 9781788780995 (E-Book)

www.austinmacauley.com

First Published (2018)
Austin Macauley Publishers Ltd™
25 Canada Square
Canary Wharf
London
E14 5LQ

Acknowledgements

I am indebted to Erich and Sepp, my brothers-in-law, who helped by supplying necessary information.

Prologue

The fringes of his scarf flapped around his ears as Rudolf fixed his gaze on the black marble headstone. A striking figure, he stood tall and erect. His hair, having prematurely lost its colour but not its volume, was being blown about in the bitter northeast wind. The candle flickered under the glass dome lighting up the gilt inscription, Johann and Josefa, his parents; Mathias and Anna, his grandparents. He bent down and placed a small wreath, paused a few moments, then turned to leave. He made his way down the church path on each side of which were similar immaculately kept graves. Some displayed photographs of the deceased and all were planted with winter blooms and conifers. Not even in death does this Germanic race allow its ancestors to escape the precision, conformity and order by which they lived. A short brisk walk brought him to the site of waste ground. His eyes moistened as he viewed the weeds and blades of grass forcing their way up through cracks in the tarmac and concrete; nature's endeavour to regain its territory from civilisation. Snowflakes landed where once a coaching inn had stood for three centuries. Now demolished, there was little evidence left of the building that had been home to Rudolf's family for almost a hundred years. His memories were being shuffled like a pack of cards and, one by one, being brought out for random reflection. All his senses were aroused as he recalled the voices, noises and smells of his childhood and adolescence, but there was nothing left to touch. The smell of his mother's freshly baked 'Zopf', the sugary brioche for Sunday's breakfast, penetrated his nostrils and he savoured the sauerkraut and homemade sausages. The sound of laughing, squabbling, crying, folk music, dancing, the clattering of kitchen utensils and the tinkling of bar glasses filled his ears. He turned around to face the direction of the small airfield adjoining the village where high-ranking Nazis landed on their way to the SS training centre at Sonthofen. His eyes stared upwards as he remembered the light aircraft in which the young Luftwaffe pilots trained. They used the back parlour for playing roulette in the evenings. Each day, the cuckoo, in its clock at the inn, announced the arrival of the pilots for lunch at precisely 12 noon. Rudolf could hear the rousing songs as they marched, swinging their arms in time, the emblem of the eagle and swastika very visible on their sleeves. He remembered he too had a swastika on his Hitler Youth uniform, as did his four brothers. Heinrich Himmler visited the Gasthof for a meal before departing to the nearby SS training camp. This rhythmic sound of leather hitting tarmac echoed in his mind to the time before his 10th birthday, but then the boots had been worn by American soldiers. Suddenly, he became aware of the density of the snow around him and he headed back to the warmth of his brother's house. On the way, his thoughts turned to the tales his father had told him of how the family had come to settle in this village. That was almost 30 years before Hitler became chancellor.

Chapter 1

Winter had been particularly cruel that year, imposing Arctic conditions much earlier than usual. It had paralysed whole communities by blocking access on all sides with an excessive fall of snow. One horse and cart managed to get through just in time by taking a longer route. Its destination was a small Bavarian village lying in the foothills of the Alps, not far from the Austrian border. It had been a long uncomfortable journey from Lindau, and Friedl, the skewbald mare, stumbled as she was pulled to a halt in the forecourt of the Gasthof. Her hooves were buried in snow which reached up to her fetlocks and her breath, like puffs of vapour escaping from a train, rose into the freezing atmosphere. When her snorting and the crunching sound of her hooves compressing the snow had stopped, an eerie silence prevailed, broken only by the muffled chimes of the church clock. The mare was exhausted, as was her driver, Mathias Birk. Molecules of ice defined his eyebrows and icicles dangled from his beard like glass droplets from a lampshade. He endeavoured to unlock his hands from the rein-holding position. Slowly, his stiffened fingers began to straighten out enough for him to throw off the sheepskin rug from his knees and wearily climb down. He slapped his arms diagonally across his chest and stamped his feet in an attempt to bring back life into his limbs. The naked trees tossed in the biting wind, casting dancing shadows on the shimmering ice covering the nearby brook. The ground was alive with whirlpools of snowflakes and the moon shone down like a huge spotlight.

Mathias ploughed his way through the snow to the back of the cart and released the flap, breaking ice which fell like a shattered pane of glass. He tugged at an old rug to reveal two small children huddled together under several layers of blankets. With barely opened eyes, they looked at him, their pinched faces drained of any colour. They clasped their hands firmly around their father's neck as he carried six-year-old Johann and then four-year-old Rosa. He set them down in front of an old oak door, which had taken on a white polka dot pattern, where the snow had clung to the metal studs. They watched him return to the cart to assist their mother, his sick wife, Anna. Draped with a blanket over an inexpensive fur coat, she levered herself up from a low stool, clutching the side of the cart to steady herself. Slowly, they joined the children, who were now shivering. As their father fumbled in his pocket for the key, they began to whimper.

The door creaked as it was opened. It was dark inside. Mathias instantly lit the candle on the table before them, which cast shadows on the sparsely furnished room with wooden floors. Mathias' dull, tired eyes did not linger on the roughly constructed wooden table and chairs, nor on the threadbare sofa, but rested on the welcome sight of a Kachelofen in the corner of the room. The stove was completely encased by pale blue tiles right up to the ceiling and there were logs stacked up beside it. Like a man possessed, Mathias leapt forward and opened the small metal door at its side. There he found kindling wood and paper. Within minutes, a fire raged, with the tiles exuding the warmth by which Anna and the children thawed their hands as they sat on the surrounding seat. Mathias returned to the cart to release Friedl from the traces and relieve her from the harness. He led her to the stable which was strewn with straw and he broke the top layer of ice in the water trough before supplying her with hay. He slid the bolt across the stable door and as he left, he gazed upwards. A shaft of light lit up the tall white tower of the village church, which was decorated with a painting of St Christopher and child. Within a few weeks, its bells would be ringing in the year 1906. Mathias offered a silent prayer.

"Oh God, thank you for bringing us here safely. Help me to make a success of this business, for my dear wife's sake. We've suffered hard times, these last four years. Bless my family. We shall continue to call this 'Gasthof Engel' in the hope that a guardian angel will take care of us and restore Anna to good health."

He turned to go inside again and found that the heat from the stove had revived the children. He could hear their excited voices as he approached. Anna had lit the oil lamps and was unpacking the food they had brought with them.

"Our new home is called 'Engel'," he told them, but they were now too excited to take any notice. Anna's smile confirmed her approval. At that time, who could have predicted that this would be Johann's home for eighty-seven years and that Anna had only six months to live.

Chapter 2

Now in 1919, Johann arrived early and sat down in the nearest pew. A Thanksgiving service was to be held for the villagers who had returned from the battlefields of WW1 and to remember those who had not. He tilted his head back and cast his eyes up to the pastel-coloured paintings covering the ceiling in this extravagantly decorated Baroque church. It was then that his mind wandered back to his mother's funeral, which had been etched on his memory for almost 13 years. She had died at the age of 34, six months after they had moved into the Gasthof Engel. The sun had been relentless on that day in June. He remembered grasping his sister's little clammy hand as they gazed at the array of large wreaths mounted on pedestals. The wide black-edged ribbon draped around them had displayed condolatory messages. Like Hansel and Gretel, they stood lost and confused among a forest of assembled mourners, mostly unknown to them. All had been dressed in black, their heads covered in shawls or trilbies. Aged seven, he had worn his Sunday best, long black trousers with black braces and a white shirt. Rosa, two years younger, had worn a white puffed sleeve blouse underneath a black dirndl with gentians and edelweiss embroidered on the bodice.

After the burial, their father had led them back to the Gasthof, where they were to experience a very unhappy and difficult period in their lives. The burden of caring for the children, coping with the smallholding and the inn's trade with very little assistance had resulted in Mathias suffering severe migraine. During these bouts, he had shut himself away, leaving the children for long periods on their own. At an early age, they had learnt self-reliance and with a child's natural resilience to crises, they had derived comfort and enjoyment from each other's company.

This had stood them in good stead when their father had married again three years later. His new wife, Klara, was the archetypical wicked step-mother. She had been widowed young and was left alone with a small son, Konrad, whom she smothered with affection. For her step-children, she had shown a distinct lack of tenderness or kindness. Her well-covered frame and healthy complexion was evidence of her farming roots. She had had boundless energy, and a sharp brain which provided her with the ability to run the business. It had been a great relief for Mathias and allowed him to spend more time with his children, when his headaches permitted.

Sitting quietly in the church, Johann's memory went on to recall at the age of 13, he had started a three years' apprenticeship. At first, to a mechanic, then later to a locksmith and finally he had learnt the art of wrought ironwork. He sighed deeply when he remembered how exhausted he had been after 10-14 hours and then to be given the task of clearing up and cleaning the workshop. He had consoled himself by treating this as an escape from a miserable home life. There would be no cheery welcome when he had returned to the Gasthof. The family had long since finished their cooked evening meal, the cold remains of which were left for him in the dimly lit kitchen. Rosa had already gone to bed, and his efforts to study after he had eaten were thwarted by Klara purposely extinguishing the oil lamps. Sometimes, Konrad, who was two years older, would provide company for him, but only when his mother was absent.

Johann looked towards the church door. There was still no sign of other arrivals. As his reverie continued, his face brightened a little when his thoughts dwelt on the sudden dramatic change there had been in their lives just before the outbreak of WW1. At very little notice, Klara had absconded to America, presumably to avoid Konrad being involved in the threatened conflict. In spite of the initial shock, the family had relished life without Klara. They had readjusted their lives and had employed a general assistant, enabling 12-year-old Rosa more time to look after their father. It must have been hard for her, he thought, when he too had left home. At the age of 17, he had been summoned to report for military service. Initially, he had spent six months in Munich with the Rail battalion, working 60 hours per week. Military training followed, after which he had been selected to undertake a four months' intensive training course on driving steam locomotives. He had learnt how to maintain the four-axel narrow gauge engines, which weighed four tons, and to stoke up their fires. Even now, at times, he imagined he could still feel the heat on his face and hands. All this had been in preparation for deployment to the battlefields of France, but not before he had received additional training with diesel and mining locomotives. These had been used to supply all heavy gun emplacements near Arras. Each wagon had carried five tonnes of yellow, green and blue cross gas grenades and each train had supplied 30 tonnes of ammunition. Undertaken at night, these deliveries had to be unloaded and out of sight before dawn. The return journey had always been fraught with the fear of being shelled. He shut his eyes and shuddered at the memory of one delivery, when a shell fell ahead of them, sending the locomotive off track, scattering its lethal cargo as it went. Miraculously, only Sigi had suffered injuries, which had not been life threatening.

At that moment, the sound of a door opening startled him. He opened his eyes and caught sight of a priest's robes as he disappeared into the vestry. *This service will provoke memories of the war and the experiences I have tried desperately to dismiss from my mind,* he thought. He had often wondered what had happened to his two mates and whether they had made it back home. Sigi was the leader of the team, Theo operated the brakes at the rear and he himself did the driving, being the one with the best eyesight. In order to see the track at night, he had to stand on the running board. This had made it easier for him to spot the craters in time and bring the train to a halt. The smaller holes they could repair fairly quickly, but if they had landed in a large one, they had to call the rescue team. Not all trains had armour plating, so there had always been the risk of flying shrapnel as well. Being targeted before unloading had been the greatest danger of all. Six nights a week they had operated from their base at Bois-Bernard. It was just across from Vimy Ridge where the Canadians and British were entrenched. His team had been well aware that they were being observed by the Allies' reconnaissance balloons. Having had to wait until the balloons had been lowered, their ten miles' trip back for reloading had been often delayed.

The sound of the church door creaking brought Johann back to the present with a jolt. The appearance of a wheelchair being pushed down the aisle was followed by a trickle of mainly young men whose injuries were very apparent. There were crutches, arms in slings, heads bandaged and eyes shielded by dark glasses or black patches. All were accompanied by relatives and friends giving support. He shifted uneasily on his seat. These images evoked more memories for him. His mind flashed back to the emotion he had felt at the sight of his comrades' limbs scattered on the battlefield. The heart rending cries for help when pain could no longer be borne still rang in his ears in nightmares. Time had been put on fast forward for these formerly exuberant teenage boys. They had to mature rapidly and faced a challenging future. Strangely, he felt a slight feeling of guilt that he had survived physically unscathed. A shiver shot down his spine when he thought of the injuries he could have suffered. His zest for life had been numbed by the surfeit of blood he had seen and the agonies he had witnessed.

During the service, many eyes were dabbed as the tears flowed. Sitting a few pews in front of him, he noticed a former school friend who, according to village gossip, had had the misfortune to be injured just as his unit had been called back in retreat only a month before the armistice had been signed. This had not signified the end of their anxiety, he remembered. A revolutionary movement, which had caused the Kaiser's abdication and escape to Holland, had prolonged the violence.

At this point, Johann was so moved by the thoughts of the horrendous journey back that he had endured and the relief he had felt when arriving at home, he decided to leave. He tucked his handkerchief back into his pocket and left the church. His reminiscing persisted as he walked slowly homewards, taking the longer route. As he approached the Gasthof, he recalled how he had staggered into the yard burdened with army kit and had surprised Rosa. She had been clearing snow that morning and had promptly dropped the shovel and ran towards him, and with her arms clasped around his neck, she had pressed her cheek firmly against his. He remembered the warm drip of her tears on his face, which she had wiped away with the corner of her apron.

"Oh, Hanni, welcome home, welcome back," she had cried. "Thank God you're safe. I must fetch Papa." Her shoulder-length hair was tied back and bobbed up and down as she had raced across the yard in the direction of the stable, slipping on the icy surface as she went.

Mathias had emerged from the barn sheltering his eyes from the brightness of the snow. With a sob catching in his throat, his father had hugged him, avoiding the two rifles which hung from his son's shoulder. He cast a cursory glance at them before he had led the way into the warmth of the kitchen.

Johann's memory continued to remind him of the enormous relief he had felt as he slumped onto the nearest chair, having first relieved himself of the rifles. Rosa had hesitated for a moment when he had asked her to put them in the loft, but he had assured her that they were not loaded. Through sheer exhaustion, he had found it difficult to speak and had just nodded in answer to their questions as to whether he would like something to eat or drink. They had respected that his recovery would necessitate several days of total rest and tranquillity and that they would have to be satisfied with the snippets of information he gave them at his own pace. His body had had no resistance against the desperate need of sleep and it was not long before he had gone upstairs to bed. His long-standing dream of feeling warm, clean water on his flesh again had to be postponed until the following day. He had taken off his boots and had been loosening his belt when the sound of a door slamming had made him instinctively cover his head and crouch down with his knees under his chin.

Shaking, he had got up and thrown himself onto the bed. Twelve hours later, he had been jolted into painful consciousness when his head had made violent contact with the floor boards. In his nightmare, he had been thrown from the ammunition train into a crater and had called out to warn the others in his team. Then, as he struggled to haul himself up from the floor, he had heard a gentle tapping on the door. Rosa had looked alarmed as she had peered around the door. She had helped him to his feet and had wondered why he had not changed into the pyjamas she had put ready for him.

"There is hot water in the wash kitchen when you want to get into the tub," she had told him, "and all your clean clothes are in the drawer." He had thanked her before asking anxiously if she had put the rifles in the loft. She had replied with a decisive nod, but her eyes lingered on his face, which had prompted him to give an explanation.

"I had to bring them. Revolutionary mobs were running riot. We'd had enough of violence and just wanted to get home," he had told her. Smiling, she had whispered that they were so pleased and grateful to have him home again, and that coffee and fresh pretzels awaited him in the kitchen, when he was ready. That she closed the door quietly behind her, had not escaped his notice.

Refreshed after a good soak and wearing civilian clothes again, he had gone down to the kitchen. His father had sat in a corner, his head bowed. He had looked up with a weak smile. Then, in a croaking voice, he had said how good it was to have him back and what a hard time they had to keep afloat, relying on the locals who at the slightest grievance would threaten to take their custom elsewhere. Thankfully, they still had Felix to look after the cows. He had no family and was quite content to live in a room in the barn. Johann recalled his father's sigh of exasperation as he had admitted that they had become almost totally dependent on Felix to do all the outdoor tasks.

Rosa had appeared at that moment just as her father had said how wonderful she had been. Ignoring the praise, she had encouraged him to eat more, saying,

"You need fattening up, Hanni." She had not understood that trauma and exhaustion had put his digestive system on hold. It needed time to be weaned back to normality.

"The locals have often asked about you," his father had said shuffling off on his tired, aching bow legs in the direction of the Stube.

"I'll come in to see them before long, Papa, but I'm not ready yet," had been his reply.

Johann had needed time to close the door of his war memories and start contemplating his future.

Chapter 3

"Was the church full?" asked Rosa as Johann entered through the kitchen door.

"Yes, it was. I left before the service ended though," he added lowering his voice. Rosa shot him a questioning glance but remained silent.

"Where's Papa?"

"In the Stube with the locals," replied Rosa, vigorously stirring the contents of a bowl.

"I think I'll go and join them."

Rosa smiled. She knew this would please her father. She had noticed that gradually, like ink seeping into blotting paper, Johann's strength and vitality were returning.

His entrance into the Stube raised a raucous cheer from the direction of the Stammtisch, a table reserved only for the regulars.

"Hello, Hanni, welcome back," they shouted, more or less in unison. They all got to their feet to shake his hand or to slap him on the back.

"Good God, you've lost some weight. Looks as if you could do with some good meals," remarked Franz, a farmer whose family had lived off the land locally for generations. He was a salt of the earth character of advancing years. He sported a bushy beard and had a weather beaten complexion.

"I 'spect Rosa will see to that," he added with a grin.

"Did you have a tough time?" asked Franz's son.

"Come and sit down with us, Hanni," suggested Gustav, the village butcher who had known Johann since he was a young boy.

"What did they give yer to eat then?"

"Our meat ration was 100gr raw and 50gr cooked meats daily and a vegetable soup, nearly always kohlrabi," replied Johann taking his place at the table

"Is that all?" asked Volkmar, a middle-aged farmer with a mop of hair showing signs of turning grey.

"We had one loaf of bread every three days. Most of us ate half of it the first day." For a few moments, they all just stared at him. Mathias sat quietly in the background, slowly shaking his head. *It hadn't been easy for civilian either,* he was thinking.

"What happened to the food parcels I sent?" Rosa enquired as she placed a full tankard of beer in front of him.

"I never received one intact. There were a couple, but it was either very damaged or the contents were already rotten. Thanks all the same, Rosa," he added looking up at her with a faint smile.

"Couldn't you buy food?" this question came from Dieter, the local cheesemaker. A loyal, trustworthy friend of the family and of a similar age as Volkmar. He had three sons.

"With one Reichsmark a day! Could only manage one schnapps with that!" exclaimed Johann. Dieter just grinned.

"All this talk of food is making me hungry. We're just going to have some bratwurst. Rosa, bring some more for your brother," bellowed Volkmar in the direction of the kitchen.

After about an hour or so of constant chatter, exchanging experiences and political opinions in a dialect unintelligible outside the State of Bavaria, Johann noticed his father hovering in the doorway. He was trying to attract his attention. Johann made his excuses and went over to him.

"Son, I don't feel too good today. Could you bring up a couple of beer barrels for Rosa, and whilst you're there, would you stoke up the boiler? You may have to go out and bring in some more wood."

As Johann lifted the logs, which were neatly piled beneath the eaves, he was reminded of the time when as a young boy, he had helped to load them on to the cart in his father's woods. Their beloved shire horse Friedl would pull them homewards, as he sat bare-footed astride her. The winters were always severe and felling, sawing and stacking had to be completed by early autumn.

Pausing at the kitchen door when he came up from the cellar, he watched Rosa bending over the cooking range, sampling the contents of a large saucepan. Johann's appetite had returned and his stomach was making repetitive demands for supplies, much to Rosa's delight.

"Cor, that smells good," he said. "I'll be back for a taster in a minute." Rosa's broad smile revealed the relief she felt, now that the full burden of helping her father had been lifted from her fragile shoulders. Johann was a good waiter and apart from serving the food, he would be able to assist Mathias dispensing the drinks.

Chapter 4

It was on a spring day the following year, when Johann sat twiddling his fingers. He laid his hands flat on the table. Thoughts that his hand were too white, his nails too clean and that he should be holding pliers or a screw driver, not a waiter's cloth, filled his mind. He was trained to be a mechanic; his hands should be covered in black grease. His ears yearned to hear the music of an engine or a machine running, especially one in discord, so that he could put it right. He would like nothing better than to watch all its mechanical parts playing like an orchestral ensemble. He longed to put on his dungarees and to have a whiff of engine oil in his nostrils again.

"Got any pushbikes you want repairing?" Johann asked as he cleared a table of well-scraped plates the following day. A couple looked up whilst the others were savouring their last mouthful.

"Come to think of it, I'ave," replied one of the old farmers. "I've got two rustin' in my barn. I'll drop 'em down next time I go to the market, unless you come and collect 'em."

"OK, I'll come," said Johann as he rushed to deposit a pile of heavy dirty plates in the kitchen.

"I've got 'un too," an old pensioner called after him. "Needs the brakes seeing to. I'll push it over tomorrow. I've heard you're real 'andy with tools."

Trudi's grazing was interrupted the following day when she was harnessed to the old cart. Similar in size, but with a lighter mane, the young shire had replaced the deceased Friedl.

"Not too heavy a load for you today, my girl. Just a couple of bikes," Johann whispered in her ear.

In the aftermath of war, there was plenty of scope for mechanics to find machines to repair. Industry had not sufficiently recovered to produce new ones. Like flood water, the news of Johann's enterprise spread around the farms. The dilemma for him was how to build it up and fulfil his duty familial. The interim solution was to work for himself in the day and to assist at the Gasthof during the evenings. This was only possible with Rosa's support and encouragement, which she readily gave.

The months passed quickly for Johann as he dealt at first with a trickle and then a steady flow of push bikes and small machinery needing attention. When required, he helped at the Gasthof, which was usually in the evening. He was having his lunch break one day when he heard the sound of a spluttering engine in the yard, which suddenly cut out. Still chewing a mouthful of Rosa's homemade meatloaf, he rushed to the window.

A young man, tall, with blond curly hair stood straddled across a motorbike. Johann wiped his mouth on his sleeve as he moved quickly to the back door and greeted the stranger.

"Hello, can I help you?"

"Hello, my name's Horst. Someone told me you might be interested in buying this," he said dismounting.

"It didn't sound too good. What's wrong with it?" asked Johann as his eyes sped over the bike's frame.

"I'm not sure, but I can't afford any more repair bills."

"May I?" asked Johann, indicating that he would like to test the engine. With approval, he drove up and down the lane, long enough for his experienced ears to detect the problem. On his return, some friendly haggling took place before an agreement was sealed with a handshake. Johann noticed Rosa watching them, half-hidden by the kitchen door. The youth saw her too.

"Hello again," he called out to her, his smile revealing a wholesome set of white teeth.

"Hello," she replied shyly. Hastily, she retired back into the kitchen in order to divert his attention from her food-splattered apron.

"Do you know him?" asked Johann when Horst had left.

"I've seen him a few times. His father has a bakery in Hegge," Rosa replied, her habitually white porcelain complexion taking on the colour of cyclamen. She was glad Johann had not noticed. His eyes were riveted to Horst's bike. He could not wait to get started on it.

The country's economy was making a gradual recovery, which, in turn, was improving the Gasthof's trade. Rosa was finding it difficult to cope, particularly as now Johann had less time to assist her. Added to this was their concern for their father's health. It was deteriorating and his absenteeism from the Stube was becoming more frequent. He suffered from severe migraine and regularly sought solitude in the quiet, cool cellar.

"I could do with another pair of hands," Rosa told her brother one morning. "I'm finding it difficult to cope."

"Me too," was his reply. "I'm sorry I can't do more for you. We've got to get some help, Rosa. I'm sure both businesses could support it."

Unemployment was still a major national problem, so it did not take long for Rosa to acquire Lisa as a general assistant. A pretty buxom girl in her late teens with plenty of stamina. Johann took on a young local lad, not as an apprentice, but one seeking temporary work, who would be useful for fetching, carrying and clearing up.

Rosa felt so much better now that she was not totally fettered to the kitchen, which enabled her friendship with Horst to blossom. She urged Johann to seek a social life as well. The war had cut a large chunk out of his adolescence and robbed him of two of his closest friends. Building up a business had become all consuming, leaving him with the minimum of time for leisure.

About a year later, an opportunity presented itself for him to add another string to his bow. He was visiting a farm to look at a malfunctioning tractor when the farmer noticed him staring at a car at the far end of the barn.

"That's an ole Buick," he informed him. "I've not use for it. D' yer want to 'ave a look at it?"

"I certainly would."

Noticing Johann's eyes light up and the way he stroked the bonnet, prompted the farmer to say, "Mend my tractor and you can 'ave it." Johann could not believe his ears.

"Wow! That's a deal then," he said taking a firm hold of the farmer's rough, grubby hand.

Johann rushed into the kitchen, his eyes bright, his cheeks glowing and his whole body tingling with excitement.

"Rosa, come with me," he grabbed her hand and pulled her towards the door. Thinking he wanted to introduce her to a special girl he had met, she resisted.

"I must wash my hands first and take my pinny off," she said.

"Don't bother, Rosa. Come on." He tugged her out to the yard. It was not what she expected. Her eyes rested on a pale beige object made of metal and rubber.

"A Buick! Rosa. Isn't it marvellous? When I've put it right, I'm going to run a taxi service!"

During the following year, many long arduous hours were spent listening to its engine, detecting faults, acquiring spare parts, repairing, spraying and polishing the Buick. The trickle of other repairs had now increased to a flow, which necessitated taking on an apprentice mechanic. By spring of 1925, the Buick was gleaming and Johann was glowing with pride when he went to register his new business at the Village Rathaus, the council offices. On the way back, he called in the Käserei to buy some cheese.

"Hello, Hanni. I see you're driving around in style today."

"Yes, Dieter, I'm going to start a taxi service." Johann took in a lungful of air reeking of sour milk before asking for, "A kilo of your best Emmentaler please."

"Certainly," said Dieter with a curious smile. "By the way, I hear you're going to have some new neighbours."

"That's the first I've heard about it, but then I haven't had much time to catch up on local news lately," replied Johann looking out of the window at a small gathering of villagers.

"He is a well-to-do miller who's retiring. Got four beautiful daughters. Got one son. Lost another son in the war."

Johann became interested and turned his head around.

"Where do they come from?" he asked.

"Not sure," Dieter handed over a small package. "Tell Rosa she can pay me this evening when I come to join the regulars."

"Thanks, Dieter."

As Johann left, he was confronted by the group admiring the Buick, which included Hilda, a well-known gossiper.

"This is for my new taxi service," Johann informed them proudly as he took his place behind the steering wheel. Driving away, he chuckled to himself. "That will save me some advertising, Hilda will do it for *me*."

His next stop was the florist's, where he bought Rosa a large bouquet. A feeling of joie de vivre had enveloped him.

Rosa was feeling very happy as well. She was in love and trade was good. Lisa had lightened her load and her beloved brother had bought her some flowers.

"How's Papa?" asked Johann as he watched her preparing the evening meal.

"Much better, thank God. You haven't seen him today, have you? He's actually thinking of buying some more grazing land and an acre of woods that's up for sale." She glanced at the clock and then continued to chop up red cabbage.

"I'm glad he's feeling better," said Johann. He pondered for a moment, I'll go and see if he's in the Stube. The usual gang's there. I expect. I saw horses tied up outside. The carts were empty, so they must have had a good day at the market."

"God, what a din they're making," he muttered to himself as he left the kitchen. There were still a few jobs he wanted to finish, so he decided against joining the regulars that evening. He glanced at them through the door. There were Gustav and his son Heini; Volkmar and his son Peter; Franz and Dieter. They were all wearing lederhosen, made from deer leather and held up with embroidered braces. Some of the other farmers present were still wearing their winter plus-fours with thick woollen socks. These were in contrast to the footless socks worn in warm weather that stretched from the ankle to just below the knee. Hanging up on the impressive wrought iron clothes stand were a row of jackets made from grey loden, with green piping on the pockets and collars. The reveres buttoned back. Above these hung their hats. They were trilby style with a narrow brim and decorated with Gemsenbart. This was the so-called chamois beard, but, in fact, the hairs were taken from the chamois' back and bound together to form a brush.

As Johann walked away from the door, he could hear them shouting like children, each one vying to be heard, their dialect like a foreign tongue to anyone outside the state of Bavaria. The Stammtisch meetings on market days followed a pattern. Urgent business first, which was ordering beer and food. This was followed by a discussion of market tittle-tattle. The

27

conversation then progressed to international affairs. As the alcohol infiltrated their blood, the more lubricated their tongues became and the volume of their voices increased. To emphasise a point, a fist would be thumped so forcefully on top of the pine table that the beer krugs would lift a fragment of a centimetre in the air, like soldiers jumping to attention. The spillage would trickle in all directions.

"Cloth needed, Lisa," bawled Gustav. Lisa wiped the table and took orders for a refill. Then, with flick of the wrist, she would make another stroke on the sodden beer mats. She knew there would be many more strokes before the time of reckoning. She did not mind. The busier, the better. She received no wage, just 10% of takings, which she kept in a leather purse attached to her belt.

There was certainly no shortage of topics to talk about. Bavaria had become a hotbed of political activity. It involved the Monarchists who supported the Wittelsbachs, the Bavarian royalty, and the Spartakists with anti-imperialist ideals. There were also the radical independents, the republicans and the increasingly popular nationalists. Irrespective of how heated the discussions became, they were always punctuated by the raising of glasses to toast each other's health.

"We are known as the Peasant State, yer know," said Heini, his voice very slurred.

"Yer right. Those Berlin bureaucrats look down their noses at us," confirmed Peter. This sentence was punctuated by a hiccup and concluded with "snooty lot".

They all joined in the conversation, which continued with the same theme.

"What yer think about the Austrian?"

"Yer mean the Schukelgruber bastard? Jumped up little twerp."

"Hitler, d' yer mean?"

"He was in the Bavarian army."

"He was only a corporal."

"But he's got his own bodyguard now."

"Has a dislike for the Jews from all accounts."

"I've heard 'is Opa was one."

"He's all mixed up."

"But says he'll look after the likes of us."

"What yer mean?"

"He says he's the champion of the middle road, like farmers and those with small properties and businesses."

"He keeps on about getting national pride back."

"We could do with that after our battering."

About an hour later of this banter, they were ready to move on to the final phase of the evening.

"Come on, time to get the cards out," demanded Volkmar.

"Lisa, we're all dying of thirst over 'ere. It's like being in the desert," roared Peter.

Raucous laughter and good humour was the order for the rest of the evening and into the next day. In the early hours, the horses were untied and those which knew the way home, plodded along to the sound of their owner's snoring. The horses not familiar with the homeward path were led to the guest stables and Johann was called upon to provide the taxi service for their owners.

"I had a chat with Herr Schnatterer this morning. He called in for a beer," Rosa told Johann as she served him a large portion of sausage, sauerkraut and boiled potatoes.

""Who's he?" he asked, relishing a mouthful of freshly made black sausage.

"A retired miller. He's just handed over his mill to his son and has bought that house where old Theo used to live. You know, at the far side of the beer garden."

"I know the one. Why does he want to live here?"

"He said he wanted to be nearer the Alps and he likes our village very much. I got the impression that he had a farm as well as a large flour and saw mill," Rosa raised her eyebrows as she placed a saucepan on the hob.

"I think Dieter told me something about it. He said we were going to have new neighbours," Johann popped in another mouthful. "He always seems to know what's going on," he mumbled.

"Herr Schnatterer said he'll bring his wife and daughters here for a meal when they come to measure up for curtains and he'll book rooms here the night before they move in." Rosa paused for a moment. "They must be quite well off," she said as she stirred the contents of the saucepan.

"Could be good customers then," Johann called out to her as he scraped his plate.

The summer was an extremely hot one. As the temperature rose, so did the stack of empty beer barrels and trade figures. With the confidence that the economy was at last fairly stable, Mathias speculated and bought more grazing land and forest. He also acquired a few pigs, which involved more work for Felix, who was quite happy to take it on.

Johann's repair business was steady and his taxi service had progressed well. The intense heat made his workshop stifling and he made frequent trips to splash his face and drink the spring water which fed the cattle trough. Returning from this one day, he saw a small family group entering the Engel. Accompanying the mature couple were four young women who were wearing pretty floral frocks and straw hats with wide brims which sheltered their faces. One of them, who was taller than the other three, suddenly looked up and caught sight of Johann. Instinctively, he looked away, conscious of his appearance with dripping hair and greasy dungarees, but the split second image of her was etched on his memory. That evening, as he sat with Rosa in the kitchen, he casually enquired if the Schnatterer family had been there at lunchtime.

"They certainly were and they enjoyed their meal," said Rosa, looking very pleased. "Their next visit will be when they move into their new house."

"Do you know when that will be?" asked Johann, trying not to look too eager.

"Not sure. Sometime in the autumn, before winter sets in."

Johann got up from his chair. "I think I'll go and turn the light off in the barn and then I'm going to join the regulars," he said. As he strode across the yard, Rosa could hear him whistling happily.

Having helped himself to a beer, Johann joined Gustav, Heini, Peter, Dieter and his son Otto.

"Hello, Hanni, my boy, how are you?"

"Fine, thanks, Gustav, and yourself?"

"Still struggling," he replied with a grin, stroking his beard. "Rosa says your trade's been pretty good lately," he took a large gulp from his beer mug. "I can remember when yer Pa first came 'ere, trade was so quiet, he had to do something about it. He opened the windows on the road side, got two young blokes to fake a fight and waited."

"What for?" asked Otto.

"For curious passers-by to come and see what it was all about," he took another gulp of beer. "Not much 'appened around here then and a little bit of excitement made them thirsty, yer see. Good idea, eh?" They all laughed.

"I hear your Pa's bought land on Hungerberg and got more cattle. Must be doing well," remarked Heini with a sideways glance in Johann's direction and his eyebrows slightly raised.

"Yeah, he got it for a good price. They were desperate for money," said Johann as he wiped over the bar counter.

"I know that feeling," said Peter. "Everyone's felt the pinch. It was all that trouble in the Ruhr."

"Couldn't blame the miners for going on strike. Some of them were shot, poor blighters," said Otto reaching in his pocket for a packet of cigarettes.

"The French should have kept out," interjected Gustav, his voice taking on a belligerent tone.

"How could we go on paying billions of gold marks?" asked Dieter, breaking his silence.

"We were already carved up," agreed Peter. "The French have always wanted Alsace and Loraine."

"And it's always been a thorn in our flesh," Heini concluded by thumping the table so hard, it startled the others.

"Our industries have had the life crushed out of them. I don't know how they thought we could pay all that," said Dieter looking serious.

"Mind you, things have got better since we got the Reichsmark, and that Ami bloke Dawes put his plan forward," suggested Otto. "Let's hope something comes of it."

Johann took advantage of the few moments of reflection that followed and asked, "Where is Volkmar this evening?"

"He's had to shed one of his workers, so had more to do himself," Peter informed him.

"Did you hear there's a nationalist in the cabinet now?" asked Heini reverting back to politics.

Seeing Gustav struggling to keep his eyes open and feeling very tired himself, Johann emptied his glass and made excuses to leave. Lisa would take over from him now. He knew the political discussion was far from finished.

The trees were turning colour and some of their leaves had already fluttered down. The Schnatterer family were due to stay that night. Mathias had a bout of migraine and had been sitting in the dimly lit cellar for hours. Expecting trade to be brisk, Johann was ready to help wherever he was needed. He took extra care of his appearance that evening. He scrubbed his hands and nails until they were sore. He washed his hair and smoothed it down with hair cream. Instead of grabbing and putting on his first shirt his hand came into contact with, he was more selective. Rosa was well prepared in the kitchen. Homemade pasta, liver dumplings, potato dumplings, sauerkraut, red cabbage and a good variety of wurst, cured, cooked, smoked and dried meats and sausages. The salads consisted of grated beetroot, radishes and carrots, all well-seasoned and dressed with oil and vinegar.

Johann dispensed the drinks at the bar. He was finding it difficult to keep his mind focused on the orders. His eyes were constantly wandering in the direction of the Schnatterers' table. Since the first glimpse of the family, the print of the eldest daughter's face on his mind had proved to be indelible. Now he had a clear picture of her raven shoulder-length hair tied back in a large bow. He noticed that she stood taller than himself. Her eyes were kind, her nose was prominent and her broad lips seemed continually stretched in a smile. She wore a dirndl. A white blouse with puffed sleeves and a pinafore type of dress with a fitted bodice.

The muddle with the orders, which resulted through his lack of concentration, irritated Lisa and was causing confusion in the kitchen. When everyone had been served and Lisa was able to cope, Johann went outside. Having had the smell of grease in his nostrils all day and his lungs full of cigarette smoke in the Stube, he felt in need of some fresh air. He made his way to the beer garden, sat down and took a deep breath of alpine air. The greyish-blue autumn sky enhanced the brightness of the harvest moon.

"Hello, it's noisy and smokey in there, isn't it? I'm Josefa Schnatterer, we're going to be your neighbours."

Johann looked up momentarily stunned. He quickly got to his feet and extended his arm to meet her outstretched hand.

"I'm Johann," he said quietly. When their hands met, it was like sandpaper touching velvet. If his heart had been the engine of a vehicle, it would have revved up to a dangerous level of revolutions.

"We enjoyed our meal very much. Your sister is in the kitchen I believe?"

"Yes," replied Johann, his heart still racing.

"I can see my family leaving. I must go. Goodnight."

"Goodnight, Fräulein Schnatterer," Johann replied, his voice slightly trembling.

Chapter 5

It was Christmas Eve before Johann set eyes on Josefa again. He and Rosa sat a couple of pews behind the Schnatterer family at the midnight mass. There had been a few sightings of them from a distance when he had been clearing snow in the yard, but not close enough to talk to them. After the service, some of the congregation gathered around the crib, admiring its beautifully carved figures. Outside, the sky was clear and the air crisp. The church bells conveyed their Christmas message and there was the usual exchanging of festive greetings. The candles flickered on the graves which were covered in a thick blanket of snow, disturbed only by the newly placed wreaths.

Making their way homewards, Johann slackened his pace, noticing that the Schnatterer family, led by Josefa, was following close behind. Rosa turned around and was the first to speak.

"A very happy Christmas to you, Fräulein Schnatterer. Err, I don't think you've met my brother."

"Yes, I have. Hello again, Johann," she replied, her eyes beaming. Rosa looked surprised. He had never mentioned this to her. Johann responded with a broad smile as he admired her winter outfit. The long beige coat reached her ankles and was worn with matching fur hat and muff. The rest of the family caught up with them and Johann chatted to the four sisters as they trudged through the snow together. Before parting, they all shook hands and once again, Johann experienced a thrill as he clutched Josefa's.

"We'll be coming to dine at the Gasthof again early in the new year," Herr Schnatterer informed them cheerfully. Rosa looked pleased and Johann felt delighted.

"I'll look forward to our meeting again soon," he said shyly, his eyes focussed on Josefa's face.

34

Johann welcomed the arrival of 1926. He felt it held a lot of promise for both his working life and personal life. His prime resolutions were to strengthen his friendship with Josefa and to expand his business. The demand for new bikes was increasing and he had decided to buy some with the money he had managed to put aside. The post-war influx of bikes needing repairs had slackened. He happened to mention his plans to Herr Schnatterer when they next met and was overjoyed by his suggestion.

"We have a lower ground floor area which we don't require. If you find yourself getting short of space, you are welcome to use it for your workshop."

"Thank you very much indeed," replied an excited Johann as he thought of the opportunity to see Josefa more often.

He cleared out his tools and machinery from the barn and moved before Easter. With Trudi pulling the cart, he collected six new motorbikes and four new push bikes which had been off-loaded at the village railway station. Having satisfied the station master's curiosity, he knew, once again, there would be no need to advertise that they were for sale. Proudly, he stored them in the barn he had vacated at the Gasthof.

The only blight on this seemingly blissful arrangement was caused by two human frailties: jealousy and pride. Johann noticed that every time Josefa visited him in his new workshop, she was immediately re-called by her mother.

"Josefa, come back upstairs, I need you to help me with something."

Her disapproval of her daughter's association with him was becoming blatantly clear. It was obvious she had higher aspirations for her daughter's future. Rosa, on the other hand, felt resentful of the time her brother spent away from the Gasthof. He was not often there when she needed his assistance and she missed his company.

The first customer for one of the new bikes came as a surprise to Johann. Returning from his workshop one day at the onset of summer, he recognised someone sitting outside in the beer garden. A well-groomed young man with sleek black hair and well-polished shoes.

"Hello, Jacob. How are you? I haven't seen you since my apprenticeship days."

"I'm fine, thanks."

"You certainly look fine," said Johann noticing Jacob's well-cut suit and silk tie. "What are you doing these days?"

"I'm doing OK, but my father died last year."

"Oh, I'm sorry to hear that. How's your brother?"

"Isaac, he went on to do a law degree. He's worked his way up. He's a barrister now. My mother's gone to live with her sister." He paused as his eyes wandered around the yard. "What about you? I heard you were selling new motorbikes, so I thought I'd come back and have a look."

"Follow me," said Johann striding towards the barn. Jacob's eyes lit up. He inspected the Ardie machine and took it for a test drive. On his return, Johann was amazed when he was asked to name the price and was handed the full amount in cash.

"You studied mechanical engineering, Jacob, didn't you?" enquired Johann curiously.

"No, I gave it up. I started another little business."

"What type?"

"Lending money." He hesitated for a moment before giving an explanation. "When we sold my father's business, I was always asked for loans. People don't trust banks anymore, you see." Johann's enquiring look prompted him to carry on.

"So I bought a shop for myself."

"What do you sell?" Johann was becoming even more inquisitive.

"I don't. It's a pawn shop. But I do eventually sell the goods if the owners are unable to redeem them."

"Oh, I see," said Johann, his eyes now fixed on the rings adorning Jacob's fingers. They looked remarkably like wedding rings. "Are you married?" he ventured to ask.

"No. How about you?"

"I've found the one I want, but I haven't popped the question yet. It's still early days." At that moment, Johann heard Rosa calling him. "I must go, Jacob. Collect it any time you like. Nice to see you again. Bye." As Johann watched his former schoolmate drive away, his thoughts turned to his other two close school friends who had emigrated to America.

By autumn, Johann had sold all the bikes, but he deferred buying more until the following spring. He was becoming a little perturbed about Rosa's attitude towards Josefa. It was civil enough, but not overly friendly. One evening, she told Johann that she had arranged to go out with Horst.

"Will Lisa be able to manage any snack orders?" he asked.

"I think so," she replied, "but if not, perhaps your girlfriend could help her. That is if she doesn't mind getting her hands a bit dirty," she screamed. Rosa knew Johann would be upset by this remark and she bitterly regretted it as she slammed the door behind her.

Josefa's visit to the workshop became more frequent and usually clandestine. It was on a day when Frau Schnatterer had gone out that Johann's most fervent hope was confirmed. As he reached for one of his tools, Josefa slipped her hand over his. An infusion of pink rose to her cheeks as their eyes met conveying their feelings for each other. As he moved forward to kiss her, there was a thud of a door closing and footsteps could be heard on the floor above.

"Let's go for a drive to the mountains this weekend," he whispered in her ear as he clutched her arms.

"I'd love to," she replied, nestling her head on his shoulder. Suddenly, she pulled away.

"Must go now. I can hear Mother calling. Let me know which day and time." She disappeared through the door.

Her mother was unpacking her shopping basket when she arrived upstairs.

"I know where you've been," she snapped. Frau Schnatterer was very well aware of the magnetic attraction the couple had for each other and her attempts to thwart their relationship were proving futile.

"Do you realise you're heading for a life of drudgery?" she screeched. "Just think! Hard work, long hours, dealing with awkward customers." Frustration caused her eyes to moisten. Her daughter was not listening.

Early one morning at the beginning of December, Josefa rushed into the workshop.

"We've just heard my sister's getting married in the spring and you're invited," she blurted out excitedly.

"Which sister?" asked Johann, looking surprised.

"Zenzi. Hilda's already married and Ida's not old enough."

Johann beamed. He was delighted. Did this mean Frau Schnatterer was relenting a little? Could he hope that his relationship with her would improve?

Christmas was spent quietly at home with his father, who was not at all well. Rosa had gone to join Horst's family. Johann seized the opportunity to break the news that he intended to propose to Josefa. His decision not to postpone doing so until spring was on account of his father's deteriorating health and Rosa's intense relationship with Horst. Both these reasons would have an effect on his own burgeoning business.

"Papa, I'm going to ask Josefa, the miller's daughter, to be my wife, but I shan't ask her till early next year."

Mathias responded with a wry smile. "As long as you're sure, son. As long as you are sure." Wearily, he shuffled off in the direction of his bedroom, mumbling, "It's not an easy life."

On New Year's Eve, Johann helped at the Gasthof. Mathias rallied and circulated, greeting the revellers. As the old year retreated, making way for 1927, the toast was for a more stable country and a brighter future. The following weeks slipped by and Zenzi's wedding day arrived. Johann bought a new suit and looked extremely smart. The reception was held at the saw-mill, the former home of the Schnatterer family. Josefa's only brother played host. After the ceremonial part of the day was over, there was much merry-making with an abundance of beer, wine and food. When the band started to play, Johann stood up, clicked his heels and lowered his head in a nod.

"May I?" he asked holding out a hand for Josefa to grasp. To the strains of the Blue Danube, they danced the Viennese waltz, steadying each other as they finished in a state of giddiness. Johann led his partner out onto the deserted moon-lit balcony. He kissed her passionately. She responded. Excited chatter from other guests seeking fresh air broke the spell. As they returned to the dance floor, Johann looked straight ahead, but he was conscious of her mother's penetrating gaze on his back. By the time they had reached home, Josefa had accepted his marriage proposal. The news was met with a mixed reaction. Delight from both fathers, resignation from her mother and his sister.

Johann's exuberance knew no bounds. He was hopelessly in love, causing a lack of concentration at the workbench and confusion in his everyday thinking. Words like political turmoil, unemployment, extremism, Ruhr conflict, inflation, anti-republicans and nationalists fluttered about in the air like autumn leaves in the wind. The euphoric couple were oblivious to their threatening message.

The two families met to celebrate the engagement. Formality had been dropped and Mathias was now on first-name terms with Agathe and Leonhard Schnatterer. Rosa was still a little remorseful for her outburst but was genuinely pleased to see her brother so happy. The wedding was planned for April the following year, 1928. Johann got on well with his future father-in-law, who was a mild mannered, eye twinkling, jovial character. Agathe shared his kindness towards others but was more of a disciplinarian.

"I'm thinking of expanding my business," Johann told his future father-in-law with the dual intention of assuring him of its stability and to impress him. "I'm going to get some more bikes. The last lot sold quite quickly. Was even paid cash on the spot for one of them."

"Not always a good sign," responded Leonhard reservedly. Johann shot him a questioning glance. As the alcohol took hold, Leonhard was beginning to sway a little, but Johann glued his eyes intently on his face, eager to learn the reason why.

"I bought my house with a suitcase full of Reichsmark because I didn't trust banks anymore," Leonhard said slowly as his eyes met Johann's. "In fact, I had enough money to buy two houses, but its value has decreased through inflation and there was not enough," he dropped his gaze and sighed. "I only managed to buy one."

The conversation came to an end when Rosa arrived handing out glasses of champagne to toast the couple's future.

Two months later, Johann spent the day with Trudi collecting one-wagon load of shiny new bikes with the cart. Once again, he was confident that the station master would spread the word of their arrival and Johann made sure he knew that hire purchase was on offer as well. The weather was fine and settled, so a row of new bikes was set up in the front yard.

The rest was stored in the barn. Rosa, who now quite enjoyed Josefa's company, joined in to admire them.

"I think you'll be getting a visit from Horst," she told her brother. "His father's bakery is doing quite well. They believe people are eating more bread because the price of meat's gone up so much."

Perhaps that's why the regulars have made themselves scarce lately. They must be having a tough time, Johann was wondering. Thoughtfully, he took a cloth to wipe away a speck on one of the new bikes. Just as Rosa forecast, Horst's appearance announced the first customer.

"I hear you're offering 'wechsel' agreement, Hanni. I'd like to take you up on that."

"I have a book here of printed IOU vouchers to be signed for each installment. Payment to be made on the first of each month. All right?" Johann asked, needing assurance.

"That's fine, Hanni. I'll be here next week to collect the bike and pay my first dues."

The following day, the appetising aroma from the large, black, cast iron saucepan rose in the air on its mission to tantalise taste buds. The kitchen door opened and Josefa poked her head inside. "Oh, that smells good," she said.

"Hello, Jo, come in," said Rosa, looking up and greeting her with a welcoming smile.

"Hanni's out there somewhere, probably in the barn."

"Yes, I know. He's busy with a customer. I've come to ask you if you'd like to come with me to look at wedding dresses. Perhaps sometime this week?"

"That would be nice. I could manage tomorrow afternoon, but I can't leave Papa for too long. These days, he gets very breathless."

"That suits me very well, Rosa."

They were both startled by Johann suddenly bursting in, his face beaming.

"I've just sold a bike," he said excitedly as he moved towards Josefa and slid his arm around her waist. "Jacob's brother, Isaac, paid me in full. Cash in hand. Yippee!" he deposited a kiss on her cheek. "It's all go here, Jo. Have you heard, my father's bought some more land and increased his herd? Lisa has been rushed off her feet as well. All this hot weather has made everyone very, very thirsty."

"You'd better get out there, Hanni," alerted Rosa, glancing out of the window. "Just look at them." She was referring to a group of locals inspecting the row of shiny new bikes.

"I shouldn't think he'll get a sale with that lot," remarked Josefa as her eyes followed Johann shooting out of the door.

"They are mostly farmers and from all accounts, they are having a tough time."

"I think they are, cos they're always moaning," was Rosa's reply as she disappeared into the larder.

"Bye, Rosa. I'll see you tomorrow," Josefa called out.

Chapter 6

The following day, they could hear the din in the Stube from outside as they returned from their shopping trip. A heated discussion was underway at the regulars' table.

"Please tell Hanni I've gone straight home, Rosa. Thanks for coming with me today. I've got plenty of ideas to think about. Bye."

"I enjoyed it, Jo," said Rosa smiling.

Volkmar stormed past Rosa on her way to the Stube. His face was red and his hands clenched. She stood in the doorway for a few minutes, watching and listening as the volcano of political views was erupting.

"Bloody politicians. How do they expect us to live? Most 'em couldn't run a bratwurst stall in a market," bellowed Gustav.

"Things were supposed to be getting bloody better, but they're getting bloody worse."

"If you're lucky enough to get credit, it's so damned expensive," moaned Heini.

"That Versailles treaty they signed has caused all the trouble," Dieter joined in. "It's one thing to lose a war, but talk about kicking a man when he's down!"

"We produce the food but get a pittance for it," said Peter forcefully, slapping his palms on the table.

Rosa chose this moment to whisper in Johann's ear and give him Josefa's message. She felt weary and did not want to get involved. As she made a hasty retreat to the kitchen, she caught sight of Volkmar returning to his seat, having relieved himself of the considerable amount of liquid he had consumed. It did not take him long to pick up the thread of the heated discussion again.

"The country's in an awful bloody mess! I've recognised one or two faces going into the pawn shop lately. More and more are out of work"

"Unemployment? I know someone who's always got plenty of work to do," muttered Rosa to herself as she grabbed an apron.

The Stube door burst open as Big Bertl, so called due to his height and broad back, strode in looking very flustered. He had a pot belly, bow legs and the sparse hair on his head hung down limply. Beneath the chin of his weather-beaten face lay folds of skin.

"I need a beer, Lisa, and quickly please," he gasped. "Just got back from market. The price of meat's gone up so much, people just aren't buying it." He took a deep breath, then carried on, "Brought me calves back home again. Couldn't get enough for 'em. What do they want to do, cripple us financially? Bloody politicians!"

"That doddery ole fool Hindenburg is too long in the tooth," said Gustav angrily as he made way for Bertl to sit down next to him. "There's a new cabinet about every two weeks."

"Yeah, he should move over. We need someone else to get us out of this muddle," Dieter said.

Johann remained silent. He couldn't express with conviction that his business was disappointing. He had chosen the route of optimism, bought new bikes and, so far, had been pleased with the response. Already on that day there had been two more customers trading in their old bikes for new ones. *Complacency, however,* he thought, *can be like a treacherous cliff path, fraught with danger and liable to give way with disastrous results.*

The boisterous discussion had reached Mathias' ears. Supporting himself on the backs of chairs, he made his way to join them. Johann pulled out a chair for him.

"Papa, I think we should cheer this bunch up with a round on the house, don't you?"

Mathias smiled weakly and nodded. Both father and son knew how dependent they had always been on local trade, particularly in winter when it became the main artery of the Gasthof's business. Johann signalled to Lisa to re-fill the

43

regulars' glasses. She had remarked lately that there were far fewer strokes on the beer mats these days.

"I've got a busy day tomorrow," said Johann getting up from his chair. "And so have you lot. Bringing your heifers down, aren't you? It's the big procession, eh? The weather should be fine, thank God." There was no response, the playing cards were already on the table.

That night, Johann lay on his bed deep in thought. He was getting very concerned about his father's health. Mathias had always been a popular landlord. He just hoped that he would live long enough to be present at their wedding. He began to think about the second-hand bikes he had taken in part exchange. There was quite a bit of work to do on them before he could sell them. The sky was clear and lit up by the harvest moon when he went to draw the curtains, but on the horizon, dark, stormy political clouds were gathering and domestic ones nearer to home.

Before he settled down for the night, he opened a little box containing a necklace he had bought on the strength of the transactions he had done that week. It was a gift for Josefa.

"Have we got an omnibus party arriving for breakfast, Rosa?" asked Johann as he heard a lot of chattering outside.

"No, we haven't, but they're all pouring into the village for today's parade. I can see quite a lot of people in the yard looking at your bikes."

Johann nearly choked on the mouthful of pretzel he was chewing. He took a swig from his coffee mug, grabbed a jacket and rushed outside. Rosa continued to decorate the torten she had baked for the expected surge of customers. She was glad Josefa had volunteered to help her.

Johan greeted the small gathering in the yard,

"Good morning all. What do you think of these then? Any customers?"

"I'll take half a dozen, Hanni," chuckled a friend from a neighbouring village. There was a ripple of giggles.

"I'll have to rob a bank first, although that won't be much good these days," called out a former primary school friend. This remark raised peals of laughter and mutterings of agreement.

"I don't think I'd get much use out of it in the highlands in winter," chimed in another. "I think I'll stick to my skis," he added with a grin.

"Can I borrow one to take me home?" called out another.

"Seriously," said Johann good-humouredly, "I'll do part exchange agreement or hire purchase."

The majority moved on to watch the procession, several of them lingered. Some seemed to think part exchange was worth considering and a couple made an instant decision to go ahead with hire purchase.

The mood in the village was happy excitement. The sun was shining and for those who lived in the upper regions, this was considered to be the last opportunity to enjoy a family day out before becoming snowbound in the winter months. The heifers were being brought down by trucks from their high summer grazing pastures, to be paraded with great pomp through the village. They were beautifully decorated with gentians and other mountainous blooms. A brass oompah band, with musicians wearing traditional Bavarian costumes, escorted them at the rear. A large marquee erected in the centre of the village offered a variety of German sausages with rye bread and a dollop of mustard, to be washed down with large quantities of the local brew. It was an occasion to wear national costume, to meet up with friends and make merry.

Johann and Rosa eventually turned out the lights in the early hours. They both felt exhausted. Trade in the Stube had been brisk and Johann had been fully occupied with his bikes. In the evening, he had helped to serve drinks in the Stube but not before making sure their own heifers had settled down back in their home stable.

As the days shortened, Johann hoped to spend more time with Josefa, when they could discuss their wedding plans and especially the guest list. It was customary to have only friends and close relatives to the celebratory meal following the church service. Afterwards, an invitation was extended to all the villagers to join them on a 'pay for your own refreshments' basis.

By Christmas, the mood had become sombre at the Gasthof, taking the edge off the excitement of the forthcoming marriage. Mathias spent most of the time in his bedroom. His

45

appetite was poor. His interest and contact with the business had become more and more remote. In the second month of the new year, 1928, Mathias Birk died. It was a funeral, not a wedding, that first brought the family members and villagers together. His popularity was evident by the attendance at the church, which was full to capacity. Rosa looked tired and drawn. The constant care of her father towards the end had aged her appearance. Horst was very supportive and she clung to him. As was customary in Bavarian villages, the wake was very well attended, where lavish amounts of food and drink were freely provided.

The day arrived for the will to be read. The immediate family members gathered in the solicitor's office. Although it was usual for the oldest son to inherit the family home, when Rosa learnt that the entire estate had been left to her brother, her face portrayed a concoction of disbelief and painful disappointment. The Gasthof, the livestock and the land now belonged to Johann. There was one clause, however, that stated how much her devotion to her father had been valued and how much the energy she had put into the family business had been appreciated.

Mathias wrote: "It is my fervent wish, and I am confident my son will carry it out, that the Gasthof will provide a home for my daughter until she marries or for as long as she needs it. She has always been a dutiful and caring daughter, putting family loyalty before her own interests."

Rosa managed to control her emotion so long as the solicitor was present, but like a festering boil, it burst when she was alone with her brother.

"Papa always implied that the Gasthof would be mine. He thought your heart was in mechanics," she said in a quiet trembling voice. She paced up and down wringing her hands. "I've put my heart and soul into this place," she continued blinking away a tear.

"You can still carry on, Rosa. You get on well with Jo. When we're married, we can all live here together quite happily," Johann took a deep sigh.

"It would never work. I know it would never work. This has been my home since I was four years old." Her voice was now raised to a loud high pitch. "We suffered real hardship during the war when you were away. I milked the cows in those freezing winters. I helped to bring the wood in. I slaved in the kitchen."

"But you enjoy cooking, Rosa, and Jo will be able to help you," Johann pleaded.

"Two women in a kitchen doesn't work. It's always been my kitchen." Rosa was becoming more and more agitated.

"Calm down, Rosa. It will be all right. Give it a chance," said Johann exasperated.

"No, I will NOT calm down," she shrieked. "All my life I've been in the company of old men reeking of smoke and beer. Always at their beck and call. Dancing to their tune when they threatened to take their customs elsewhere. Waiting for them to finish playing cards so that I could go to bed halfway through the night!" Her face was contorted in rage and scarlet in colour. Johann did not attempt to interrupt her. He just stared at the floor.

"I've fed the pigs, the geese and mucked out the stables. Other girls of my age had their freedom. Don't you think I would have liked to join them sometimes? Now when things are getting easier, I'm replaced," she burst into tears.

Glancing out of the window, Johann spotted Josefa. "Here comes Jo. Don't let her see you so upset."

"She can bring in the wood when you're selling bikes. She can sweat in the kitchen and lift those heavy pots. She can stoke up the stove and clean and clean and scrub for evermore. She can also order from the brewery when you're busy, keep the accounts and replenish the provisions, because I WON'T BE HERE."

She was shaking as she delivered these words at the top of her voice. Josefa entered through one door as Rosa stormed out of the other.

"Let's go in the Stube for a drink, darling," whispered Johann, giving Josefa a big hug. They sat at a table in the corner, unnoticed by the regulars who were busy solving other problems, like troop movements, brown shirts, unemployment and the American Owen Young's salvation plan. Johann decided to bide his time before telling Josefa about their problem: Rosa's outburst.

The pony waited patiently as Horst carried out the last box of Rosa's possessions to put in the trap. No amount of reasoning could make Rosa change her mind. Her anger had taken her to the point of no return and for the last couple of days, the atmosphere had been very tense. Johann's thoughts were in a turmoil as his sister walked slowly down the stairs and through the kitchen, without a backward glance. Her face was drawn, her eyes red and puffy. Johann watched her silently with Josefa by his side. He resisted the impulse to move forward and hug her, fearing her reaction might cause more upset. Horst helped her into her seat and went back to the kitchen. His embarrassment was obvious, making it clear that he wanted to remain neutral.

"I'll be back soon to pay my next installment," he said with an awkward smile before returning to the trap to take up the reins. Johann seemed stunned. It was almost like another cause to mourn. Josefa took hold of his arm and gently squeezed it. She knew exactly how distressed he was. The situation, however, had presented her with a challenge. Spurred on by her love for Hanni and her determination to prove to her parents that she had made the right choice, she was going to grasp it. In six weeks' time, they were due to get married and by then, she would make sure she was fully prepared to take on her new role at the Gasthof. Whilst she put on her apron, Johann braced himself to go to break the news to the regulars. His eyes were troubled and he looked distant. He was wondering how they would react. They were all very fond of Rosa. Gustav was the first to enquire.

"Hello, Hanni. What's happened to Rosa? Haven't seen her since yer father's funeral."

The explanation was greeted with silence until Volkmar spoke.

"Well, these things happen in families, don't they? She'll be back, you'll see." After a moment of thought, he added, "Anyway, it'll be your wedding soon. She won't want to miss that." Not knowing what else to say, the subject was dropped, beer was ordered and a pack of playing cards appeared on the table.

Josefa's sister Ida was enlisted to help and together with a local girl Heidi, they managed in the kitchen. Johann assisted

Lisa in the bar and took over the ordering and paperwork. This extra workload resulted in the motorbikes, which were taken in part exchange, gathering dust. Some, he knew were almost beyond repair, but in his eagerness to clinch a deal, he had lent a sympathetic ear to hard luck stories and had accepted them. Pleased with the hire purchase sales though, he lined up the remaining bikes in a prominent position in the yard. By the time the wedding day arrived, he had only three bikes left.

Once again, within two months, the church was packed with a large assembly of relatives, friends and villagers. Josefa, a few inches taller than her husband, wore a fashionable off-white, calf-length lace dress. Her raven hair hung loosely, her curls dancing beneath her short veil as they walked down the aisle and out into the spring sunshine. Johann stood erect, a trim figure with prematurely greying hair, his Charlie-Chaplin moustache a shade darker. His ready smile exposed a set of small even teeth and when he laughed, his eyes were barely visible beneath the lids. From the breast pocket of his smart new suit dangled the chain of Mathias' watch. The newly-wed couple led the way back to the Gasthof. A colourless procession of close relatives followed, traditionally wearing black, out of respect for the church. The wedding breakfast awaited them, but before going inside, the custom of sawing a log took place. With a two-handled saw, the newly-wed couple cut into the wood, signifying pulling together along life's path.

As the guests took their seats, Johann's eyes scoured the Gasthof's function room in search of Rosa or Horst. He allowed himself a few moments of disappointment before taking his place beside his new wife and entering into a pervading happy mood. Johann made a short welcoming address before a traditional celebratory meal was served. It consisted of consommé with veal and pork liver dumplings, followed by roast veal, roast pork, homemade pasta and mixed salad. From then on, it was 'Open House'. Anyone in the village, who wished to join in, was welcome. It was during the afternoon when a variety of torten and coffee was on offer that another custom took place: the stealing of the bride. She was whisked away by a few close friends of the bridegroom in a car. They visited as many inns in the neighbourhood as they could before the bridegroom caught up with them. It was in his interest to do this as quickly as possible, because he was presented with a bill for all the drinks they had consumed during their escapade.

Towards early evening, pork chops with mixed salad was served. Following this, a local band started to play and dancing went on until about 11 p.m. For those there, still with an appetite there were large platters of a variety of thinly sliced dried and smoked sausage meats. At around 1 a.m., the bridal couple retired, leaving the stalwarts to continue celebrating.

A notice hung on the Gasthof's main door. It stated 'Closed Tomorrow'. They had one day's honeymoon. It had been the happiest day of Johann's life, blighted only by Rosa's absence.

Ida returned home, knowing that Josefa and Heidi had established a happy relationship and a good routine. A few weeks passed, the days were getting warmer and the trees were blossoming. The heifers were getting fidgety in the stables, sensing that it was time for them to go up to the high summer pastures. The snow had melted, laying bare a table of lush, vivid green spring grass for them. If they were let out too soon, it could lead to disastrous consequences, as Gustav related in the Stube that evening.

"I let them out too early this year. Had to plunge a knife in one to let the gas out. She was blown up, but it was too late. I took her to the Freibank (meat bank). At least it helps those poor blighters out o' work. They can get meat there, very cheap, at a giveaway price. Things are getting worse," he said lifting his shoulders with a look of despair.

"What yer think about the election next week?" asked Volkmar.

"Some o' the youngsters are turning to the commis," said Franz thoughtfully.

"Everybody's getting fed up waiting for this Owen Young bloke's plan," remarked Dieter, struggling with the pronunciation of the name. "Supposed to solve all our problems. Let's hope he can get us out of this mess."

"He'd better move fast, or it will be too late for the likes of us. Prices are dropping like stones," warned Walter.

"Don't think that Hitler stands much chance. Surrounds himself with them brown shirts (SA). They are always causing trouble. Rowdy and violent lot!" Volkmar took a quick glance around him to make sure there were none present.

So much has happened in his own personal life recently that Johann had not really taken enough notice of the wave of political unrest of tsunami proportions that was about to swamp his country. The following day, he had even more on his mind. Josefa told him she was pregnant. He was ecstatic.

The news was received with a loud cheer in the Stube, an excuse to raise glasses was always welcomed. Reasons to celebrate were becoming increasingly scarce due to the country's economic deterioration.

"Here's to the expectant Mama and Papa," said Dieter. They all raised their beer tankards in Johann's direction, muttering, "Good health to you all."

"And if it's a boy, to our future landlord," added Volkmar. This brought a smile to all their faces as once more the tankards were raised.

"I don't know if I'll still be around then," concluded Gustav, his voice very slurred.

Before a light-hearted comment could be made to this statement, the Stube door was forcefully opened and two SA members entered. They swaggered to a table, threw their caps down on the bench and loosened their thick leather belts for comfort.

"Service! Service!" one bellowed, thumping on the table with his clenched fist. Lisa hurried over to them.

"Well, my pretty wench, we'd each like a litre of your best local beer," said the other as his companion's leering eyes followed the contours of Lisa's body.

"Yes, sir, of course." She wasted no time in bringing their order, giving them priority over another customer she was serving.

An uncharacteristic silence befell the regulars' table, where Franz had joined them. They cast furtive glances in the direction of the two uniformed men. Johann remained watchful behind the bar. Dieter launched a bit of small talk about Rosa's continued absence and how they were coping. The others joined in. No one ventured to discuss anything political. Suddenly, Heini rushed in looking very agitated, with blood dripping from his lip and one eye half closed.

"My God, what's happened?" asked Gustav looking very alarmed and endeavouring to focus his bleary eyes on his son.

"Just a scrap, Papa. A difference of opinion with a couple of commis."

"The bastards! We'd better get you home, son." He got up, tottered and would have fallen had Dieter not steadied him.

On hearing this conversation, the two SA members had jumped to their feet, tightened their belts, donned their caps, threw a bank note on the table and made a swift exit.

"It's all right for them to loosen their belts, but we farmers have to bloody well tighten ours to the last hole," said Volkmar forcefully, making sure they were out of earshot.

"Think it's time I went 'ome. Money's 'ard to come by these days," murmured Gustav.

"I'll take you and your father in my van," Dieter told Heini. "He can fetch his cart and mare tomorrow. Hanni will put her in the guest stable."

Feeling the mood had become sombre, the others drained their tankards, too, mumbling excuses for leaving early. There would be plenty to discuss after the election results.

Josefa studied her hands. Formerly soft, white and slim, they were now rough, red and chapped. She was relieved that the morning sickness she had initially suffered had been superseded by an infusion of energy, in spite of the summer's relentless heat. Shy by nature, it suited her to be out of sight of the Gasthof's clientele. Her sister's presence had helped to boost her confidence and she now felt in control of her domain in the kitchen. Johann, on the other hand, liked meeting new people and enjoyed chatting to the regulars, most of whom he had known all his life. Certainly, there had been a great deal to discuss during the last two months, since the general election. The outcome was the formation of the Grand Coalition of the democratic parties. This result, together with the expectations of the American, Owen Young's plan, had released an air of optimism in the country. The Nazis had received little support, with only 2.6% of the votes. The communists fared better with 10%.

Chapter 7

One morning, Johann rushed into the kitchen.

"I need some more ice. Here are some orders, Jo. Are you OK?" She nodded.

"Whew! It's hot in there. We've got several of those posh people from the big houses. You know, the ones who usually go to the hotels in town."

He quickly filled a bowl with chunks of ice, but before disappearing with it, he added, "They must be feeling the pinch like everyone else."

Back in the Stube, Johann recognised one of his new customers. He was a director of a local saw-mill and his colleague, Johann thought, was in management at the glue factory not far away. They were sitting by an open window. A sudden influx of dust-filled air and the rumbling sound of trucks startled them. The occupants of the trucks were singing stirring, rousing songs. Everyone stopped talking and turned their heads towards the road. As the noise faded, Johann moved forward.

"I'm sorry about that," he said.

"No need to apologise," was the mill director's reply.

"I've heard there's a communists' meeting planned in town today. I bet those brown shirts (SA) are on their way to sort them out. Thank God," he added.

"It's the youngsters, mostly students turning to the extreme left. Bloody troublemakers," uttered his companion as Johann went to fetch their orders from the kitchen.

It was later that afternoon when Dieter's son Otto appeared with a few friends, all looking dishevelled.

"Hasn't my father turned up yet, Hanni? We arranged to meet him here."

"No, not yet. He's usually earlier than this on market day."

Otto and his friends sat down. "We could all do with a beer, Herr Birk, please," said one of them. Johann was just about to move away when Otto's news stopped him.

"There was a real ole fisticuffs in town today. SA versus commis. Most of the shops are closed."

"It got a bit nasty, so we left," butted in another.

Waiting to hear more but mindful of customers waiting to be served, Johann hurried to get their beers. When he returned with them, Otto had some more news.

"You know Jacob, don't you, Hanni? A stone was thrown through his pawn shop window today. A farmer saw his family heirlooms up for sale and decided to snatch them back. The police were called in. There was plenty of activity in there today."

Their experience had made them all very thirsty and they were about to order a refill when Dieter poked his head through the window.

"Come on, boys. Let's go home. Can't stop now, Hanni. I'm late. See you soon," he called out. Quickly, they settled their bill and were gone, leaving Johann with a worried frown.

Having sold two more bikes, Johann made the decision not to buy any more for several reasons. The winter was approaching, he needed to repay some of the loan from the incoming installments and as Josefa's pregnancy advanced, she would rely more on him for assistance. Besides this, the heifers would be brought down soon and since the farmers were not spending so much these days, he wanted to cultivate the custom of their new clientele. Also, Ida had implied that she was hoping to get engaged soon, which meant that next year, they would have to look for another general help.

It was a morning in November when Johann looked out of the window, he saw a motorbike in the yard. One that he recognised. He was not expecting a payment that day. *Just a social call,* he was thinking as he went to investigate. It came as quite a shock to him when his eyes scanned the message attached to the seat. It read: "Johann. I'm sorry. Just can't find work. I'm desperate. I can't pay you anymore. Returning bike. Sebastian."

Johann went inside, stunned. He was glad Josefa was upstairs resting. He decided he wouldn't tell her causing her to worry. He would spruce it up and sell it on again when he had the chance. In need of a stiff drink, he went into the Stube. Only Dieter, Otto and Franz sere sitting at the regulars' table. He felt compelled to tell them.

"I don't like the way things are going," said Dieter solemnly. "We can't seem to rely on the Reichstag to get us out of this mess. There're so many out of work." He sighed deeply. "The only hope is the Ami Young's plan. We should know about that early next year."

"There's a lot of violence these days," muttered Franz drowsily.

"Well, desperate times bring out the worst in man and there's always someone lurking to exploit it. Come on, it's time we went home," said Dieter before draining his tankard. He grabbed his coat.

Johann had a great deal of respect for Dieter. He possessed all the good qualities: honesty, loyalty, wisdom and a sense of fair play. When they had left, he unhooked the wooden frame holding the newspaper, sat down for a few quiet moments and started to read. One headline caught his eye.

"Adolf Hitler's ban on public speaking lifted. His oratory drawing crowds."

Christmas and the arrival of 1929 were spent quietly with Josefa's family. They remained mostly indoors, apart from going to midnight mass on Christmas Eve. Josefa clung to Johann as she trod carefully in the snow and at the church, she had difficulty squeezing into the pew. This problem did not present itself a couple of months later, at their son's christening. Dora, the local midwife, had delivered a baby boy on January 31. One of Johann's first reactions was to share their joy with Rosa. He sent a message with Horst when he came to pay an installment on his bike the following day.

"It was 'drinks on the house' for the regulars and they were in high spirits."

"So what is your young son's name?" asked Volkmar.

"Hans," replied Johann proudly.

"The word 'young' reminds me of another bit of good news," said Dieter smiling. "Did anyone else read that we Germans will be represented on the committee to discuss the Owen plan?"

"Yes, I did," answered Heini. "There's been some fierce negotiating about how long we should go on paying reparations, but I think we're going to get control over our railways and banking again." He picked up his glass and raised it high. "That calls for another round, don't you think?"

There was unanimous agreement and they all emptied their glasses.

"And they're persuading the French to vacate the Rhineland this year. That calls for another drink, too," said Gustav jovially, raising his beer mug.

They were all feeling very happy.

Baby Hans lay in deep slumber in his cot next to the bed where his mother was sleeping. Johann crept out of the room and went downstairs. He had been awake for some time, reflecting on the events of the last six months and contemplating the future. His mind wandered to the row of returned motorbikes out in the yard. Never could he have imagined such a bleak situation. The majority of bikes had been returned. Only one or two had defaulted in payment and kept them. He had put these in the hands of a lawyer, Isaac, Jacob's brother. Those two had been the only ones who had paid for their bikes outright. Now he had to think of a way to raise money, having accepted that not only had he invested and lost his own savings, but also money he had borrowed as well. He would have to clean up the returned bikes, of course, and attempt to sell them on, salvaging as much as he could to pay back the loan.

The Gasthof's trade was not doing so well these days. Certainly, the farmers were not drinking as much. The brewery was pestering him for payment of barrels received, which were still full. Regarding the cattle, milk would always be in demand, but the price had dropped dramatically. Felix, his herdsman, was indispensable. He slept in a room above the cattle stalls and was not paid much anyway. Now that Ida was getting married, Lisa could help in the kitchen, as there was not so much to do in the Stube.

Johann yawned. He was tired, but he knew the turmoil in his mind would not allow him to sleep. His thoughts turned to the Buick. Perhaps he could do some excursions to Oberammergau. He had heard that desperate people were visiting the passion play in the hope that their fortunes would change. Then another idea entered his head. A skittle alley. People surely needed something to take their minds off the daily depressing economic news. A baby's cry broke his chain of thoughts. Josefa appeared with Hans in her arms.

"He wants a feed. Will you hold him for a minute?" she said handing the baby over to him.

Ida's marriage to a magistrate a couple of weeks later was not a lavish affair. It was just a bright, happy interlude from worry. As far as Johann was concerned, the Gasthof was closed until the evening, allowing them to enjoy a family meal in privacy and without interruption. There were just the bride's and bridegroom's parents and their sibling with spouses. There was a small gathering of villagers outside waiting to wish them well when the bridal couple left for a short honeymoon. Much to Johann's relief, Herr Schnatterer settled the bill promptly before the door was opened to the public again.

"What's that you're building at the back there, Hanni?" Otto enquired as the regulars took up residence at their table and Lisa responded to their urgent request for beer.

"A skittle alley," Johann replied enthusiastically, "I'm using the wood from the land my father bought. Had it cut at the saw-mill. The owner's brother is giving me a hand to put it up."

A skittle alley, eh? mused Gustav, stroking his beard.

"That sounds interesting."

"Well, I have to try to keep the wolf from the door somehow," replied Johann with a big sigh.

"And there are plenty of wolves about these days," confirmed Dieter. "The economy's sliding backwards. There are two million unemployed now." He paused a moment. "At least the midwives' job is safe, thanks to Hanni and the like." This statement induced broad smiles around the table. "How is the baby by the way?"

"Fine, thanks, Dieter," replied Johann beaming. Lisa arrived with their beer order, which provided the fuel to launch a political discussion.

"Can you imagine, a billion Reichsmark are spent on pensions for war invalids and dependents of those killed? Where's the money coming from?" questioned Volkmar, raising his voice. "We've got a chancellor who spends it as if there's no tomorrow and an octogenarian president." He shrugged, emptied his beer mug and raised his arm for a re-fill.

"I don't like the sound of this right-wing front," continued Dieter, his brow furrowed in thought. "Four main nationalistic parties have ganged up and they're fiercely against the Young plan. They say it won't work and they're trying to make everyone else think so, too."

"Well, it hasn't been accepted yet." Heini took a gulp from his glass before adding, "We should know next month, in August. If it means getting the French out of the Rhineland next year, I'm all for it."

There was a unanimous mumble of agreement from the others.

"What's happened to Franz?" asked Johann, not wanting to get involved in a political discussion. "I haven't seen him for a while."

"He's heavily in debt and hanging on by a thread, poor blighter," replied Dieter. "The farm's been in the Schmidt family since 1800s."

Johann felt tense. He was all panicky inside. He would not let it be known that his situation was becoming dire as well. It would not be good for trade, but he thought he could risk asking if they knew of anyone who wanted a motorbike at a bargain price. They made no comment, just said that they'd ask around.

It was not long after this discussion that Johann visited Isaac. He needed to supply him with the necessary information of those who had defaulted on payment for the bikes.

"I'll see what I can do for you, Johann. If there's no money there, not much can be done, I'm afraid. By the way, I'm thinking of going into farming," said Isaac nonchalantly as he opened a drawer in his filing cabinet.

"Really?" Johann looked very surprised. He couldn't imagine Isaac in muddy boots. Noticing the evidence of affluence, he thought an expensive car, handmade suits, silk ties and gold cuff links were more his scene.

"You probably know the farm I'm going to buy, Johann," Isaac said shutting the cabinet drawer. "It belonged to Franz Schmidt."

Johann was shocked when he heard this. Franz's family had farmed it for generations. What would Walter, his son, do now?

Shortly afterwards, having made no comment, he made his excuses to leave promptly.

During the following weeks, in desperation, Johann sold several of the bikes at half the value. It was a necessity in order to settle the brewery bill and to pay back part of his loan. The increase in trade through the skittle alley was not significant and with the trips to Oberammergau, he had come across competition. Then he heard a rumour that planning had been submitted to make an airstrip in the fields on the outskirt of the village which would be for recreational glider flying. He had rooms he could let to the men working on it, he thought, but it would take time and money to renovate them. He was beginning to suffer from his nerves. He lost his appetite and endured restless nights. All the time, he tried to conceal his anxiety from Josefa. He became tetchy and hated himself for speaking sharply to her on occasions.

Then it happened one October day. The Wall Street crash. Germany faced financial collapse. America had withdrawn all her support. There was no longer surplus funds to invest in Germany. Consequently, industrial production spiralled downwards. Agricultural prices plummeted and investments went into freefall. Johann was distraught. He had lost his direction and did not know which way to turn. He was besieged by his creditors. He was sliding uncontrollably towards the cliff's edge and into the sea of bankruptcy. A life belt was thrown to him just on the point of drowning. It came from someone with whom he had always had a fragile relationship: his mother-in-law. He was not aware of it at the time, but several years later, he learnt that the raging inflation which followed, spreading like a plague, had robbed his father-in-law of his suitcase of money. The money Herr Schnatterer had saved for his retirement was then worthless.

There was a distinct chill to the response Johann received when he gave his mother-in-law a hug of gratitude.

"Thank you," he whispered.

He knew from her expression that she was thinking, *I did it for my daughter, not for you. She should never have married you.*

He turned to Josefa and they clung to each other for a few moments as the stress and tension they had been suffering were being slowly released.

"The wheels were coming off our livelihood, Jo, but I'm a mechanic and I'll put them back on. Trust me. Everything will be all right now. You'll see." Without a word, Josefa just smiled at him fondly.

The next few days were spent settling the accounts of the creditors. The loan for the bikes was paid off, but there was not quite enough to totally pay off the brewery. Knowing there would not be another lifeline, Johann decided reluctantly to sacrifice his free house status and become a tied house. Some of the customers would be upset about it, but this way, the brewery would turn his debt into a loan and would replace any refrigeration used for their supplies. It was up to him now to sell off the rest of the bikes and get the guest rooms ready before work started on the airfield. Women had been the first to lose their jobs in the unemployment crisis, so it would not be difficult to acquire more help for Josefa, enabling her to spend more time with baby Hans.

The year progressed and an early fall of snow created the extra daily chore of keeping the access to the Gasthof clear. There was not much cheer at Christmas and it was little Hans who played a big role in lifting the adults' spirits. It was difficult to have optimism for the New Year 1930, but Hans' first birthday provided the occasion for a happy family gathering.

When it was time for his grandson to go to bed, Leonhard went into the Stube and joined the regulars at their table. The proud grandfather paid for a round of drinks to toast his first grandchild before engaging in more serious conversation.

"Many thanks, Herr Schnatterer," said Dieter. "It's nice to have something to celebrate. There's not much good news about these days."

"No, nothing seems to be getting any better now," agreed Volkmar. "Unemployment's reached three million and there's a contagious feeling of unrest everywhere."

"Yeah, and the army chiefs are a bit worried about how things are going, too," said Gustav before emptying his glass.

"General von Schleicher seems to be edging his way into civilian politics these days," remarked Leonhard as he raised his arm to order another round.

"All those politicians from all those parties just can't get their act together," an embittered Franz raised his voice in sheer despair, having just lost his farm.

"You're right. They're at loggerheads the whole time over everything and the country's going down the drain!" Heini thumped the table, fortunately, just before Lisa arrived with a tray of full glasses.

There was a short interlude of silence whilst they satisfied their thirst until Otto carried on.

"They bicker all the time on how they're going to support the unemployment fund, whether to increase taxes or cut government expenditure and what's worse now, they're thinking of reducing welfare benefits."

"That certainly won't be popular," said Peter. "That's the trouble with coalitions."

"We need just one party," concluded Otto.

"That's all right, son, if it has a good leader," replied Dieter who had been listening very intently.

At that moment, the door opened and Hermann appeared. Everyone knew him. His family owned a large bakery in a nearby village. He was on the parish council and had a finger in most of the parish pies. A portly man with jovial expression and an air of self-importance. Johann had known him since their primary school days.

"Good evening all," he said pulling out a chair.

"Evening, Hermann. How are you these days?" replied Dieter.

"Can't grumble, can't grumble," he repeated. Then turning towards Johann, who had just joined them, he said, "I saw Rosa the other day, Hanni. She asked me if I'd seen you lately. I said I hadn't. But I'd be calling in this evening. She looked well."

Johann averted his eyes for a moment before asking, "Beer, Hermann?"

"That's good of you, Hanni. Yes please. Is there a cause to celebrate?"

"My son's first birthday."

"I'll be glad to drink to his health and his future. It's not rosy at present for some. I've just been to a meeting to discuss the problem of beggars in the village. There have been quite a few punch-ups. Poor blighters can't support their families. There's no work." Hermann raised his glass and toasted the new baby before taking a large gulp.

The continuation of their conversation was interrupted by the sound of a commotion in the entrance hall. The Stube door opened and five inebriated SA brown shirts stumbled in. They slumped down at a table, one jerking the arm of a customer and spilling his drink as he did so. Offering no apology, he proceeded to yell out for service. Lisa hurried over to them.

"Bring us a two litre krug of your best, blondie," he said ogling at her trim figure clad in an attractive blue dirndl and casting admiring glances at her blonde plaits. As she turned, she was startled by the sensation of a hand grasping her buttock. Without looking back, she continued to the bar. This incident did not go unnoticed by Johann. He looked anxious and was on the point of getting up to move in their direction, when Hermann put his hand on his arm.

"Stay sitting, Hanni. They don't mean any harm. Just having some fun, that's all. I'll go and calm them down a bit. You stay here with your friends." He strolled over to them.

"Have a round on me, fellas. May I join you?"

Judging by the banter and raucous laughter as they passed the krug around for each to have a gulp, he entertained them well.

Johann sent Lisa into the kitchen to help Josefa whilst he went behind the bar, where he cast nervous glances at the SA members. Out came the playing cards on the regulars' table and about an hour later, the brown shirts left. Hermann, a little unbalanced, returned to the regulars' table.

"Good night all. I'm going to toddle off home now. Enjoy your cards," he said as he put on his overcoat. "By the way, Hanni, I'm going to stand for Bürgermeister when Herbert steps down." He paused a moment fixing his eyes on Johann's.

"I hope I can count on your support." Not waiting for an answer, he turned towards Leonhard. "Perhaps you'd consider being on the council, Herr Schnatterer."

Leonhard forced a weak smile, muttering, "I don't think so. Good night." He waited until Hermann had made his exit before reaching for his overcoat, saying, "Those bloody Austrian corporal's thugs! They are a menace. They ran over my neighbour's dog with their truck last week. They didn't even stop. Good night all."

With the arrival of the March winds, a whirlwind of discontent, disagreement and failure took place within the government, resulting in the resignation of the Chancellor Müller's cabinet. President Hindenburg appointed Heinrich Brüning to take his place but retained power of parliamentary decision making for himself.

Johann was so focused on keeping the Gasthof afloat, that he relied on snippets of conversation and newspaper headlines to inform him of what was taking place in the Reichstag. He knew full well that the farmers and small businesses surrounding him were in a desperate situation. He was also very much aware of the presence of the SA at clashes which took place with the local government tax collectors. There were disturbances in both towns and rural areas, which were becoming more and more violent. There was one piece of happier news, however, which alleviated these worrying thoughts. Josefa announced that she was expecting another child.

Dora, the midwife, was alerted, dates were put in her diary and visits were made to check the expectant mother's well-being. There were still bikes that remained unsold even at a reduced price, but Johann did not allow his disappointment to undermine the excitement of Josefa's pregnancy. Instead, he immersed himself in creating guest rooms up in the Gasthof's vast attic space. He worked tirelessly using the wood which he had inherited and gratefully accepted offers of assistance from experienced electricians and plumbers in the village. When he had learnt that the construction company was making the final arrangement to erect the glider hangars on the airfield, he wasted no time in informing them of the completed guest rooms. He did not have to wait long for a favourable reply. He was told accommodation would certainly be needed for the foremen and some of their workforce. Understandably, the company was eager to get as much of the construction done by autumn, before the onset of unfavourable weather.

Johann was exhausted. The pressure to get the rooms ready had been enormous, particularly as Josefa's assistance had been naturally limited. It was a morning in August when Dora came down the stairs hurriedly.

"It's another boy! Herr Birk, it's another boy!" Johann came up the cellar stairs.

"Is she OK?" he asked anxiously.

"Yes, they are both fine," replied Dora beaming. "I understand the name is going to be Erich. Is that so?"

"Yes, that was the name for a boy, yesterday. I don't think there's been a change," he replied with a grin. He went into the kitchen, washed his hands and rushed up to the bedroom, two steps at a time.

"He's got Birk eyes," Johann said as he stared proudly at his second son.

"So what's he got from the Schnatterers?" asked Josefa with a smile.

"We'll have to wait and see," was the reply.

"How are you coping down there?"

"We're just managing. It's all right for some having a day off in bed," Johann said with a giggle as he left the room. He ducked just in case something was thrown at him.

Chapter 8

When the leaves turned colour, signifying the change of season, so did the election results signal the change in the Reichstag. The reaction of the Gasthof's customers were various. Some were delighted, mainly the younger voters, some were disappointed and others were just simply stunned in disbelief. Johann returned to his place behind the bar, having just shown a guest to his room. He could hear Volkmar's voice clearly above the rest as he came downstairs.

"The Nazis have 107 seats. That's a hell of a jump from 12 in just two years."

"The commis got 77 and as long as Adolf keeps that lot out, I'm happy," said Dieter. "Anyway, Hindenburg's appointed Brüning as chancellor and he's not a bad bloke."

"I've voted for Hitler," joined in Kurt, Otto's friend. "He's promised to help the farmers. I know what a tough time my father's had. Hardly gets anything for his milk." Kurt could feel the colour rising to his cheeks as he struggled to control his anger.

"I voted for him, too, much to my papa's disgust," muttered Otto self-consciously, glancing in his father's direction. "We need a strong leader, not a doddering, senile, old fool presiding over a bunch who're bringing this country to its knees."

"The trouble is, son, that there are about four million unemployed and the strong leader you're talking about gets his support through the bully tactics of his thugs."

Dieter rendered this information as calmly as possible and then took a deep breath. "Coercion and terror. That's his policy! The scum always rises to the top in bad times." By now, Dieter had also become quite agitated.

"Well, Hitler says he'll get rid of those corrupt republicans. Weed them out and clean it up," replied Otto fighting back.

"The judges certainly need to be weeded out," agreed Kurt, his cheeks now a deep shade of pink.

"Some have been there since the Kaiser's time. You could laugh at the sentences they give the criminals. The right wing ones of course. A murderer could get away with murder!" he bellowed.

The others silently stared at him as he emptied his beer mug. He took advantage of their attention and had more to say.

"Papa went to a lawyer about money owed to him, but they're not bothered with likes of us. The buggers just drag their feet."

"There's some truth in the saying," chirped in Peter, "Nowadays, those with money don't spend it; and those who spend it, don't pay."

The statement was acknowledged by a general nod of heads. Listening to this conversation led Johann to think he had not heard from Isaac either, when, at that moment, the bell rang and he jumped to his feet to greet another guest.

The autumn turned to winter and the arrival of deep snow. Lisa helped Heidi take all the rugs outside to clean them and restore their colour before the festive season began. They lay them topside down in the snow and beat them, leaving dust-blackened patches in the white landscape. Christmas was expected to be a much more relaxed and happy occasion this year, now that the income from the guest rooms and the formation of a skittle club had eased Johann's financial situation.

On Christmas Eve, Hans watched his mother intently as she placed the hand-carved figures around the crib in the open-sided wooden box strewn with straw. His present from the Christ Child was his first pair of skis. The following morning, he tried them out, whilst his bemused baby brother Erich watched from his pram. In the afternoon, Josefa took them to visit their grandparents. She pulled them along on a wooden sledge made by their neighbour, a wheelwright. Hans clutched Erich tightly, shrieking with glee.

Josefa welcomed the arrival of spring of 1931. She had decided she was going to get some chicken and eider ducks.

We can offer our guests fresh eggs and I'll be able to collect the down feathers from the ducks like I did when I was a child. My mother always made our feather bed covers, she thought. At the first opportunity, she told Johann about her plan.

"We have our own milk, we have pork and bacon from our pigs, and we could almost be self-supporting."

"Sounds like a good idea. I'll leave it to you," he replied as he carried a crate of bottles into the bar.

On the day the birds were being delivered, the sound of a noisy locomotive in the yard caused a tremendous commotion. There was screeching of birds and a flapping of wings. Johann stared in amazement at the vehicle.

"What do you think of my tractor, Hanni?" yelled Heini. "It's the first in the village. It has 6-8 horsepower and travels 6 km an hour. Papa and I reckon it could save us a lot of time and money."

Johann's eyes remained wide open and the sound of this engine made his heart beat a little faster.

"The trouble is, Hanni, it has one or two little problems and I wonder if you could sort them out."

"I'll have a damn good try, Heini," replied Johann excitedly, desperate to inspect the engine. "Jo, come and have a look at this," he called out in the direction of the kitchen.

"What is it?" she asked when she appeared at the kitchen door, thinking her husband looked like a child who had been given a box of toys.

"A tractor, Heini's. He wants me to do some work on it."

Josefa smiled, waved to Heini and then withdrew to the kitchen. *I think he's had enough excitement for one day. I'll keep my news until tomorrow,* she thought as she gave her stomach a gentle tap.

It was on a day when Josefa had taken the children to visit a friend. Johann was in the barn when he heard a truck being driven into the yard at speed. The brakes were slammed on, creating a cloud of dust. He peered out from the barn and saw three SA members clamber out. They noticed Johann and went over to him.

"Good day, Herr Birk. We've just called to see if you've ever considered joining the Nazi party?"

"Err, no. I don't really belong to any party," he answered as he shut the barn door. "It's not always a good idea to get

67

involved in politics when you're in a business like mine." Their eyes remained focused on his face. "Anyway, I'm always so busy," he added hastily.

"Do you have a family, Herr Birk?" asked the spokesman of the three.

"Err, yes. I have a wife and two children, with a third on the way," he replied, his face lighting up.

"Then perhaps we could persuade you to become a member."

"I don't know," said Johann, beginning to feel very uncomfortable.

"We understand you have a tied house. Suppose the brewery refuses to supply you anymore."

"Oh, I don't think they'd do that," replied Johann becoming rather tense.

"Oh yes, I think they would," said another emphatically, "and I also think your milk churns would not be collected."

Johann stared in disbelief. What did this mean? What were they talking about?

"We'll leave you to think about it, but we'll pay you another visit."

They climbed back in the truck laughing and drove off knocking over an empty milk churn as they left. Johann was bewildered. He had to tell someone. He wasted no time in going to see Leonhard Schnatterer, his father-in-law. In answer to the knock on the door, Leonhard opened it. He was surprised to see Johann breathlessly asking if he could come in for a few moments.

"Of course," he replied, standing aside for him to enter. "What's the matter? What's happened?" he asked anxiously.

"I've had a visit from the SA," Johann blurted out.

"Oh, they are all over the place," Leonhard said, relieved that nothing had happened to Josefa or the children. "There are 300,000 of them now. They multiply like rats."

"They're threatening to ruin my business if I don't join the Nazi party."

"Don't stress yourself too much, Hanni. They could be just idle threats, although they're not known for them. The Nazis draw their SA recruits from the young unemployed and put them in uniform. It's then that they believe they can throw their weight around. It's intimidating and it's very unnerving."

"They haven't got the power to carry out those threats, have they?" asked Johann, his voice trembling a little.

"It can happen, I'm afraid, Hanni. You see, the youngsters are looking for a political messiah to get this country on its feet again and they think they've found him in Adolf Hitler."

Leonhard took a deep breath. "They believe him when he says he can lead us all out of this mess and he gets them to enroll more members for his party." Leonhard paused and cleared his throat. "But there is a glimmer of hope that things might get better now," he continued. "The British and allies have agreed for the reparation payments to be waived, so now we must just put faith in Chancellor Brüning." Leonhard stood up. "Would you like something to drink, Hanni?"

"No thank you, I must get back. I expect Jo and the children are home by now. I shan't say anything. She's got enough on her plate, without extra worrying. Oh, I almost forgot to tell you. Jo's expecting again. Due in December, I think." Leonhard's face lit up. "I'll tell Aga. She's always hoped that Jo would have a little girl. We'll just have to wait and see, won't we?"

Erich was crying for his feed and Hans was running around excitedly when Johann returned.

"Did you have a good time?" he asked.

"Yes, we did," replied Josefa raising her voice above the baby's cries. "We watched the bees. It reminded me of my childhood. I'd love to have some hives again."

"That's fine by me, Jo, as long as you know how to cope with them."

"Of course I do. I'll wait till next spring though."

"That makes sense. You've got a more important project to think about," said Johann with a knowing look. Josefa smiled.

"Well, right now, I must feed the baby and get them both to bed. Say good night to Papa, Hans."

Having watched them disappear up the stairs, Johann went to see what business there was in the Stube.

Otto was sitting alone with a beer mug in his hand.

"Hello, Otto. Where's your Pa?"

69

"He's coming along later. I'm waiting for a friend. We're going to a Nazi torchlight rally." He averted his eyes before taking a gulp from his tankard. "Pa's not very happy about it, as you can imagine."

"What do you hope to gain from it?" asked Johann as he took a seat at the table.

"Any party, in my opinion, that can push the Reds back is worth supporting." Otto wiped his mouth with the back of his hand, then carried on. "Hitler's promised to do that and help the farmers, and by God, they need it!" Johann remained silent and waited whilst Otto took another gulp.

"He said he'll protect them against cheap imports, especially from Poland, and that he'll get the economy back on track again." He wiped his mouth again. "Who would have thought one of our biggest banks would collapse?"

"I hear people moaning all the time about welfare cuts," said Johann glancing around at just a handful of customers.

"I should think they are! Unemployment benefits are down and public employees have had their pay reduced by 23%—" Suddenly, he stood up. "Oh, there's my friend. Have to go, bye, Hanni."

Johann was feeling tired. He was used to hard work, but this was something else. He put it down to nervous exhaustion. He waited for Josefa to come downstairs. They needed to fix a date for Erich's christening.

A couple of weeks later, Horst called to pay an installment on his bike. He was one of the very few who were still managing to keep up payments. He told Johann that he and Rosa were planning to get married later in the year and it was going to be a very small gathering, with just his parents and his sister present.

"How's business?" asked Johann, suspecting a change in their circumstances.

"It's the cost of grain that's the problem, Hanni. As you know, our wheat comes from the large estates in the eastern provinces." Johann nodded as he listened intently.

"Most of them are managed by incompetents, but in order to keep them afloat, the government has put heavy duties on imported grain!" Horst was becoming quite agitated and paused for a few seconds to calm down. "And do you know why,

Hanni? Because our dithering old president hails from East Prussia and owns an estate there!"

Johann had never seen the characteristically quiet Horst so worked up.

"So that is why the prices for our bread and cereals are kept at such an inflated level," continued Horst. "When I tell you that grain in Germany is 25% more than we could buy it from on the open market, you'll know what I'm talking about. Whew!" He took a few deep breaths but was not finished. "Still, we're not the only ones who're suffering. The poor farmers' agricultural prices have fallen like a stone. They used to get 20 pfennig for a litre of milk, now they get 8 pf."

Johann shrugged and shook his head, but before he could say anything, Horst looked at his watch. "Wow! Rosa will wonder where I am. I must go. Anyway, Hanni, we're struggling, but as long as we don't have children, don't buy clothes, eat basic food, don't keep pets or go on holiday, hopefully, we'll get by."

"Most of us are in the same boat, Horst. We've all just got to keep going," Johann hesitated for a moment, "It'll be Erich's christening next Sunday. Any chance of you and Rosa coming?"

"I'm afraid I can't say," was the reply as he mounted his motorbike. "This is my only luxury," he said patting it. "It's essential for our transport. Bye, Hanni." With a wave, he was gone.

Johann was disappointed but not surprised that Rosa was not at the service. The priest, in his address, welcomed the newly baptised member of the parish. He then proceeded to offer prayers for the farmers and others in the community who were suffering severe economic hardship. As the family trudged back home in an early fall of snow from the previous night, the sun shone brightly in a peaceful pale blue sky. The spell of this magical scene was suddenly broken by two truckloads of SA brown shirts speeding through the village. Josefa looked in dismay at Hans' best coat splattered with discoloured snow from the road. Erich, startled by the sudden noise, began to cry and Johann felt a shiver of apprehension.

Dora made regular appearances at the Gasthof, checking up on the expectant mother's well-being.

"If the baby is a few days late, Frau Birk, it could be a Xmas day baby." Josefa smiled as she thought a baby girl would be a wonderful Christmas gift. Her wish was granted and baby Helga was born on the day predicted. The family celebrated her safe arrival just prior to the Christmas and New Year festivities of 1932.

Chapter 9

The new year was still in its early stages, Josefa and the baby were visiting her mother and Leonhard had taken his two small grandsons on a sledge to a gentle slope in an adjoining field. Johann was collecting logs from the yard when he received a second visit from the SA. This time there were five brown shirts, four youths in their late teens or early twenties, and the other a little older.

"Have you thought over what we proposed last time, Herr Birk?" asked the more senior one in an intimidating tone.

"Err, no. I haven't had a chance yet to discuss it with my wife yet," replied Johann tensely.

"Well, we give you a little longer to decide, otherwise, you might find your liquor licence withdrawn. That would be dreadful, wouldn't it?" said the Storm Trooper sarcastically. Johann looked stunned as he stared at the row of smirking faces. For a few moments, he stood motionless. He felt as if he were nailed to the ground as he watched them drive away. Then he moved instinctively towards Josefa when he heard them returning.

"What was that about?" she asked.

"Nothing really. Just an enquiry."

The following day, whilst Josefa was busy in the kitchen, Johann made his way to the parish council offices, where he asked if he could have a word with his councillor friend, Hermann. He was not a particularly close friend, but Johann had known him for most of his life. He was a little younger than Johann and his father had been a very good, loyal customer at the Gasthof when Mathias was alive. Johann was fully prepared to support Hermann in his bid to become mayor the following year.

"Hello, Hanni. Nice to see you. What can I do for you?"

"Can we go somewhere private, Hermann?" Johann asked, his eyes scanning the reception hall.

"Of course, let's go in here." He led the way to a small adjoining room.

"I've had a couple of visits from the SA. They haven't actually threatened me personally, but they suggested that it would be very difficult for me to run my business if I didn't join the Nazi party. I'd just like your advice. I'm so confused."

Hermann sat looking down at his desk, wanting to take in everything Johann had to say, before commenting.

"I don't have a lot of time to get involved in politics, as you know," continued Johann. "Both our fathers supported the Bavarian Monarchy, I remember, but I've always kept, more or less, to the middle of the road. I just don't like to be persuaded in this manner." Hermann lifted his head and their eyes met.

"They can't really do any harm, can they? I couldn't have my licence revoked, could I?"

Hermann waited a few moments before replying as he studied his friend's pained and desperate expression.

"No. The only way that could happen is if there was continually rowdy and violent behaviour at the inn. They've earned themselves a bad name because some of them have stepped out of line, I admit, but what is the alternative, Hanni?"

Johann looked solemn and moved uncomfortably in his chair.

"There's a real threat of the Reds taking over the country and the SA do help to keep them at bay. On the other hand, we've got a senile eighty-four-year-old president who's given himself social powers and can override cabinet decisions. Take your pick." he took a deep breath and shrugged. "First and foremost, you must think of what is best for Josefa and the children."

"Yes, you're right, Hermann. Thank for your time. I won't keep you any longer, I know you're busy."

"Good bye, Hanni. I'll be along to see you sometime. By the way, I haven't had an opportunity to congratulate you and Josefa on the arrival of number three." They shook hands with reciprocal smiles.

Johann returned home. The fact that it was a beautiful spring day, did not lift his spirits. His mind was in a whirlwind recalling the conversation he had had with Leonhard, Otto, Horst and Hermann. The last one was still fresh in his mind. The thought that the SA could easily cause disturbances at the inn was beginning to worry him a great deal. Otto had told him about the farmers facing ruin. The inn had always relied so much on their custom. His leaning was towards the republicans and Chancellor Brüning, like Leonhard. After all, Brüning had managed to release the country from the reparation payments. He went into the deserted Stube and took down the newspaper from the stand to read the result of the presidential election. He read, "President Hindenburg re-elected. Chancellor Brüning seeks to suppress the power of the SA."

Johann rose early that morning. He had slept soundly these last six weeks, since Chancellor Brüning had imposed a ban on the SA. The violence had abated considerably, but the country was still in a turmoil politically and economically with a restless current of Nationalism. Hindenburg had managed to scrape in enough votes to become elected for another term.

Having torn off the month of May from the calendar, Johann realised it was one day too soon. Josefa was still upstairs dressing the children. He made some coffee and buttered a freshly baked pretzel, which Lisa had just fetched from the bakery. His breakfast was disturbed by the arrival of the brewery delivery lorry. He drank the rest of the coffee before going out to the yard.

"Morning, Herr Birk. Have you heard the news?"

"What news?"

"Hindenburg's given Brüning the boot, or 'dismissed him from office' as the newspapers say."

"Good God, what for?"

"He hasn't been able to deliver the goods. The country's in a hell of a mess. Couldn't get a safe majority. Sign here please," he said handing Johann the delivery note. "I'm not surprised he was called the Hunger Chancellor. There are a lot of hungry people about." Johann opened his mouth to speak, but the delivery man had more to say.

"A bloke was telling me about someone he knew who went to a restaurant and the price of the meal had doubled by the time he'd eaten it. That's raging inflation for you! Not only is the economy depressed, so is everyone else. Nothing to laugh about these days." By now, all the barrels were unloaded.

"What—" was all Johann could utter before the man continued.

"I'm only too pleased if people drown their sorrows and drink beer. It keeps me in work. It's been nice to chat to you, Herr Birk. Bye now." Within a couple of minutes, he was in his cab and ready to drive away.

Josefa and the children were already having their breakfast when Johann went back inside. Thoughts of the news he had just heard were soon banished by the distraction of the children's excited chatter.

"Finish your breakfast, Hans. I want to see it all gone when I come downstairs." Then turning to Johann, Josefa said, "I'm just going to put Helga in her cot. She still seems a bit tired."

"I could take these two over to see Oma and Opa. How would you like that, boys? They can see how Erich is beginning to toddle." Squeals of delight answered his question. The children knew Oma had a secret cupboard where she kept sweeties.

Johann carried Erich for most of the short distance to their grandparents. Aga said she would amuse the boys in the kitchen, which gave Johann the opportunity to have a few words with Leonhard.

"I expect you've heard the news," said Johann.

"Yes, I certainly have," replied Leonhard, staring reflectively out of the window. "I'm afraid this might lead to the collapse of our democracy."

"Why's that?" asked Johann, who was prepared to hang on every word of the reply. He had a great deal of respect for his father-in-law's reasoning. Leonhard turned his back to the window and faced Johann.

"It all depends on who influences our president. He's getting on in years, which is sometimes a drawback to his judgement. He has listened to all those around him saying Brüning had lost public support. Also, the government's plans for his home territory in the east worried him. The plan being, to break up those large bankrupt estates and turn them into small holdings for the unemployed," he took a deep breath before adding, "of whom there are now six million, one in three of the workforce!"

"But Brüning suppressed the SA activities. Everyone was fed up with all the violence and rioting," Johann pointed out.

"Well, there's certainly been less truckloads of hooligans racing through the village, Hanni, but in unsettled times like these, there's always someone waiting in the wings to step in. I just hope his successor Franz von Papen will have the solution and be able to do something."

Suddenly, Hans burst through the door, followed by a tottering Erich. Their mouths showed traces of chocolate. Their appearance brought the discussion to a close, and it was time to take them home.

"How's my little granddaughter?" Aga asked, her eyes twinkling.

"She's doing very well," replied Johann. "Pop in to see her again soon."

During the afternoon, Josefa went to hang out the washing in the garden, which billowed gently in the light summer breeze. The two boys played happily giggling when Hans became wrapped in the sheets and lost from view. Johann was at his desk sorting out bills when there was a tap on the window. When he looked out, he was confronted by a family of Gypsies, the parents and four children.

"Please, do you have any food to give us?" the woman asked.

Johann's gaze rested on the pale, drawn, little faces of the children, with dark brown, sad, pleading eyes. He went to the kitchen and bundled some hard boiled eggs and a large loaf of bread into a bag. There was no meat to give away. That had become a rarity for their own family meals. They only had chicken when one of their hens stopped laying and occasionally a duck for roasting. The pigs were sold to provide extra income.

"Thank you, thank you. God bless you," the man said as Johann handed it to them. They moved away, with the children tugging at the bag.

It was about two weeks later when Josefa had taken the children to visit an aunt and Johann was outside behind the barn. He heard a truck pull into the yard. The screeching of brakes and the sound of the occupants jumping to the ground made his pulse quicken. Keeping out of sight, he watched them peer into his workshop and then go into the Gasthof. After a few moments, they came out laughing and jostling with each other, their raucous banter clearly audible above the sound of the engine as they drove away. When they were out of sight, Johann hurried inside.

"What did they want, Lisa?" he asked anxiously as she filled a beer tankard.

"They were looking for you. I didn't know where you were, we haven't seen them for a while, but a customer tells me the ban on them has been lifted." Johann's face was one of horror. "Oh, no! Oh my God, No!" he exclaimed, putting his hands to his head as if in pain.

The sound of Josefa screaming one evening a few weeks later sent Johann racing outside to where she was getting in her washing from the line.

"What's the matter, Jo?" he yelled.

"Look, come here quickly. Look, look, oh, how horrible." She turned her head aside. Johann cringed as he saw one of the ducks with its head flattened, either by having been stamped upon or by a heavy object having been dropped on it. There was no sign of blood trails or blood-stained feathers being scattered, so that Johann knew at once it was not the work of an animal. This was the first of a series of incidents that were to plague their lives. Windows were broken, chicken disappeared and a milk churn awaiting collection was tipped over, creating a white pond. The tyres of his Buick were slashed, causing him to let down taxi service customers, who became very disgruntled. In spite of the perpetrators leaving no evidence, Johann knew who was responsible. His suspicions were confirmed when he had another visit from the SA.

"Are you ready to join the party yet, Herr Birk? Do you still need persuading?" As no reply was forthcoming, the more senior of the four Storm Troopers carried on, "We're thinking of holding a party at your Gasthof and inviting several of our friends. I hope they will behave themselves and not be too rowdy."

Johann's stomach muscles tightened and the feeling of nausea overcame him. He and Josefa were at the end of their tether, there was always the fear for the children's safety. The sleepless nights of worrying were taking their toll. Nervous tension was making them both very short tempered with each other and with the children. Johann was suffering an agonising moral dilemma.

"How could he?" Leonhard asked his daughter.

"He had no choice, Papa, for all our sakes. We could have lost everything, our customers, our health and, worst of all, through strain, each other!" Her eyes searched her father's eyes for understanding. "You should have seen their grins of achievement and satisfaction when his membership badge was pinned on. It was sickening," Josefa's voice was quavering.

The following month, the Reichstag elections took place. Von Papen still held the chancellorship. The Nazis gained 230 seats, a massive increase from previously. There was a no-confidence vote in their leader from the cabinet. Three months later, this led to the nation walking the well-worn path to the polling stations again. The Nazis support dropped to 196 seats. Von Papen resigned and shortly afterwards, Schleicher, the former military leader, took his place. This sparked off collaboration between the Nazis and the communists, which resulted in organised strikes, savage acts of violence and sabotage.

"What do you expect when you get bed-fellows with that political libido?" asked Dieter rhetorically, "A hell of an explosion!" He had just joined Leonhard in the Stube.

"What hope have we got with a senile eighty-four-year-old and two men who are trying to get the better of each other because of their mutual loathing of each other? It will probably lead us all into an inferno," Leonhard replied forcefully.

Two months later, Schleicher resigned. Oskar, Hindenburg's son and a friend of Von Papen, persuaded his father to overcome his dislike of the former Austrian corporal and offer him the chancellorship. It was readily accepted, and on Johann's 34th birthday, January 30, 1933, Hitler came to power.

The day after that, Josefa had announced some more earth-shattering news. She was expecting their fourth child.

Having wiped the condensation from the Stube window, Johann stood staring out for a few moments. Since the early hours, the heavy fall of snow had kept the snowploughs busy. He caught sight of Hermann treading carefully as he made his way along the narrow clearing on the pavement. The white thick blanket covering everywhere had muffled all sound, but, suddenly, the peaceful winter scene was shattered by rumbling Lorries driven at speed. As the noise of the engines and the shouting of the vehicles' occupants grew to a deafening pitch, Hermann stopped in his tracks. He turned towards the road, straightened up and stretched his right arm out high. The Nazi salute was reciprocated and followed by a chorus of cheers from the cargo of brown-shirted youths. *Is that a sign of allegiance,* Johann wondered, *or has Hermann also heard about a man in Berlin who was beaten up by the SA?* He'd been looking in a shop window and hadn't saluted them when they'd marched past. A few moments later, the Stube door opened and the newly elected mayor stumbled breathlessly through it.

"Hello, Johann," he gasped in a forced jovial manner. He hung up his coat on the ornate wrought iron stand and cast a sideway glance at the Nazi party membership plaque on the wall.

"Good morning, Hermann, or should I address you more formally now, Herr Bürgermeister? Congratulations. What would you like to drink? It's my birthday today."

"Thank you very much. My best wishes to you, Hanni. A schnapps would be a welcome warmer."

Johann joined him at the table and Hermann raised the small glass, saying, "Here's to your good health, Hanni," before emptying it in one gulp.

"Thank you," said Johann raising his glass, "and here's to a successful term of office for you."

"Thank you, thank you, Hanni," repeated Hermann, his ruddy complexion having taken on an even deeper shade of pink. "Well, what do you think of the national election results and our new chancellor?" he asked enthusiastically.

"I don't know, Hermann. We've been through some bad times and something had to change. Inflation can't get much worse than when a man steals a wheelbarrow and leaves behind the cash box bulging with money, because the barrow was worth more!" Johann took a quick breath. "Did you hear about that?" Not waiting for a reply, he carried on. "I just hope things will start to get better. Only time will tell," he added nervously.

"Good morning, Hermann, you're about early on such a cold morning." Hermann turned his head to see Josefa standing in the bar doorway.

"Good morning, Frau Birk. This is just a courtesy call to thank all those who have supported me."

"Has Hanni told you? We're expecting our fourth."

"No, he hasn't. There's no danger of not having an offspring to take on the business then," he said smiling broadly as he raised his glass in her direction. At that moment, a blast of cold air heralded the arrival of Ludwig, known by his nickname Luggi. He came regularly to wind up the cuckoo clock.

"Good morning all. It's snowing quite hard now. I made sure I shook my coat outside," he said hanging it up. Melting snowflakes dripped from his beard as he removed his mitts and balaclava. He slapped his hand against his thighs in an effort to get some feeling back in them. Advanced in years, Luggi's life of clockmaking had left him with an arched back and a slightly slanted shoulder. He was a gentle, polite, kind man who had experienced military service stretching back to the last century, when Bavaria was a kingdom.

"Good morning, Luggi. Your usual?"

"Yes please, Herr Birk. What a din there's been along the road. Military convoys charging about. Anyone would think we're preparing for war." He shuffled towards the clock and gently pulled the chain with the weights up.

"It'll be nearly ten minutes before the cuckoo makes its appearance, so I'll thaw out a bit by the Kachelofen," he muttered. He sat down on the seat encircling the stove. The heat they absorbed made it a popular place to sit. Johann put down half a litre of lager on the table beside him, which was all Luggi asked for in return for his services. A schnapps was placed beside it.

"It's Johann's birthday," said Josefa smiling as she saw his eyes widen at the sight of the additional glass. Luggi immediately stood up again and stretched out his ice cold hand to offer his congratulations. Hermann had got up, too, and was putting on his coat.

"I must go now. It's a busy day for me. Thank you, Hanni. Good bye, Frau Birk. All the best to you." He nodded in Luggi's direction and as he went to the door, it opened and Leonhard stepped in.

"Good morning, Herr Schnatterer, I was just about to leave."

"Good morning, Herr Schäfer. I hear you're our new mayor."

"Yes. That's so. I'm afraid I'm in rather a hurry, Herr Schnatterer. Please excuse me. Good bye." Without any more eye contact, Hermann stepped out into the snow.

"He's in a hurry," chuckled Leonhard. "He's well aware of my opinion of the election results. God help us all." Having taken off his coat, he went over to Johann, shook his hand and patted him on the back. "Congratulations, Hanni. It's all happening on your birthday. The SA have planned a colossal torchlight procession in Berlin tonight." Johann pursed his lips and slowly shook his head. "What would you like to drink, Leonhard?"

"I can see the schnapps bottle there. That would warm me up nicely." Seeing Josefa, he asked, "Are you coming to join us, Jo?"

"No, Papa, I've got plenty to do. I must go to see the children now. They can't wait to get out in the snow." Her voice trailed off as she disappeared in the direction of the kitchen. Leonhard was just about to toast Johann's health when the sound of shoes being scraped and Dieter's recognisable voice was heard at the Stube door.

"I expect you've heard he's in," he called out to them, regaining his balance after slipping a little. "The dithering imbecile Hindenburg has made him chancellor. Does he realise what he has done?

"Yes, we've heard all right. Take your coat off and come and join us. It's Hanni's birthday," replied Leonhard. Dieter shook hands with Johann, expressing good wishes, and then sat down with them at the regulars' table, where he readily accepted a schnapps.

"It's the youngsters. They idolise Adolf. False promises and bully tactics is how the Nazis get their recruits." Dieter was very agitated as he spoke.

Johann cast an anxious glance around to see if anyone had come in unnoticed. A thought flashed through his mind. *Is this how it's going to be? Will people not be able to speak freely anymore, like they have always done at the Gasthof?*

"Have you read what General Ludendorff said when he heard what Hindenburg had done? I'll read it out to you." Dieter cleared his throat as he unfolded a newspaper.

"This accursed man will cast our Reich into the abyss and bring our nation to inconceivable misery. Future generations will damn you in your grave for what you have done."

The silence which followed, as Dieter re-folded the newspaper, was broken by the cuckoo announcing the hour. Then all eyes turned towards the door, observing the entrance of two youth in high spirits, slapping each other's back. Dieter's contorted face expressed a concoction of emotions. Disbelief, disappointment, dismay and despair. Peter, Volkmar's son, and his own son, Otto, stood there dressed in brown shirts, the uniform of the SA. The others were struck dumb, overcome by surprise and shock.

Johann and Leonhard made eye contact and nodded simultaneously, prompting them to make an exit. They muttered excuses about wanting to see the children and need to get the wood in. They had barely reached the kitchen door when they heard Dieter's raised voice aguishly repeating, "Why? Why? Why?"

Otto's reply was calmer. "Papa, you've got to understand, I'm almost 20 years old and was born just before Europe was turned into a blood bath. I've experienced the consequences of that war all my life. The worst was seeing you and Mama clinging onto the business, which has been in the family for generations. Can you imagine the frustration I've felt, not being able to find a job when I was old enough to help you and Mama? With six million unemployed, there wasn't a chance. Even if I'd found one, the contents of my pay packet would have been gobbled up with raging inflation."

"But son," interrupted Dieter.

"Papa, just let me finish. Young people like me need someone to lead us out of this mess. Someone strong. I want to belong to a country I can be proud of and it's up to my generation to make sure it happens. There're nearly 750,000 young men who have joined the SA. They can't all be wrong!"

"But make sure you get the right leader," retorted his father, "not one who gets his followers like Adolf Hitler does, through violence, intimidation and whipping up mass hysteria."

"But, Papa. It's a bit like a revolution. You can't change things without people getting hurt."

"But you must allow people to think and choose for themselves. Hitler wants total control. He's a good orator. I'll give you that," replied Dieter.

"We've had a choice before, Papa, and where did it get us? Doddery old men bickering with each other, ousting each other out of office every five minutes. We need a strong leader. I'll follow anyone who'll help the farmers, and he's promised to do just that." Otto took a deep breath and glanced around the Stube, allowing Volkmar's son an opportunity to continue.

"He says, for farmers in debt, he'll ban creditors from foreclosing on them until October," said Peter, his voice several decibels quieter. "He's going to protect the home market by increasing the import duty on major agricultural produce and to help the dairy farmers, he'll cut the production of margarine by 40%." Otto wanted the last word.

"Papa, let's give him a chance. It's the only straw we've got left to grasp," he pleaded.

Chapter 10

Johann was out in the yard looking for his large wooden shovel to clear the snow when he saw Luggi trudging homewards. *He's cut his visit short today,* he thought. *Normally, he likes to linger in the warmth, enjoying the company, although he rarely enters into the conversations, particularly if it's political.*

Luggi was a widower, childless and lived alone. His visits to the Gasthof brought mutual delight to him and the children. He always had sweeties in his pocket. A few minutes later, Johann noticed Dieter and Otto leaving. He smiled when he saw they had their arms around each other's shoulder. He knew that their bond was so strong, there could never be a serious rift between them.

Josefa called out from the kitchen, "Hanni, we need some bread. Could you go and get some and take the boys? I've got so much to do."

"Yes, all right. Hans can go on his skis and I'll pull Erich on the sledge," he called back. The children's excitement at his suggestion hindered the process of putting on snow boots and dressing up warmly. Eventually, they set off, their scarves, mitts and pom pom hats striking a colourful contrast to the snow. They arrived at the Bäckerei having met one or two villagers on the way, who stopped to exchange a few words with the children. As they left the shop, Johann held the shopping basket containing the loaves in his left hand and gripped the rope of the sledge tightly in the other as Erich scrambled on-board. As he was about to pull the sledge, Johann became alarmed when he heard the rhythmic crunching of marching feet approaching. Without hesitation, he freed his right hand and quickly hustled the children back into the shop.

"I've forgotten something," he said rather sharply as they protested in their state of confusion.

"I think we need a few more bread rolls," he said nervously to a surprised shop assistant. He knew they were not needed, but he would not risk the consequences of failing to give the Nazi salute whilst the children were with him. Through the shop window, Johann could see one of Otto's friends marching in the column. He engaged in idle chat with the shop assistant until he was certain the column had passed.

There were still remnants of snow drifts and a chill in the air when spring arrived. One evening at dusk, Johann went out into the yard to collect wood from the neatly stacked pile. He heard an unusual sound. He paused and listened, his eyes scouring the yard. Through the barn's small window, he caught sight of a movement. *Wild cats,* he thought until he heard the sound again. *Psst.* He peered through the barn door cautiously. His mouth fell open and his eyes widened as they rested on a bedraggled figure cowering like a cornered animal.

"Hanni." He heard his name whispered. "It's me, Jacob. I need your help."

"Good God. What's happened?"

"Isaac's had his car smashed and all his law books burnt. He's taken off to America." Johann looked horrified as Jacob continued.

"I've had SA men outside my shop for weeks, telling people they mustn't give Jews custom and if they do, they're in for a good beating."

Johann stood dumbstruck as he absorbed what he was hearing. After a pause to take another breath, Jacob carried on.

"They're out to get us Jews. My shop windows have been smashed and everything looted. I've just got enough money to get me over to Isaac, but I'm not sailing for another two days. I can't take the risk staying at the shop any longer."

He looked down on the floor as he added, "They'd probably kill me." He looked up with pleading eyes. "Can I stay here in the barn?" he asked desperately.

"Of course, Jacob. This is terrible. You're welcome to come inside."

"No, I daren't. I don't want anyone to see me."

"I'll get you some blankets."

"Don't bring them in here please. Hang them over the washing line. I'll get them when it's dark," he whispered nervously.

"Have you eaten?" asked Johann. Jacob shook his head.

"Could you spare some bread for me? Please don't arouse suspicion. Put it on top of the wood pile. I'll get it from there. God bless you, Hanni."

In the dim light, Johann could just see his former school friend's watery eyes glinting. As he carried the logs through the kitchen and down the cellar steps, he made a decision not tell Josefa. She had enough to worry about.

"I've just found two empty beer bottles in the barn. Don't tell me you've taken up secret drinking," Josefa said with a smile as she came in the back door a few days later. "You could at least bring the bottles back."

Johann immediately tried to disguise the alarm he felt by flippantly replying, "Oh, I expect some of the lads must have finished bottles outside and chucked them in there."

To avert any more discussion on the subject, Johann hurriedly left the kitchen and headed for the Stube. He felt so relieved that Jacob had managed to get away without being discovered. He didn't know what the punishment would be for helping a Jew. The possible consequences triggered off a sensation of fear and he shuddered. Josefa calling to him released him from any more worrying thoughts.

"Hanni, will you take this dough to the baker please. I was going to bake some bread myself, but I need the oven for something else. We're short of bread again. I can't understand it."

"OK, I think I'll call to see Luggi as well. He hasn't been in for a while." Within minutes, Johann had put on his jacket and made an expedient exit, avoiding any more questions regarding the bread shortage.

A few rays of sunshine provided a welcome respite from heavy showers, enabling Johann to push the trolley carrying the tins of dough without getting wet. It was the last week of April and he was surprised to see the village being decorated with banners and flags of many colours. Garlands of evergreens, spring blooms and ribbons hung outside the houses around the doors and windows. He racked his brain wondering for what reason. As he entered the baker's shop, Gottfried appeared from the baking parlour at the rear, where a radio could be heard.

"Hallo, Hanni," he said with a large grin.

"Morning, Gottfried. Jo wants to know if you could bake these for her."

"Certainly. Will early tomorrow morning do?"

"I can't hear with all that din. Did you say early?" Johann asked, his voice raised. Gottfried nodded.

"I'm sorry, I'll turn it down," he said and disappeared for a moment. Then making sure there were just two of them present, he continued.

"Since the government took control over broadcasting, there doesn't seem to be anything else but", he lowered his voice to a minimum, "propaganda. It's Adolf Hitler's birthday in a couple of days, you see." His eyes searched Johann's and his voice was reduced to a whisper again.

"Radios have become very cheap. You can't tune into a foreign station though." Johann stared at him for a moment as he realised the reason for the bunting. Then turning to leave, he said with an awkward smile, "I'll see you tomorrow."

Having deposited the trolley under cover in Gottfried's back yard, he trudged up the hill towards Luggi's modest home. He noticed the community buildings, such as the parish council offices, the fire station, the post office and the railway station flew flags emblazoned with swastikas, but there was no evidence of the national black, red and gold flag. When he reached Luggi's house, he stood transfixed. It was boarded up and the front door was daubed with yellow paint in the shape of a star. A neighbour's head appeared at an upstairs window, which she cautiously opened when Johann beckoned her to speak to him.

"Where's Luggi?" he asked. The woman looked up and down the hill before answering.

"They've taken him."

"Who? Why?" Again, the woman scoured the street before answering, "It was in the night. Brown shirts bundled him into a car, shouting, 'Dirty bastard. Filthy Jew.' Someone told me they'd heard Dachau mentioned. I don't know anymore," she said before forcefully closing the window.

It was the noise of a convoy of armoured vehicles which jolted Johann out of his trance as he made his way back down the hill. "What's happening?" he muttered to himself. "Our village has always been so peaceful and tranquil. Now, not a day passes without it being disturbed." When he reached home, the children came running out to meet him.

"Mama told us you were going to see Luggi. When is he going to come again and bring us some more sweeties, Papa?" they asked excitedly.

"He says he'll come to see you as soon as he's better. He's not very well at the moment," was his reply. Then, with a sideways nod, he indicated to Josefa to follow him into the Büro, where he told her about what had happened. He noticed that it upset her and he regretted having to tell her, especially at a time when she was emotionally charged.

Business continued to be brisk, and Josefa, now heavily pregnant, found working in the kitchen in the early summer heat very tiring. Ida came as often as possible to help lessen her sister's workload and Dora made regular check-up visits. Johann was kept busy in the Stube, where he noticed a change in the behaviour of their cliental. There seemed to be a general affliction of not entering into conversation before turning their heads to make sure they could not be overheard. Some just sat and said nothing. Others left their tables in the Stube now and again for the privacy of the corridor, where they huddled in a corner talking in hushed tones. An anti-social mistrustful atmosphere prevailed.

It was during one busy evening that a young man entered the Stube alone. He sat at a corner table and ordered a beer. As the evening progressed and the air had been thickened with cigarette smoke, several customers were settling their bills and preparing to leave. Suddenly, the door burst open and three uniformed members of the SS rushed in. All conversation froze and all eyes rested on them. No one noticed the young man in the corner at the far end dart under the table and crawl behind the bar to make his exit. A frenzy of searching by the three SS took place. Chairs were pulled out from tables and hurled about. Customers' legs were violently kicked if they impeded their progress through the Stube. Bottles and glasses toppled onto the floor, causing splinters of glass to fly. A customer's dog squealed when a chair landed on top of it. As the SS left to go outside, a few moments of stunned silence preceded a general decision to leave. Hesitation followed when they heard screams and yelling coming from the yard. A man appeared at the door in a very distressed state.

"Please come and help. They are beating him up. Call the police quickly."

"They are the police," someone shouted at him. "Himmler's in charge of our police force now. Those are his men. That poor devil must be a commi. God help him."

A child grizzling drew Johann's attention. Josefa stood at the bar door in her nightdress hitched up by her enormous bulge, little Helga was in her arms.

"What's going on? I heard a lot of commotion. It woke Helga up." Johann took Helga from her and escorted them back upstairs. "I'll explain tomorrow," he said quietly.

There was no opportunity to give an explanation the following day. Josefa went into labour and Dora was summoned.

The sound of a newborn baby's cry rang through the upper floor of the Gasthof. Shortly afterwards, Dora hastened downstairs. Johann was out in the meadow adjoining the yard, with the children.

"Herr Birk. You have another baby son," she announced breathlessly. "I understand he's going to be called Josef. Am I right?"

"I believe so," he replied with a broad grin as he rounded up the children, urging them to wash their hands before going to see their new little brother.

As soon as the news reached them, Agatha and Leonhard wasted no time in visiting their new grandson.

"He'll probably be called Sepp," predicted his grandfather.

"I expect so, Papa. That's usual for a Josef."

Noticing his daughter was in need of a rest, Leonhard suggested that he and Johann should go for a stroll, leaving their grandmother to amuse the children.

"Let's walk where we can talk," said Leonhard glancing behind them. They remained silent until they reached the boundary of the village and the wide open space allocated to the proposed airfield. Having reassured himself once more that they were alone, Leonhard was first to speak.

"Have you heard about Otto's friend?"

"Which one? You mean Kurt? The one who joined the SA and persuaded Peter and Otto to follow suit?"

"They found out he has had Jewish blood, so they chucked him out of the SA." Leonhard stood still a moment, looked around, before adding, "They gave him some farewell gifts though."

Johann shot him a questioning glance.

"A swollen face, two black eyes and a couple of broken ribs."

"Good God!" exclaimed Johann. "What made them join that lot?"

"When there's massive unemployment, it must be easy to convince a youngster. They're at a very impressionable age. They put him in a uniform which instils a feeling of worth in him and he thinks he's doing something for his country. They feed him on propaganda which makes him feel more important, toughen him up, roughen up the smooth edges, so to speak, and he becomes aggressive."

Leonhard stopped short and his eyes conveyed a message that someone was catching up with them. They quickly changed the subject to the family's new addition.

"Good morning, gentleman, beautiful day." Keeping his eyes to the ground, a man walking his dog moved swiftly ahead of them.

"He always used to stop for a chat. Have you noticed that's a thing of the past now? No one stops to talk," remarked Johann. Leonhard shrugged and sighed.

"Everything's changing," he said quietly. "There's so much violence and it's escalating. Every day, there are demos, boycotting and beatings. Judges are being dragged out of courts. In fact, all Jews are being hounded out, the uni professors, the museums directors, the civil servants, the lot!" He took a deep breath, "And what's more, the trade union offices have been rampaged."

As Leonhard became more vocal, it was Johann's turn to make sure they were not overheard. He took a nervous look behind them before saying in a hushed tone. "And in the one party state like we're living in, there's no one to stop them, is there?"

Receiving no answer from his father-in-law, Johann looked up at him. Leonhard just shook his head slowly. They arrived back home. After a few moments, he said, "I wonder why it has been decided to have an airfield here. Perhaps pilots enjoy a bird's-eye view of the Alps. Anyway, it will provide entertainment for the village, watching the light aircraft take off and land."

Early one morning about a month later, Johann was clearing out the empty bottles from the bar. The door burst open and big Bertl rushed in.

"Cor, you're early," remarked Johann

"Have you heard the news, Hanni?" he blurted out.

"I haven't been up long enough," replied Johann, blinking as if still half asleep. "The Reichstag's been burnt down! They've arrested a young Dutchman." He paused to get his breath back. "They're not sure who put a match to it, but they're blaming the communists." Bertl swallowed hard. "Give me a beer please, Hanni. I'm parched."

"Sounds serious," muttered Johann reaching for a glass.

"I wouldn't like to be in those poor blokes' shoes. My God, there'll be a purge on the commis and they'll get no mercy."

Bertl picked up his beer glass and drank until it was empty.

"Thanks, Hanni. I'll settle when I come in this evening." He left as quickly as he had entered.

The news spread as fast as the Reichstag's fire, in the wake of which, the Gasthof's trade increased. Apart from those seeking to quench their thirst in the late summer heat, there prevailed a noticeable need to be among others who were also apprehensive about the future and needed to be reassured by those who held an optimistic view. The atmosphere at the Gasthof had become considerably quieter though. Small talk about health and family matters had replaced political discussions such as Himmler taking over the Bavarian police, that there were now 50,000 SS and that the Enabling Act had given Hitler total power. Airing an opinion about any of these had to take place behind closed doors and in whispers. The flood gates had burst and the whole populace was being swept along in a deluge of Nazi fervour. It was becoming common knowledge that any attempt to swim against the swell, could result in severe punishment or death.

Chapter 11

A few weeks later, Josefa set off to take the children out in the autumn sunshine. Little Helga wanted to help her mother push baby Sepp's pram, whilst Hans and Erich ran ahead gathering armfuls of fallen leaves to throw at each other. They began to lag behind.

"Come on, boys. Let's go to the lake where you like to throw pebbles in," she called out to them, knowing it would be a very popular suggestion.

They had left Johann behind the bar. Volkmar came in on his way back from market, looking weary and forlorn. Dieter arrived soon afterwards.

"I hear you're in difficulty, Volkmar. Let's have a chat," he said as loud as a whisper would allow. Volkmar, with tired eyes and face drawn, nodded in agreement. "But not here," he muttered.

"May we go into your private room for a while, Hanni?" Dieter asked.

"Of course, the children are out with Jo, so it will be nice and quiet." They followed him to the Büro. With the door tightly shut, the two men felt they could now speak freely.

"It's the Entailed Farm Law, isn't it?" asked Dieter.

Volkmar nodded. "It all sounded good at first," he sighed staring at the floor. Then looking up, he pushed back a lock of hair from his face and carried on.

"Foreclosing was banned until October. For those of us who had debts, it gave us a breather. Now we've got the sting in the tail." He emptied his beer mug and wiped his mouth with the back of his hand before divulging the sting. "With this new law, it's almost impossible to get credit, because we can't use the farm as collateral. That means we can't buy new machinery or buy small pieces of land adjoining our farms that come up for sale. What's worse, we can neither sell, nor split up our farms, and our children can't inherit them. How bad can it get?" he said in exasperation.

"So it can't be used as security on a loan," said Dieter as he mulled over the information he had just heard and tried to grasp the terrible situation his friend was in. At the same time, he was thinking how fortunate he'd been to stay out of debt, but only just.

"The worse thing of all is, we mustn't open our mouths and protest for fear of someone grassing on us, we'd probably get arrested, as we haven't any legal standing anymore. It's bloody frightening!" Dieter sat quietly, listening intently.

At that moment, the door opened and Otto appeared.

"Ah, I've found you two. Hanni told me you were here. I just wondered if you'd heard about the plans to build motorways. That will sort the unemployment problem out. Didn't I tell you, Papa?" Noticing Volkmar's tense reaction to this statement, Dieter welcomed Johann's timely call that three beers awaited them in the Stube.

By the beginning of December, the first fall of snow barely covered the ground. It was time for St Nikolaus to visit all the children in the village. Dressed in medieval clothing complete with mitre and staff and with his knave Ruprecht carrying a small broom made out of birch wood twigs, the two went on their mission. Good children received a gift and naughty ones received punishment in the form of a light tap on the behind with the twigs. According to their consciences, the children either received the two visitors with excitement or severe apprehension. Josefa's good report on her brood resulted in each one receiving a small toy.

The snow was several inches deep at Christmas, which delighted the children. Hans and Erich raced outside to play with the neighbour's children and wasted no time building a snowman in the field. They had great fun throwing snowballs and sledging down the nursery slope at the rear of the Gasthof. There was the usual visit to church with Oma and Opa, who also joined them for a happy family lunch on New Year's Day 1934.

Sadly, shortly afterwards, the happiness changed to anxiety. Helga's health became a cause of extreme worry. The doctor prescribed medicine for her feverish condition and emphasised that if she showed no improvement, they should not hesitate to call him again. Johann hurried to the chemist and on his way back, he noticed an old man shuffling a few yards ahead of him. The soles of his shoes had all but parted company with the uppers, exposing his bare feet to the crisp snow. His clothes were in tatters and certainly not adequate for mid-winter. His white hair hung around his shoulders and, when Johann caught up with him, he saw that his eyes were bloodshot, his lips swollen and his beard reached down to his waist. His lower jaw dropped to reveal broken teeth amid spaces of inflamed gums. There were weals on the back of his hands. He held a small branch from a tree which provided him with a little support.

"Luggi!" Johann's breath carried the word out barely audibly. He made to put an arm around the old man's shoulders, but Luggi tried to avoid it and stumbled. Scrambling to his feet, he resisted, as forcefully as he was able, any assistance. In his attempt to help him, Johann dropped the packet containing Helga's medicine. He knew how anxiously Josefa was waiting for it. He picked it up and took a final glance in the direction of the old man for whom he had always held affection. Now as he stared at him, he had the image of a human being broken in body and spirit and consumed by fear and mistrust.

Josefa held the hands of her two elder sons and Johann carried eight months old Sepp as they followed the small coffin being taken slowly down the centre aisle. Little Helga's favourite doll and teddy bear sat amidst the abundance of spring blooms adorning the coffin. The village church, with its rich Baroque interior, was full to capacity. The congregation, all clad in black, stood with heavy heads. Only the sound of sobbing broke the painful silence. Gusts of the March winds blew around the mourners as they stood huddled at the family grave. Helga was to take her place next to her grandfather Mathias. Following the burial, the family, together with close relatives, returned to the Gasthof, which had been closed since Helga's death.

It had been a few days after Johann's visit to the chemist that she had been admitted to hospital where meningitis had been diagnosed and, from which, she had died a few days later.

The impoverished communities of South Germany had always been very religious and to overcome her grief, Josefa relied heavily on her faith. She had disciplined herself to believe it was God's will to take away their beautiful daughter and that it was futile and irreverent to dwell on the reason for His action. The only way to start the healing process was to immerse herself in caring for their three beloved sons and helping Johann to run the Gasthof.

She had been shocked when she heard Hanni's account of his meeting with Luggi. At the time of her preoccupation with her sick child, she had felt indifferent to what was happening outside of her four walls, but now she found herself with many unanswered questions. Her place in the kitchen meant that the snippets of news she received from the Stube were always second or third hand and she intended to become more informed. She heard the government had subsidised the manufacture of six million cheap radios, so she suggested to Johann that she should have one. He agreed.

During the lunch period, about three weeks later, Johann took an order into the kitchen.

"Two bratwurst and sauerkraut, please, Jo," he said pinning the order onto the board. "They've been talking about Himmler being made chief of the secret police."

"You mean the Gestapo. Yes, I know," replied Josefa stirring the contents of a large saucepan. "The SA needs to have their wings clipped. They're getting too violent and too powerful."

Johann lifted his eyes from the pan where four large bratwurst were sizzling and looked in amazement at his wife.

"How'd yer know, Jo?"

"I heard it on the radio and now I know that Hitler would not like this delicious goulash I've just made, cos he's a vegetarian. I heard all about him. He's kind to animals and loves children."

"I've got to get another order. I'll be back in a tick," said Johann still with the look of surprise on his face. Within minutes, he was pinning another order on the board.

"Dieter's just come in and here's something you can't possibly know. Otto's left the SA. He says they're a bunch of thugs and sadists hell bent on causing havoc."

"What's he going to do now?"

"I'll tell you in a minute. I'm busy," said Johann disappearing again.

During the lull that followed the lunch trade, Johann was able to tell Josefa that Otto had thought of joining the army following its big recruitment drive but had opted for the newly formed air force instead.

I expect Dieter's very pleased about Otto, mused Josefa as she finished her lunch. *I heard a lot were leaving the SA. Strange, not so long ago, the manufacturers couldn't keep up with demand for cloth to make brown shirts!*

The parched earth cried out for moisture as the intense heat continued into the last week of June. An overwhelming amount of traffic was passing through the village. Lorries, trucks and cars carrying SA members sped down the main street.

Clouds of dust entered any open windows along their route with very intrusive noise. The brown-shirted youths lived up to their reputation of being rowdy, foul-mouthed and heavy handed. Early one morning, a car swerved into the Gasthof's yard and stopped inches from the water trough stocked with fresh trout. All four car doors opened and the occupants spilled out. They were highly inebriated and staggered into the Stube, where Johann, not wanting to aggravate them, supplied their demand for four krugs of his best beer.

"Where is everyone?" yelled one of them, causing a spillage on the table top as he turned towards Johann.

"It's early yet," was the reply.

The sudden dash for the door by one of his companions and the sound of retching in the entrance hall caused Johann to close his eyes in dread. Hearing Josefa's scream of repulsion, he shot through the door after him. He was confronted by the sight of vomit strew across the flagstones. The other three had followed him and seeing Josefa, one of them sidled up to her and put his arm around her waist. Seized by anger and revulsion, Johann grabbed the back of the offender's collar, swung him around and, with surge of strength, fuelled by rage, pushed him through the door with the sole of his shoe. When the other three went to pick him up, Johann slammed the door shut and bolted it. He felt relief when he heard their car's ignition.

Two days later, Josefa was hanging out the washing when she noticed two men dressed in black from their trilbies to their shoes. Her pulse started to race and she looked nervously at the children. A very long half hour passed before she saw them depart seemingly in haste. Then Johann appeared in the garden, nervously looking to make sure they had departed.

"I've had a visit from the Gestapo. Those louts reported me. I had to explain the whole incident."

"What did they say? Did they believe you?" Josefa asked anxiously.

"I've been let off with a warning. They seemed to be in a hurry. Had to get to Munich for some reason."

That reason became clear when Josefa switched on her radio. It was reported that 3,000 SA members had rampaged through Munich. Chancellor Hitler had become personally involved when he wrenched off the epaulettes from the uniforms of the high-ranking riot leaders. The Nazi leader had taken action after an announcement that if the activities of the SA were not curbed, the president would declare martial law. The Stube became a hotbed of whispered rumours about the high-ranking SA members who had been sent to prison and about those who were given a good beating from the SS.

"What did the regulars say about it?" Josefa asked.

"From behind cupped hands, they said they reckon the lucky ones got shot," replied Johann looking very serious.

Since the discussion of political matters was kept to an absolute minimum in public places, Josefa became the main provider of information gleaned from her radio, which was mostly in praise of the Nazi party. There was also a broadcast by Hitler attempting to justify the bloodshed in Munich, which had become known as the 'Night of the Long Knives'. A month later, the usual propaganda was interrupted by an announcement.

"President Hindenburg's died," she told Johann when he next appeared.

"Yes, someone's just told me. There's a rumour circulating that he'd become so senile that by the time he passed away, he addressed Hitler as 'Your Majesty'. I suppose he thought he was the Kaiser!"

In autumn, another event took place which dominated the conversation.

"Can you imagine, Hanni," Josefa said, "500 trains carried half a million people to that rally in Nürnberg which lasted a week. A special railway station had to be built and there was a city of tents!"

"Just think of all the food and drink they would need," said Johann thoughtfully.

"It makes me feel weak just thinking about it," replied Josefa as she peeled the potatoes.

"Someone must be doing good business there. I wouldn't say no to a small fraction of it," Johann muttered stroking his chin.

"There's one more bit of news for you," said Josefa casually.

"Yeah?"

"We're expecting another baby."

"Wow!" His eyes lit up.

"Have you told the boys?"

"No, not yet."

Josefa closed the lid of the little cardboard box containing the carefully chosen seasonal spice biscuits, meat loaf, stollen, all of her own making, together with a small bottle of pear schnapps and some sliced salami. Johann was outside with the children and she could hear the squeals of delight as their toboggan careered down the slope.

Josefa had decided to grab this opportunity to take Luggi an early Christmas parcel. It had been preying on her mind that she had not managed to visit him sooner, but her conscience had been reconciled by the tragic loss of her daughter and the worry of the Gestapo's visit. Aware that she could easily slip and lose her balance with her present miss-apportioned body weight, she took her steps carefully. The hill which led to Luggi's cottage seemed steeper than ever. The gate squeaked when she opened it and before she could knock on the door, the neighbour's head appeared over the fence.

"He won't answer it. He doesn't talk to anyone. Hardly ever puts his head out of door."

"I've brought him a little box of goodies," Josefa replied softly.

"I'll put it on his back door step if you like," the neighbour suggested. "I do little bits of shopping for him and if I leave it there, he takes it in when I've gone. I usually put any leftovers from our meals there for him, too, cos he's got very little money." She paused and studied Josefa's face for a few seconds. "You're from the Gasthof, aren't you?" she said.

"Yes," replied Josefa handing over the box. "Thank you very much. You're very kind. Christmas greetings to you and every good wish for the year to come."

Without a word, just a slight nod, the woman turned and disappeared behind the cottage. Retracing her steps, Josefa reflected on Luggi's former visits to the Gasthof, his sparkling eyes, benign smile and the children's happy faces when they saw him. Reaching the main street, she became aware of how much quieter the village was since the night of the Long Knives, but the fear of talking outside the privacy of one's home was still very evident. She received only cursory greetings from the villagers.

As the first Christmas without little Helga drew near, both parents and grandparents made a concerted effort to disguise their sadness.

"I wish Helga was here as well, Mama," said Hans. Josefa looked away fighting the ever-ready tears as she enclosed her eldest son in her arms.

"I want you to help me get the box out today with the manger and put the animals around in the straw. The Christkindl is coming this evening." Hans' face lit up. "With some presents?"

His mother nodded as she wiped her eyes.

"Our crib has always been one of the best in the village. The one in the church, of course, is the most beautiful, but our lovely carved figures are pretty god as well. We'll put the whole nativity scene on that little table in front of the crucifix."

"Will Papa be with us, Mama?"

"Yes, the Gasthof's closed today. Oma and Opa will be here too."

The excitement was almost unbearable for the children as they had waited to be called in to receive their presents. Laid

101

out in front of the crib was an orange, a mechanical toy, a piece of clothing and homemade biscuits for each one of them. When it was time for the three tired little boys to be tucked up in bed, Hans asked. "Do we have to go to church tomorrow, Mama?" Josefa turned to answer the question, but Hans was already asleep.

Chapter 12

During the first month of the new year, Hans started school just prior to his sixth birthday. The village primary school was only a short distance from the inn. He settled in happily and talked incessantly about his new friends and his teacher Fräulein Müller. One morning, as the two younger boys were playing, Josefa began to prepare for the lunchtime trade, she needed to make some soup and there was always a demand for Spätzle— her homemade pasta. She put on her apron and turned on the radio. Half listening, she gathered that there was a general relief that Hitler had acted against the brown shirts, making the streets safer from drunken and disorderly behaviour.

I can vouch for that, she thought. *It's much more peaceful.* The commentator carried on in the usual vein.

"We must be grateful to our Führer, who has the common touch and cares for his people. He is one who is fond of children, kind to animals and has dealt compassionately with comrades who have fallen on hard times—" At this point, Johann burst through the kitchen doors, carrying empty beer crates to put outside for collection.

"I seem to hear the same thing every time I come in here," he muttered. "Perhaps the needle's got stuck."

Josefa leant over to turn it off as her mind flashed back to Luggi.

"We're going to be busy, Jo. D' yer think you can cope?"

"I think so, but I shall have to get Lisa to help. She's upstairs cleaning at the moment," was the reply as she laid her hands gently on her bulge. "Mother's coming to take Erich and Sepp out for this morning," she called after him as he rushed back to the Stube.

"I'm here," she heard Aga's voice.

"Hallo, Mama, thanks for coming."

"I would have been here earlier, but I stopped to read the *Daily* to catch up with the news. I didn't know Hitler had already chosen Gŏring as his deputy."

"Yes, Mama, that was before Christmas," said Josefa, slightly agitated as she glanced at the clock.

"We're glad to see you, Oma. It's all go here," said Johann, picking up a tray of clean glasses and narrowly missing a collision with his sons who came charging towards their grandmother.

Josefa collected the boys' boots and anoraks. She took a second glance at the clock, but not taking the hint, Aga persisted to relate what she had been reading.

"The SS were threatening people who wanted to do their shopping in Jewish stores. A man who insisted on shopping in one was told he'd have his welfare payment stopped if he did."

Not being aware of Josefa's efforts to dress a toddler in warm clothing, Aga continued. "An Aryan toy shop selling models of the SA and SS was ordered to get rid of them. I don't know what's happening these days. Every poster, every magazine says how marvellous Hitler is. Let's hope they're right."

As her daughter started to usher her and the boys out of the door, her voice dropped to a whisper. "You know what your father thinks of him, don't you?"

"Yes, Mama, but one good thing Hitler's done is to make Mother's Day a national holiday. Unfortunately, he also said a woman's place is in the kitchen and that's where I happen to be! See you later. Be good, boys."

Josefa turned the radio on again, hoping to hear some relaxing music, but instead, they heard that the unemployment figures had fallen like a stone to less than half what they were when the Führer came to power. The whole of the building industry had been mobilised by the manufacturer of aeroplanes and cars. Added to the delight of the industrialists was the construction of the Autobahn. It was expected to provide employment for at least 600,000 men. "Who would have thought", concluded the newsreader, "that when our Führer turned the first turf in September 1933, we could soon enjoy driving on dual carriage ways through scenic routes. This accomplishment will compete with the world's most marvelled achievements." Josefa took another fleeting glance at the kitchen clock.

"Well, the Führer won't come to help me if I'm not ready when the first orders come in," she uttered between her teeth as she turned off the radio.

There were a lot of new faces appearing in the Stube during the early months of 1935. Although they did not divulge much information, Johann understood that they were working in factories that supplied all manner of components for the construction industry. There were also those who were starting work on the airfield adjoining the village. The farmers, however, were still struggling and the regulars' table was not often fully occupied. It was during one quiet evening that Johann had a chance to sit and chat with Dieter and Volkmar.

"How's Otto getting on?" asked Johann.

"Oh, fine. He loves flying and really enjoys the good company. What a difference from the other lot." Instinctively, he looked around, even though he had spoken quietly. "He told me he had to swear allegiance to Hitler. It's compulsory for all troops now. An oath of unconditional obedience to him." He looked over his shoulder again, a movement that had become known as the German affliction.

"And how's Peter?" asked Johann turning to Volkmar.

"He's OK. He's in Frankfurt. He's been taken on to work on the motorway." Also showing signs of having the German affliction, he continued in a hushed tone. "Did you know that to be a member of the SS now, you have to have proof of Aryan ancestry as far back as 1800? That's for rank and file, 1750 for officers." After a gulp of beer and another symptom of the affliction, he whispered, "If you want to get married, you have to have special permission and your girl has to be Aryan, too."

"No wonder Kurt was thrown out of the SA with a half Jewish grandfather," said Dieter resting his elbow on the table and covering his mouth with his hand.

"By the way, how's Josefa bearing up?" asked Volkmar reverting to a normal voice. "I expect she's hoping for another girl." Ignoring this suggestion, Johann replied, "She's all right, thanks. Gets very tired. Dora's keeping an eye on her. It's due fairly soon now."

He rose from his seat to welcome other customers, not realising how soon it would be.

"It's another boy! Frau Birk," announced Dora the following morning. She searched Josefa's face, but there was not the slightest hint of disappointment that it was not a girl. On the contrary, her face expressed only joy and relief.

"What's his name going to be?" asked Dora handing over the new bundle.

"We haven't decided yet. Would you go and get Johann. I'll let him choose this time," she said with a smile.

"Rudolf," said Johann breathlessly, having charged up the stairs in between serving customers.

"What made you decide on that name, Hanni?" asked a puzzled Josefa.

"I recently saw a poster with a picture of Mayerling, which made me think of Prince Rudolf. Then I thought that a name good enough for a Hapsburg prince is good enough for our son!"

Chapter 13

The family left the church and returned to the Gasthof for the Rudolf's christening tea party, after which the children played until Josefa whisked them away at bedtime. The Stube was quiet, being Sunday evening, and Johann left Lisa in charge. He collected another bottle of wine from the cellar before joining his parents-in-law in the Büro.

"So you have four sons now, Hanni," remarked Leonhard.

"It will save a few pfennigs on buying clothes. They can be handed down," reflected the forever parsimonious Aga, who had brought up four daughters. "They grow out of them so quickly."

"They wear them out quickly, too," said Johann as he re-filled the wine glasses.

"Talking of clothes," continued Leonhard, "we went to Munich to buy Aga a new coat the other day. We had a terrible time. I shan't go there again in a hurry."

"Why not? What happened?" asked Johann.

"It seemed there was a general boycotting of Jewish shops. Plain-clothes SS were outside them, harassing would-be customers. There were scuffles and windows broken. Then they started beating up the shop assistants."

"One brute knocked the manager down and kept kicking him," interrupted Aga.

"The bastards. If I'd been younger, I'd have—" Leonhard clenched his teeth.

"It was terrifying," interjected Aga. "On the way back, we saw a synagogue that had been completely vandalised and the SS were throwing books on a bonfire."

"Where's this all going to end?" said Leonhard pensively. "I heard that Jewish companies which have put in tenders for making uniforms and Jackboots have been turned down. They must be colossal orders."

"But the unemployment figures have tumbled," mused Johann enjoying the evening of relaxation.

"I know, but it's swings and roundabout, isn't it? Now the small businesses are finding it difficult to get staff. They've either been conscripted or they're working on the motorways." Leonhard took a deep breath. "That's—" He was interrupted by Josefa's appearance. Johann poured out a glass of wine for her.

"Are they all tucked up, Jo?"

"Yes, Mother. Thank goodness. It's been a tiring day," she sighed as she raised the glass to her lips.

"Well, we ought to be making a move. Come on, drink up. Let these two have an early night," urged Aga, handing his coat to her husband.

"Yes, dear. By the way, Hanni, did you hear that the Ordensburg they're building at Sonthofen should be finished in the spring next year?"

"Yes, I did. There's a hell of a lot happening in that direction. I've been told it's massive. It doesn't bring us any business though. It's almost 30 kilometres from here," replied Johann stifling a yawn as he opened the door for them.

"Thanks for your help with the children today," he said sleepily.

""What is the Ordensburg exactly for?" asked Josefa when they were alone and finishing the contents of their wine glasses.

"I'm not really sure. I heard someone say they're for training the graduates of Adolf Hitler schools, to be our leaders in the future." Josefa raised her eyebrows and took another sip from her glass.

"Probably, they'll be stuffed with ideology and toughened up with discipline and dangerous sports, because in their view, physical achievements account for more than intellect." Johann emptied his glass and gathered the empty bottles together. "There's one thing for sure, there won't be any religious instruction."

"I wouldn't like our boys to go to one," mumbled Josefa as she struggled to stop her eyelids from dropping.

"There are only three being built at the present, all located up high in remote areas. Supposed to last a thousand years. I shan't be around then and I shan't be around tomorrow morning if I don't go to bed now. Come on, Jo, let's call it a day."

A few days later, it was announced that the first stretch of motorway from Frankfurt to Darmstadt had been completed. There was no letting up of the surge of movement on the road. Lorries were transversing the country, racing to satisfy the motor industry. The sky was busy with small light aircraft and gliders, training pilots for the newly formed Luftwaffe. It had become a common sight to see columns of marching children, members of the Hitler Youth and the BDM (League of Girls). They held their heads up high and looked smart in uniform. With ages ranging from 14–18 years, there were now almost four million. All this activity contributed to the gradual transformation from the feeling of despair to a general mood of hope. Not least at the Gasthof, where Johann turned part of the yard into a small Biergarten, hoping to increase the sale of liquid refreshment during the long hot summer months.

It was one day in the autumn when Aga called to see her daughter. She sat down and gratefully accepted a drink as she complained about being showered by the clouds of dust created by the Lorries charging through the village. What she said next left Josefa with her brow in a deep questioning furrow. She just looked at her mother as if she could not grasp what she was being told.

"Do you mean to say that we have to be careful what we say in front of our own children?" she asked her mother with a look of disbelief.

"My neighbour asked me to warn you. She meant well. Strange things have been happening in the schools," replied Aga as she went over to shut the door leading to the corridor. "There have been Jewish teachers thrown out and the Nazis are trying to get a grip on the schools."

"What do you mean, Mother?"

"If a child repeats an anti-Nazi view he's heard at home which a pro-Nazi teacher overhears, he or she would report it and the parents could be in trouble."

"Informers you mean?" Josefa looked aghast.

"They're planting those in the schools as well, just in case the teachers express any anti-Nazi ideas. There are informers simply everywhere now. You just can't trust anyone and certainly not someone who bears a grudge against you."

Aga allowed her daughter a few moments to absorb what she had just heard. She could tell by Josefa's pained expression that she had realised the effect this would have on their business.

"Something else Frau Schumann told me," said Aga as she prepared to leave, "Someone got rid of a neighbour he didn't like. He informed on him, but he'd made it all up! The neighbour was arrested."

Josefa shuddered. "How awful. What sort of society are we living in, Mama? We have to be careful what we write in letters, we can't talk freely on the phone and we're even scared to talk to neighbours."

Aga sighed deeply and nodded. "I know. Everyone is suspected of being an informant," she said quietly. "Sometimes those we've known and trusted all our lives, and then we're tortured by guilt for being suspicious."

"I'll warn Hanni about what you've just told me. I must do some cooking now."

After her mother had left, Josefa went into the kitchen and put on her apron. She found it difficult to concentrate. This information had sent her thoughts in a spin. In order to calm down, she sought some soothing music on the radio. The Walküre Opera blared forth.

"Oh no, not Wagner again," she moaned. "He may be the Führer's favourite composer, but he's certainly not mine!" She lowered the volume and looked up to see Johann standing in the kitchen doorway. His face was almost hidden by a newspaper.

"Some Catholic priests have been arrested for not giving the Nazi salute."

"What? Where? Not our Father Theodor?"

"No, up north. There are allegations of sexual offences and financial corruption is being investigated as well. Wow!"

"I'll read about it later. Mother called in and I'm all behind now. I've had enough bad news for one day. I'll tell you what she told me later, preferably when we're in bed, where we can't be overheard."

"OK. I'll wake you up if you're already asleep when I get up there," was Johann's reply as he returned to the Stube, looking puzzled.

When Hans arrived back from school, his mother noticed he was trying to conceal that he had been crying. She took hold of his shoulders and turned him around to face her.

"What's the matter, Hans? Have you been squabbling with your schoolmates?"

"No, Mama. I just don't like our new teacher."

"I didn't know you had a new teacher. What's happened to Fräulein Müller?"

"She's not there anymore."

"Is she ill or has she left?"

"I don't know, Mama. No one said anything."

"Well, I'll come to the school and find out what's happening. Now cheer up. We've got some of your favourite sausages for supper."

Still upset, Hans found it difficult to fall asleep that evening. Consequently, he was tired the following morning and Josefa had difficulty in getting him ready for school on time.

"You'll be late and miss prayers if you don't hurry up," she told him.

"We don't have prayers anymore, Mama."

The head teacher ushered Josefa through the door of her office and turned the key in the lock. Tall, slim and with hair tied back in a bun, she greeted Josefa with a shy half smile, offered her a seat, lifted her eyes in Josefa's direction before taking her place at her desk.

"Frau Hoffman, Hans has been rather unhappy, mainly because Fräulein Müller has not been at school recently. I'm wondering if this is temporary or permanent. He also told me that Father Theodore doesn't come to hold morning prayers anymore. I was rather shocked to hear that. I'd just like to know what the situation is."

"I understand your concern, Frau Birk," she said fixing her kind pale blue eyes on Josefa's face. There was a moment of hesitation before she continued. "Fräulein Müller will not be returning. It became necessary for her to leave her post." Frau Hoffman paused again, her eyes now fixed on the floor as if she were choosing her words carefully. At this point, she began to

111

speak so quietly that Josefa found it almost necessary to lipread.

"When Father Theodore was advised to refrain from holding morning prayers, or indeed giving anymore religious guidance and instruction, Fräulein Müller refused to omit what she considered to be vital part of the children's education. She continued to say prayers and to encourage them to abide by Christ's teaching."

There was a pause when Frau Hoffman fidgeted in her chair, looked downwards and held her chin in her hand. Josefa felt sure this was an effort to conceal her moistening eyes. She looked up again. "A new member of staff reported her to the Reich Education Ministry and she was forced to resign. Sadly, in consequence, my staff now avoid the common room where they've always happily socialised."

Josefa listened intently, astounded by what she had heard and reluctant to interrupt.

"We are fortunate that we are not a denomination school. Father Theodore has told me that parents who send their children to church schools have been accused of being state enemies. I understand a protest has been made directly to the Führer by one of the cardinals about this." Josefa looked dazed.

"Thank you for explaining everything to me, Frau Hoffman. I just hope Hans will settle down with his new teacher. I know he's looking forward to his brother joining him next year."

"I'm afraid I shan't be here then, Frau Birk. I shall be retiring at the end of the summer."

"Oh, I'm very sorry to hear that. Who will be your successor?"

"I don't know yet. There have been changes there, too. Normally, the new head would be appointed from outside."

Before Josefa could utter another word in response, Frau Hoffman stood up, pushed back her chair and moved towards the door. Turning around, she said with an awkward smile, trying to disguise her uneasiness, "I would like to assure you, Frau Birk, that I personally will keep an eye on Hans."

Still, with many unanswered questions, Josefa took her leave, expressing regrets and gratitude. She did not wish to probe Frau Hoffman any further about matters which were obviously embarrassing and emotional for her.

Later that day, when they were alone together, she related to Johann the content of the conversation she has had with Frau Hoffman. He sighed and shook his head.

"I read in the paper today that some schools have had to remove their crucifixes. Many elementary schools have unfilled posts." After a moment's thought, he added, "I think teachers are becoming disillusioned. Let's hope our school can manage to get staff."

"Well, they can't stop us celebrating Christmas and influencing our children as we—" Before she could finish her sentence, an agonising expression crossed Josefa's face. Johann stared at her for a few seconds. Without another word, they knew both their minds had reverted back to Aga's warning. The year progressed and there were excited reports on the radio and in magazines about the forthcoming Winter Olympics which were to be held in Garmisch-Partenkirchen. They would commence in the new year of 1936 on February 6th. One day, shortly before the opening, when Hans was at school, baby Rudolf was asleep and the two other brothers were at their grandparents, Josefa switched on the radio. She listened to the following announcement whilst she was waiting for lunch orders.

"In just a few days, Adolf Hitler will be making his way to Bavaria to open the Winter Olympics. Our Führer, who comes from a humble background, has retained the common touch and encourages simple folk to achieve. He is particularly an admirer of excellence in sports and the arts, to which he has always given his support and shown a great interest.

"Ja, ja, ja. Let's have some music."

"Who are you talking to?" asked Johann appearing with an order for Wienerle sausages. "We're going to be busy, Jo. So there's no time to have a conversation with yourself," he chuckled. "I'll be back again in a tick."

In the Stube, the farmers had returned from the market and the regulars' table was fully occupied.

"Whew! There's a hell of a lot of traffic heading for Garmisch," said Gustav, eagerly awaiting his tankard of beer.

"The market was busy, too," said Volkmar. He took a good gulp of beer before continuing to tuck into a large portion of potato salad, sauerkraut and bratwurst. With his mouth full, he added, "God knows we've waited long enough for it to perk up."

"Well, if they wanted us to produce more food, they knew they bloody well had to give us a bit of help," Heini pointed out emphatically as he impatiently looked for his refill of beer to arrive.

"Yep, and cheap loans for machinery was a good start, but the incentives to grow crops hasn't really helped us in the south though, has it?" questioned Dieter.

"A friend of mine told me he's going in for flax. He says the price of fertilisers has really tumbled," replied Gustav already raising his tankard for a refill.

"Of course, the problem now is to get anyone to work for yer. The youngsters are called up for national service, now that it's compulsory, the ship yards are busy, new cars are being churned out and all these new roads are being built," complained Volkmar as he wiped his mouth and pushed his empty plate aside.

Johann was smiling. He was glad the gang was back again and faring better, but, of course, they always had something to moan about. He noticed they were much more relaxed. Their loud raucous voices were almost back to their former decibel level, accompanied by thumping on the table to emphasise a point of view. This, he realised, was due to the Stube being packed to capacity with winter sports enthusiasts, whose excited chatter minimised the risk of being overheard.

Four days after opening of the winter sports, those who were not caught up in the Olympic frenzy were probably the first to realise the seriousness of a new law that was passed. The Gestapo were taken out of the jurisdiction of the courts and could not be held to account for their actions. There could be no appeal.

About a month later, the children were playing outside in the spring sunshine. Josefa and Johann were just finishing their breakfast when Johann picked up the newspaper.

"That's interesting," he mused.

"What is?" asked Josefa.

"An English minister is being entertained by Adolf at his Berchtesgaden pad."

"What's his family name?"

"Lloyd."

"And his first name?"

"George." At that moment, Hans came rushing in.

"Papa, can you help me find my ball please. It's gone into the barn."

"I've just finished my breakfast and I've got some important writing to do. I'll come out later."

"Ooooh," moaned Hans. "How long? What sort of writing?"

"I have to fill in a form all about our family."

"What sort of things, Papa?

"What colour hair we have, what colour our eyes are, which church we go to and where your Opa and Oma used to live. All sorts of things. Now run along and I'll come when I've finished."

`"Who wants to know all this, Papa?"

"A man called Heinrich Himmler."

"Who's he?"

"He is a very important policeman." Hans turned on his heel and ran out of the room, his curiosity satisfied, but his face expressing confusion.

Johann put the completed form into the desk drawer and went out to the yard. He found Josefa plucking a duck. A large sack was at her side in which she stored the fine down until she had collected enough to fill a duvet. The lighter feathers that escaped in the breeze flew about like bubbles, delighting the children.

"Has Hans found his ball, Jo?"

"I don't know. He's gone off with the neighbour's children to the Hitler Youth Sports Centre. I must say, they do provide a lot of exciting activities for the youngsters. Hans is a bit too young yet though."

"He used to like to go the church's sport club, didn't he?" said Johann holding out the sack for her.

"Yeah, pity it had to close down. Hanni, you'd better go and help Lisa. It looks like it's getting busy. I must get back in the kitchen."

115

Johann found a family in the Biergarten waiting to be served. The couple had three children. Two boys, around ten and eight years, and a younger girl. Johann took their order for drinks and Käsespätzle. The family were unanimous in their decision to try Josefa's homemade pasta topped with grated Emmentaler cheese and crispy fried onions. It was whilst Johann was clearing their plates and accepting their compliments to be conveyed to his wife that he saw Hans returning. He waved to his father as he walked by with the neighbour's two boys who were dressed in the Hitler Youth uniform.

"Are they all your children?" the mother asked.

"No, just the small one," replied Johann, "but I've got three younger boys." The woman glanced at her husband and then cast her eyes downwards before continuing.

"It will be a few years before they will be all in uniform then," she remarked.

"Well, that's if they want to," was Johann's reply. Then reassuring herself that the only two couples sitting on the far side were well out of earshot, she stood up and took Johann aside.

"Just a word of warning. Don't discourage them from joining the Hitler Youth. Our older boy didn't want to go their meetings. We were accused of deterring him from going against his wishes and we were threatened with arrest."

The woman looked around anxiously, her voice, now emanating through a thin line between her lips, was barely audible. "Someone we know up north refused to let her boy go on weekend camps and she was told that if she persisted, the boy would be taken from her."

Johann felt his muscles tighten. He just stared at the woman, momentarily stunned.

"May we have the bill please?" The husband's request jolted Johann into action.

"Of course. I'll get it for you."

He disappeared inside. Later that evening, he related the conversation to Josefa, who listened with a look of fearful apprehension.

The summer's intense daytime heat had turned into a very warm evening. Lisa and a part-time helper were serving in a full-to-capacity Biergarten. Johann stayed in the Stube dispensing drinks. The farmers were the only ones who preferred to be inside, having spent the whole day out of doors. It was fortunate that they were alone, as the excessive heat had given them an insatiable thirst for beer, which loosened their tongues and they spoke more freely.

"The Catholic Church is taking a bashing, ain't it?" said Gustav, his voice already slurred. "The clergy 'ad better look out, Himmler's really got his knife in them."

"Clamping down on the Catholic Church won't make him very popular here, that's for sure," responded Dieter. He raised his eyes slowly and a suggestion of a grin crossed his face as he added, "I can't imagine there could be a whiff of scandal around Father Theodor."

"You're right, but he'd better look out though. He's so anti-Nazi, he absolutely refused to give the salute. Don't blame him." Volkmar paused to take a few more gulps of his lager.

"Did yer 'ear Wolfgang 'as got two extra helpers?" Asked Heini as he wiped beer froth from his mouth with his sleeve.

"Yeah, he says they work OK. Poor blighters. They seem to 'ave been knocked about a bit. They don't say a word though cos they know they'd be straight back in Dachau," said Gustav picking up yet another full tankard.

"What are they in there for? Are they Jews?" asked Dieter.

"One is, I think. The other's a commi or maybe a Gypsy," said Heini.

"I've 'eared they'll only let them out to clear land like moorland for cultivation."

"I could do with some help now that Peter's working on the motorway, but he's expecting to be called up any time," Volkmar said with a sigh.

"I'm missing my boys, too," said Dieter. "I never thought I'd see all three in uniform. One in the Luftwaffe, one has got his marching orders for the army and the youngest in the Hitler Youth. I'm not very happy about him," he grimaced, "but he loves going, especially as they're let off from school to go on outings. He enjoys the camping weekends, too, with lots of sport and singing, I think it makes him feel important being in uniform, like his brothers."

"A customer told me you can find yourself in trouble if you stop your kids joining," butted in Johann, who had been listening from behind the bar.

"Yes, I've heard that, too, and it's almost impossible to get an apprenticeship if you're not a member," replied Dieter.

"I met Frau Zimmerman the other day," said Heini raising his hand to settle up. "I was told someone grassed on her for giving food to a Jew. She had a visit and a warning from the SS." He paid Lisa and stood up. "Come on, Pa, let's get you home."

"What sort of country are we living in?" pondered Dieter when they had left. "We don't trust anyone. We live in fear of informers, making a wrong move and getting arrested. Our freedom's become eroded." The others nodded in agreement. They had a lot of respect for Dieter, who was not afraid to express what they all felt.

"We can't even rely on the Church. Every day on the radio, there are reports of corruption, fraud, sexual abuse and homosexuality. The lot! All trumped up charges, of course, I suspect." Dieter's eyes were focused straight ahead as he spoke, but the others instinctively looked about anxiously.

"There's one bit of good news," chirped in Johann.

"What's that?" they asked in unison.

"Unemployment's down to below a million."

"That reminds me. I've got to work tomorrow. Time to pay my dues, Hanni," said Dieter as he moved towards the bar. "Good night all." The others soon followed suit.

Chapter 14

With Rudolf in his push chair and Erich and Sepp in tow, Josefa made her way to the school. Usually, Hans came home on his own, but today was the last day of the summer term and she wanted to wish Frau Hoffman a happy retirement. Excitedly, the children poured out of the school building and into the brilliant sunshine. Josefa waited until they had all nearly dispersed before going inside. Frau Hoffman was just leaving her office. Josefa wished her well and expressed her disappointment that she would not be there when Erich started in autumn. Unlike her usual jovial self, Frau Hoffman looked sad and serious. She retreated to her desk for a moment, scribbled something on a notepad and came towards Josefa with an outstretched hand. As she clasped it, she could feel something pressed into her palm.

"Thank you for coming, Frau Birk, and for your good wishes. I hope all your boys will be happy here in future."

Josefa clenched the hand firmly until they were at home again. She opened up the crumpled piece of paper and read the message. "Be careful. Informers have been planted in the school. Please destroy this note."

Now three months had passed since Frau Hoffman had handed the note of warning to Josefa. Johann had read it and straight away burnt it in the stove. They agreed then that they would never again discuss politics or current affairs when the children were present.

Hans and Erich had just left for school and Josefa was taking the opportunity to relax with another cup of coffee, whilst the two younger boys were happily occupied.

"What was their reaction when you told them?" enquired Johann, peering above the newspaper.

"They said they hoped he would like playing football."

"They don't even consider it might be a girl then," chuckled Johann.

"Apparently not," Josefa grinned. "Did you know our four boys are known as the Engel boys?"

"Angels! They're more like little devils," he replied. "But we can't change Gasthof Engel to Gasthof Teufel, can we?"

They both smiled at the suggestion. Taking a quick glance at the clock, Johann stood up hurriedly. "I must go and stock up the bar now, then I'll go and get the cheese. We may get some pilots in. It's really busy, busy over at the airfield."

Later that morning, when Johann was returning with the cheese, he became fascinated by the activity above him. Walking with his head tilted back, gazing at the light aircraft buzzing about like bees, he almost collided with someone.

"Good morning, Herr Birk."

"Oh, good morning, Father Theodor. I'm sorry, I wasn't looking where I was going."

"How are your boys? Erich started school this term, didn't he?"

"Yes, he did, he hasn't told us much about it yet though."

"I miss seeing the children at the school and the sports club," commented the priest; suddenly, he became fearful and leant his face nearer to Johann's ear. "It's been a difficult time," he whispered, looking around. He hesitated for a few moments before continuing. "There have been many false accusations made against priests and harsh sentences handed out, which you may have heard about."

"Yes, Father, I have. It's terrible."

Father Theodore shuffled a little nearer and lowered his voice even more.

"I think the church is being infiltrated by those", he hesitated again, "who oppose it." He looked around once more. "I feel as if I'm being observed all the time." For a moment, their eyes locked in mutual understanding.

"Please convey my best wishes to Frau Birk," he said in his normal voice.

"No doubt I shall see her on Sunday." With his eyes cast downwards, he hurried away in the direction of the vicarage.

Johann put the cheese in the larder as Josefa came in through the back door, having hung out a washing line of boys' clothes.

"I've just met Father Theodor, Jo. He sends his best to you."

"How is he?"

"He looks so drawn and pale, I had quite a shock when I saw him. He's lost weight and looks older."

"I'm usually the last to get to the service on Sundays, so I'm always right at the back. Then I have to rush home afterwards, so I don't get much chance to speak to him," said Jo putting her laundry basket down and hanging up the peg bag.

"His sermons have been sort of different lately. More like urging us to stand firm, support each other and to believe in the Catholic Church." Placing a large saucepan on the stove, she added, "Well, we wouldn't be in the church if we didn't, would we?"

Johann nodded in agreement. "I can hear Volkmar's voice. He must have just come in," he said heading for the Stube.

"Only popped in for a quick one, Hanni," said Volkmar taking a swig of his beer. "Got to get back to those gormless gits. They're too young, too weak and haven't got a clue."

"What yer mean? Who are you talking about?" asked Johann.

"The authorities that have drafted youngsters on the land. Admittedly, there's a dire shortage of labour on farms, but most of them are useless. They've been trained to march like soldiers, sing patriotic songs and keep their pitchforks gleaming."

Volkmar emptied his tankard and grabbed his hat. "But that isn't much good when you have to muck out pig sties and milk cows, is it, Hanni?" Johann just shrugged and shook his head. "We'll all be in later, Hanni, and no doubt, we'll be comparing our new farmhands. Bye for now."

The trade at the Gasthof remained steady and showed an increase during the following months and into the new year of 1937. Josefa's pregnancy was now advanced and Dora came regularly to check up on her. Aga helped with the children, but it was clear they needed to employ a child minder.

One day, when he was walking towards the Gasthof, Leonhard saw his grandsons returning from school.

"Hello, boys," he called out cheerfully. Then, as he got closer to them, he noticed a graze on the side of Hans' face.

"What have you been up to then? Been in a scrap, eh?"

Hans looked down at his feet, but Erich looked up to his grandfather.

"Opa, what's a Jew?" he asked with a furrowed brow.

"What you want to know for?" Leonhard replied gingerly.

"Some of the boys called Hans' friend Paul a dirty Jew and punched him and they said Hans shouldn't be friendly with a Jew." Leonhard looked alarmed. He didn't know what to say. He was saved from explaining by an acquaintance calling him a few yards away.

"I'll see you in a few minutes, boys," he said hurriedly, relieved to have the excuse to move away at that moment. By the time he had caught up with them at home, they were engrossed in playing games and the question had been forgotten.

With the arrival of spring, Dora was summoned to the Gasthof, where she delivered yet another boy, Gerhard. His four brothers took a quick look at him. Then the two older ones decided it would be some time before he could play football with them and ran off to join friends outside, closely followed by Sepp. Only toddler Rudolf remained with his father for a longer inspection of the new family member.

"It's nice for some to have a rest up here in the bedroom whilst we slave away downstairs," joked Johann a couple of days later.

"I know how to swing it," replied Josefa with a giggle. "Seriously, how busy are you?"

"I'm not telling you. You'd only worry."

"Oh, come on. I'd only worry more if you don't tell me."

"All right. Suffice to say we're coping quite well. Your papa's been telling me there's a huge increase in investment and industry's doing fine, so I suppose that's what's helped to boost our trade. Anyway, you'll be up and about when we start catering for the pilots. Must go." With a peck on Josefa's cheek and a gentle rock of the cradle, Johann left and went downstairs.

It was a beautiful summer's day when Josefa put baby Gerhard outside in his pram. Rudi and Sepp were at their grandparents'. She switched on the radio and was relieved to hear some cheerful music. It was a welcome change from the surfeit of propaganda she had endured on the radio during her confinement. She set about preparing the variety of salads to accompany her homemade meatloaf which was called Leberkäse. It was the day of baby Gerhard's christening and close family members were coming to lunch afterwards. The Gasthof would be closed for this Sunday afternoon and a few close friends had been invited to join them later for torten and coffee. Johann popped his head around the kitchen door.

"Everything OK, Jo?" She smiled and nodded. At that moment, the music was interrupted by an announcement.

"NOW FOLLOWS A BROADCAST BY HERR GOEBELS."

Josefa turned her head towards the radio and Johann walked slowly into the kitchen. They both stood in silence, listening intently, their eyes fixed on the apparatus from which an intense onslaught against the Catholic Church and its organisations poured forth. They had never before heard such venomous criticisms against their faith, which included claims that their souls were being poisoned by their church leaders and local priests. The radio was turned off.

"I must go and get myself and the boys ready now," said Josefa resolutely. "We mustn't be late for the service."

The three brothers looked smart as they followed their parents. Josefa pushed Gerhard in his pram, with Johann by her side holding Rudolf's hand. They had only walked a few yards when a column of Hitler Girls (BDM) marched towards them along the main street. All were in uniform, holding heads high and with their eyes focused straight ahead. When they had passed, the family crossed the road. It was then that they could see Hermann, the mayor. He was speaking to a large gathering of Hitler Youth boys in the village centre. With a semi smile, he nodded sheepishly in their direction and then continued to captivate his audience.

A few days later, Johann dashed through to the kitchen sink to swill out the beer spillage container. Josefa was frantically kneading and punching the dough. She glanced at the time.

"The hands on that clock whiz around like blades of a windmill in high winds. The boys will be back soon. They just have to wait for their lunch. The Spätzle are not ready yet."

She let out a long frustrated sigh.

"Don't worry, Jo. That lot from the airfield aren't in yet. It's filling up though." His voice trailed off as he raced back to the Stube. Trade had been very brisk of late, evidently, the result of unemployment dropping to below a million. The whole country seemed to be active and mobilised, bringing about a feeling of burgeoning prosperity. Since the completion of the airfield, the Gasthof had secured the custom of the training personnel who were already installed and waiting for the arrival of the young pilots. The increase in their income enabled Josefa to employ a young girl Emma to help with the children and for Johann to take on a young lad David to assist Felix, the herdsman, and to help generally, mainly outside. David Kuhn was from Berlin. His father had been brutally arrested in the middle of the night, for a reason unknown to David, apart from being a Jew. His distraught mother, now the sole bread winner, persuaded her son to go to stay with his grandparents who lived in the south, not far from the Gasthof.

The tone of the boys' voices, as they returned from school, prompted Josefa to look up. Hans was frowning.

"What's the matter? Hungry?" she asked.

"My new teacher's nasty, Mama. I don't like her."

"He got smacked," chirped in Erich, with a suggestion of a grin spreading across his face. "He didn't put his arm up to say Heil Hitler." Josefa's face took on a worried frown, but she said nothing.

"I know we've got to salute at the Hitler Youth, but I didn't know I had to at school. I wasn't watching. I picked up my pen from the floor," grumbled Hans.

"You'd better do what you're told, Hans, and watch the others. Now wash your hands and sit down for lunch. Your favourite today," said Josefa cheerfully in an endeavour to lift his spirits. Johann popped in at that moment and pinned an order on the board.

"Hello, boys."

"Papa, I was—"

"Can't stop now. Tell me later." Turning towards Jo, he continued in a lower tone. "Strange things happening out in the road."

"What sort of things?"

"The lamp posts are being taken down."

"What on earth for?"

"Smelting. They are going to be replaced by wooden ones."

"Why?"

"Cos the metal's needed."

Josefa just shrugged her shoulders. She had enough to think about. She didn't manage to get further than the clothes line these days. With five boys, ages ranging from four months to eight years, there was always plenty of washing.

It was on the following Sunday, however, when she went to church, that she saw the wrought iron gates leading into the graveyard had also been removed.

"My protests", the priest told his mystified congregation, "resulted in my being pushed to the ground by the uniformed SA thugs. I was threatened with arrest if I persisted in harassing them." This statement was met with sympathetic murmurs from the horrified parishioners. As she walked back home after the service, Josefa kept wondering why there was this sudden desperate need for metal.

About a week later, she was surprised to see three teenage boys climbing up the cellar stairs. They were all dressed in Hitler Youth uniform.

"What have you been doing down there?" she asked sternly.

"If you are looking for toilets, they're at the end of the corridor." Then she noticed they were holding a poker, a shovel, some metal hooks and the brass fittings from an old window frame.

"What are you doing with those?" she asked, her dulcet voice rose to its limit. At that moment, one of them dropped a bunch of keys.

"Where did you get those keys?" her voice was now bordering on the hysterical.

"Your boy gave them to us," was the reply. Josefa became very agitated. At that moment, Hans' head appeared at the top of the cellar stairs.

"Did you give them these keys, Hans? Where did they come from?"

"I found them in a drawer, Mama. They're old and rusty. I didn't think you needed them anymore."

"We were told at the last Hitler Youth meeting to collect metal and search cellars for old radiators, tin plate and things," said one of the teenagers. Josefa was shaking with anger as Johann came out of the Stube.

"What the hell's all this noise about?" he asked abruptly. "You're lucky it's being drowned by the din in there," he said pointing to the Stube.

Josefa could hear the baby screaming and promptly left Johann to cope with the situation.

That evening, when the last customer had departed, Josefa and Johann sat and drank a glass of wine together and discussed the cellar episode. Johann explained that he had dealt leniently with Hans because he felt that he had been intimidated by the older boys. "We'll draw a line under it," he said wearily. "I don't think Hans would try it again."

To divert from the subject, Johann began to tell Josefa about what he had heard in the Stube that day.

"Volkmar says the farmers are becoming desperate. There's a dire shortage of farm-hands. The factories are gobbling up most of the workforce and the Arbeitsdienst youngsters, the farmers were provided with, are leaving to join the army." He emptied his glass. "Dieter says the police have been rounding up tramps and beggars in the town today and he thinks perhaps they should put them to work on the land, instead of locking them up." Johann yawned. Looking at Josefa's half-closed eyes, he stood up and said, "Come on, Jo, let's get some sleep now."

Two months later, in September, Hans and Erich had just set off for school, Sepp and Rudi were playing and Gerhard was asleep in his cot. Josefa joined Johann at the breakfast table, where he held out a piece of paper in a shaking hand.

"What's the matter, Hanni? You look as if you've had a shock."

"I have. This is a notice ordering Aryan employers to dismiss all Jews. It says it's on record that I have an employee from Berlin with Jewish parentage." They both stared at each other for a few moments, both with similar thoughts. How could they do this to David? He had been working so hard and conscientiously. How were they going to tell him? Always very subdued and quiet, they knew he was constantly worried about his mother and he missed his father terribly. What would he do? Would he try to find a Jewish employer, go back to his mother or stay with his grandparents?

It was a great relief to them both that, although visibly very disappointed, David's submissive acceptance of the news was proof of his anxiety about his mother. He felt, in his father's absence, he should be with her.

After David's departure, they tried to cope without a replacement, but when Klaus Schulz, a young boy from the village, knocked on the kitchen door a month before Christmas, they gave him a job.

"Please give me some work, Herr Birk," the boy pleaded. "The long-term unemployed are being rounded up. I haven't been able to work for a bit and they're checking records at the labour exchanges." He stopped to take a deep breath. "Some of my mates have been called up for Arbeitsdienst and sent to training camps, but I'm not old enough yet."

At first, Johann hesitated because of his age, but with the proviso that if he didn't pull his weight, he would have to leave, it was arranged for him to start the following week. This allowed Johann enough time to check the boy's family, fearing that if he fell afoul of the law again, he would have a visit from the SS.

One morning, just ten days before Christmas, Josefa was busy in the kitchen making Christmas biscuits. She had been very upset to learn that the school had decided not to have a nativity play that year. Switching on the radio, she hoped to hear some carols, but there again she was disappointed. There was an announcement, however, of a decree that had just been issued, which allowed for the arrest of the following: Gypsies, prostitutes, pimps, tramps, vagrants, beggars, hooligans, long-term unemployed or anyone else with an anti-social attitude. By

Himmler's orders. They would be detained in a camp at Dachau.

Chapter 15

Leonhard and Agathe celebrated Christmas and the 'slide' into the year 1938 with Johann, Josefa and the boys. Several incidents during the period prior to this had left the adults with a feeling of uneasiness, which they had tried to conceal from the children.

Just few weeks earlier, Hans brought home a half-burnt book which he had found behind a bush. An unbefitting end to possibly years of work by a Jewish author. They had also received a letter from David in Berlin in which he had told them that his mother had been in a state of hysteria recently when she had visited the cemetery and found his paternal grandparents' grave desecrated. The following week, Johann had overheard in the Stube that Isaac and Jacob's family home had been confiscated and had been given to an Aryan family. On hearing this, Johann had to muster all his self-control to conceal his anger. He knew, that if reported, any protest against an injustice towards Jews would be a punishable offence.

Now with the Gasthof's doors firmly closed and the children in bed, they were able to speak more freely.

"We're finding ourselves in a situation," said Leonhard pensively, "that in order to survive, we have to hear nothing, see nothing and speak nothing. Just like the three monkeys."

He let out a long sigh before taking another sip of wine. "Anti-Semitism is spreading like poison in a festering wound."

"With seven mouths to feed, Papa, we must be grateful that our business is doing well," said Josefa patting her father gently on his back.

"I thought the airfield was to be for private planes and leisure flying. They're military pilots training for combat," said Leonhard forcefully.

"There's nothing we can do about that, Papa. They are nice young chaps and there's no risk of us not being paid." The bottle was empty and Leonhard's voice had become slurred.

"Like every other family, the surest way to avert harm coming to us is not to question anything, give an opinion or—" He could not manage to finish the sentence. He laid his arms on the table, rested his head on them and closed his eyes. This brought the conversation to an end and it was not long before Johann was accompanying his parents-in-law homewards.

The mountain peaks were still covered with a plentiful layer of snow, even after Gerhard had celebrated his first birthday in March. The rays of weak sunshine did not provide enough warmth for the boys to want to play outside, and so they amused themselves in the Büro. Gerhard was having an afternoon nap and Josefa took the opportunity to have a rest. Johann went into the Stube to have a chat with Heini, Bertl and Volkmar. The farmers were much more relaxed these days now that the labour shortage on the land had been solved by releasing some of the detainees from the prison camp at Dachau to help them.

"They work like blazes or as well as they're able," said Volkmar lighting up a Virginia which he'd just accepted from Heini. "There's certainly no time wasted through chatting. They just don't say a word." He blew out a trail of smoke.

"They're too scared. They'd be taken back inside again, I 'spect," said Bertl. "I 'eard the Gestapo are rounding up all the work-shy, too. The camp must be getting pretty crowded."

"Yep," confirmed Volkmar. "They look as if they've been knocked about a bit, poor blighters," he shifted uneasily in his seat, before adding, "but they woof down my wife's cooking as if there's no tomorrow."

"Which is probably the case, poor souls," said Heini. Johann took advantage of the momentary pause in the conversation.

"The next round of drinks is on me now. I've got a bit of news."

"Don't tell us you're expecting another," chuckled Heini.

"We sure are," replied Johann, "in the autumn. Jo's determined to have a little girl to replace the one we lost. She spent a couple of hours in town yesterday just looking at baby

130

girl clothes. She said the shop she used to go to has closed down."

Without saying, they all knew this must be the large Jewish-owned children's wear store in the centre of the town. Johann indicated to Lisa to bring another round of drinks. "Jo said", he went on, "that there were colonnades of troops marching through town, causing chaos."

"There's certainly something up. The amount of traffic through this village has become intolerable," complained Dieter, who had just joined them. "Armoured cars and troops everywhere. All heading south."

"Not only on the roads either. There were many light aircraft up above a couple of days ago. They looked like a swarm of flies. What's going on?" Heini's eyes scoured their faces, but he got no answer.

"Don't the pilots tell you anything, Hanni?" asked Dieter.

"No, nothing at all."

"Did yer 'ear about ole Fritz over at Lindenberg?" asked Heini as he stubbed out his Virginia. "As if life ain't 'ard enough for him," his voice had dropped to a whisper, "now he's been threatened with 'aving his winter aid withdrawn cos he's been using a Jewish dealer to buy and sell his livestock. Can you believe that?" He thumped the table just hard enough not to draw attention.

"I heard he was 'aving a hard time, too," said Volkmar, his voice adopting a similar, low, quiet tone.

"His two teenage sons have been collared for Arbeitsdienst, he told me," butted in Heini. "It's bloody tough in those training camps. They wear military uniform, but instead of rifles, they carry spades over their shoulders when on parade." Heini paused and took a gulp of beer, giving Volkmar the opportunity to carry on.

"I know, and they have to keep the blades so sparkling, that they can use it for a mirror when they shave."

As they were grinning at the thought, there was suddenly a loud rumbling sound which got them scrambling to their feet and rushing towards the window. Four excited little boys came charging through the Stube and joined them, standing on the window seat to get a better view. Little Gerhard, having completed a marathon crawl, tried unsuccessfully to climb up beside them. A cavalcade of army Lorries filled with military personnel was racing through the village. Josefa came looking for the boys, just as the regulars were disappearing through the door, heading for home. She rounded the boys up and they followed her back to the Büro.

"What have you been playing at? Just look at this floor. It's covered with bits of paper. Clear it up at once, boys; otherwise, it's early to bed!"

"Mama, Erich and I made some planes out of an old cardboard box," explained Hans. "I asked one of the pilots yesterday what he'd been doing and he told me he'd been dropping pieces of paper out of his plane." Josefa looked puzzled as she fixed her eyes on her eldest son's face.

"We were only copying them, Mama," protested Hans. "Sepp and Rudi tore up the paper for us."

Without further comment, Josefa returned to the kitchen. The following day, they learnt that Austria had become annexed to Nazi Germany and Adolf Hitler was on his way to Vienna. They also learnt that the 'pieces of paper' released from the planes had been propaganda leaflets.

Out of all the seven pregnancies, this one seemed to be the longest. The onset of the summer's heat sapped Josefa's energy and she was glad of a village woman's help in the kitchen. One afternoon, she was sitting outside watching the sheets on the washing line swaying in the light breeze. A woman approached her, whom she recognised as Luggi's neighbour. She drew quite close to Jo, then whispered,

"Frau Birk, I have some bad news. Luggi died last night." Josefa gasped with a look of horror.

The woman glanced around and took up Josefa's offer of a seat beside her before continuing.

"I'm not sure how the news reached him, but he heard that his brother's shop in Vienna had been ransacked. When his brother tried to stop the looting, he was beaten up and arrested." She looked around again before continuing, "Luggi knocked on my door late in the evening. He was devastated by the news." She fumbled in her bag for a handkerchief. "I have known him for a long time, but since his release from Dachau, he has been consumed by fear and has been very mistrustful. He didn't share his thoughts, even with me."

"Who found him?" asked Josefa, her voice quavering.

"When I took some food this morning, I could see him through the window on the floor. I believe he'd just given up and couldn't take it anymore. He was so fond of his brother." Like raindrops on a window pane, tears trickled down Josefa's cheeks. The woman, overcome with emotion, gave Josefa's hand a gentle squeeze, got up and left.

News of such a tragedy would have spread rapidly around the village before the Nazis came to power, but now anyone who heard about it, would be reluctant to pass it on. After a couple of days, however, Josefa felt compelled to go to tell her neighbour. It would be an opportunity, also, to enquire about her husband's health. He had not been well at all lately.

"Is your husband feeling better?" Josefa asked as she sipped a cup of coffee in her neighbour's kitchen.

"Yes thank you, although we have had a spot of trouble getting a diagnosis. We had to find another doctor. When we went to our usual Dr Rosenbaum's surgery, we were told that he could no longer treat us. There was a large notice on the door of his surgery, saying:

MR ROSENBAUM WILL BE TREATING JEWISH PATIENTS ONLY IN FUTURE. HE WILL NO LONGER USE THE TITLE 'DOCTOR'."

The two women stared at each other for a few moments, then Josefa dropped her gaze, biting her lower lip. Her emotions surfaced very easily during her pregnancies and once again there was cause to shed a tear. Dr Rosenbaum was a customer of theirs, a highly respected and well-liked member of the community.

At the beginning of September, the three words, "it's a girl", released a flood of joyful tears. Blinking to clear her vision, Josefa gazed down at the small bundle which Dora had carefully laid down on the bed beside her.

"I'm going to call her Helga, just like our first little girl," she told the smiling midwife as she gently stroked the baby's head.

It was not long before five little pairs of eyes were staring in wonder at the doll-like figure their mother was cuddling.

Johann, holding Gerhard in his arms, was beaming, relief and happiness etched across his face.

"Come on, boys, we must leave our girls in peace now. Emma's got tea-time ready for you lot."

When they were alone again, Dora put the baby back in the cot and sat down on the side of the bed.

"I would like you to have seen Dr Goldberg, Frau Birk, just to check everything is OK, but I've heard he's no longer there."

"Oh, what a pity. He's such a lovely man, with all the best human qualities."

"It will be a hard task for them to find someone as well qualified as he is," said Dora getting up.

"Like Dr Rosenbaum, I expect it's because he's a Jew," said Josefa thoughtfully. "Oh, Dora, what's happening?"

The midwife just shook her head, sighed and began to pack her small hold-all. After a short pause, she said, "Well, when you feel stronger, in a couple of days or so, perhaps your husband could bring you to the out-patient surgery."

Josefa nodded. As Dora was about to leave, she turned towards her patient. With a grin and twinkle in her eyes, she said, "I've brought all seven of your babies into this world, Frau Birk. I wonder if you will ever need my services again." Josefa replied with a peal of laughter and shaking her head vigorously.

One afternoon, when Helga was just five days old, Josefa was taking the advice of the new gynaecologist and having a regular afternoon rest. She was listening to the radio when her father arrived.

"Just popped in to see my new grandchild," he said excitedly. "I have to report back to your mother. She can't manage to come today."

As Josefa leant over to turn the radio off, she felt her father's hand restraining her.

"Wait a minute, Jo. What's that he's saying? Herr Hitler reviewing 100,000 troops in Nürnberg! God forbid, that sounds like sabre rattling to me. He's not preparing for war, I hope. The pompous little upstart from Braunau!"

Josefa looked anxious and Leonhard regretted that he may have worried her.

"I've been listening to the BBC on my radio," he said in a quieter tone. "There was a report this morning that the British Minister Neville Chamberlain is coming to visit Hitler later this month. Perhaps he can knock some sense into him."

Suddenly, Hans and Erich appeared, having heard their grandfather's voice. They rushed in to see him. They were both wearing their HY uniforms.

"Hello, boys."

"Hello, Opa. We're going to come to see you and Oma later. We want you to teach us to play cards so that we can play with the pilots."

"I'd love to teach you," replied Leonhard smiling. Then looking sternly at them, he added, "but I do not want to see you in my house in those uniforms."

They looked startled, then they both replied meekly, "All right, Opa."

"Ernst's papa won't let him wear the uniform either or come to the meetings," Hans blurted out. "Ernst said his papa had a visit from the police and it made his papa very worried and nervous afterwards." At that moment, the two younger boys appeared.

"Emma says you've got to come and finish your Brotzeit, Hans," said Sepp tugging at his arm. Hans swung around and gave him a hefty punch.

"Stop that, Hans, and go and do what Emma says," said Josefa crossly.

"We've been told at HY that we've got to be as tough as leather and as hard as Krupp steel. What does Krupp mean, Mama?" asked Hans.

Before Josefa could answer, they both ran out of the room, yelling, "And as swift as a greyhound."

"They're at a very impressionable age and ready to believe anything they're told," said Leonhard looking very concerned.

"That's the trouble, Papa." Josefa sighed deeply. "One of the teachers at school told them that the Führer is the most important person, even more important than their mother, father and families." She adjusted the baby's shawl, trying to conceal her moistening eyes.

"Don't worry about it too much, Jo," Leonhard whispered. "You concentrate on getting your strength back. I must go now. Your mother will be here tomorrow."

The brewery's lorry pulled into the Gasthof's yard to deliver the large quantity of beer Johann had ordered to satisfy the demands of the thirsty pilots.

"What's happened to Max?" he asked the unfamiliar driver as he jumped down from his cab.

"He had his driving licence taken away.

"What happened? Did he have an accident?" The man remained silent until he had unloaded and climbed back into the driver's seat. "Cos he's a Jew," was the brusque reply before he drove away.

Johann was stacking the shelves with beer bottles and was so deep in thought about what he had just heard, that he wasn't aware of Dieter approaching the bar.

"Any chance of a beer?" he asked looking down on Johann as he crouched to fill the lower shelves. "I've just been chatting to your competitor about the notice on his door."

"Who? Ole Albrecht at the Hirsch?" Johann stood up and poured out a beer.

"Yep, it's an Aryan-only Gasthof now. He doesn't serve Jews."

"Albrecht? He's always been a happy-go-lucky chap. Believes in live and let live. What's changed his mind?"

Dieter looked over his shoulder and around the Stube, making sure there was no one within earshot, before replying,

"He's not anti-Jews. He's done it for his own good. The other day, an old Jewish couple were having a drink there. Two SS came in and rough handled them before chucking them out. One of his regulars who tried to protect them got beaten up and was arrested. Another customer got caught up in the affray and was taken to hospital."

Johann looked horrified. "What happened to the old couple?" he asked.

"They got carted away by the SS."

On hearing this, Johann stared at Dieter with a tornado of thoughts in his mind. Could it happen to him? What should he do? Surely, the SS wouldn't cause trouble if his Luftwaffe clientele were around. He served some more customers, which temporarily took his mind off this disturbing piece of news. Then Dieter changed the subject.

"Have you got a new girl working in the kitchen?"

"Yes, called Emma. Jo needs someone to help her with the children, do the washing, etc. It's too much for her with the baby as well."

At that moment, Heini appeared and joined Dieter at the regulars' table. Heini's lips were moving, but there was no sound. Dieter nodded, obviously having understood. *We have such fear of being overheard,* thought Johann, *that we're all becoming accomplished lipreaders.* He looked at Dieter intently as Heini's lips delivered the next piece of news that Jewish lawyers were allowed to take Jewish clients only.

With the arrival of more customers, Dieter resumed the usual form of communication.

"The British Minister Neville Chamberlain has been back here again," he told Heini. "The Führer showed him around München. He must like it here."

"Who wouldn't?" mused Heini. "Adolf's got a nice little pad up in the mountains and a smart apartment in München."

A few weeks later, Dieter was sitting in the Stube, looking towards the window.

"Volkmar's a bit late today," he said. "Ah, there he is, just coming."

"Hello all. I'm gasping. A beer as quick as you can, please, Hanni," said Volkmar imitating a panting dog. After several gulps from his glass, he lapsed into such a quiet whisper that their lipreading skills were put into use again.

"Have you heard?"

The regulars around the table lowered their eyes and slowly nodded. They were already aware of the onslaught on Jewish places of worship. So many synagogues had been desecrated and streets were littered with so much glass that it had become known as the 'Night of Crystal Glass'.

"Read all about it! Read all about it! Sudeten welcome our troops," bellowed the newspaper vendor on the town's main high street as Leonhard walked by. On his return to the village, he headed briskly towards the Gasthof and searched for his son-in-law.

"Ah, there you are, Hanni. What did I tell you? He's up to—"

"Let's go in here," said Johann looking around nervously and ushering him swiftly into the Büro. He shut the door firmly behind them. He knew his father-in-law well enough to realise he was about to speak his political mind. He never resorted to lipreading or miming, which gave Johann constant cause for alarm. Leonhard's father had served in the last king's Bavaria's cavalry and had brought his children up with royalist ideals which clashed with the existing regime's.

"He's up to no good, I tell you. That bastard Hitler is preparing for war."

"But he's just signed a peace treaty with the British," retorted Johann, and, anyway, the Sudeten want to belong to Germany."

"So you think he'll stop there, do you? It's in the air. I can feel it." Leonhard clenched his hands to endorse his fears. "I had hoped never to see this country in combat again. It's only 20 years since—" Their conversation was interrupted by the boys rushing in.

"Papa, Opa, come and see the procession." They charged out again, leaving the door wide open. The two men followed them as the sound of lightweight leather on tarmac approached. They witnessed columns of young adolescents, boys and girls in uniform, shoulders back and heads held high, marching with pride.

"I can recognise some of them, don't you, Hanni? Look, there's Stefan's daughter and I can see Max's son. It makes you realise how much influence and control the Nazis have over our youngsters. This is like a prep-school for the armed forces. I'm just glad yours aren't older." Johann remained silent, but the anxious look in his eyes revealed his thoughts.

"Well, I'm off home now. Bye, boys."

"Bye, Opa," they called out in unison. Johann just looked at him with a weak worried smile.

Josefa found Emma to be a great help, especially with the child minding. Emma's fondness for the boys was reciprocated and having younger brothers herself, she knew how to cope with them, which was to be firm but to have fun. Her presence allowed Josefa to plan a visit to her sister, who was anxious to make the new baby's acquaintance.

Chapter 16

Helga was a few weeks old when Josefa boarded the bus with her for the hour long journey. The day passed very pleasantly, relaxing and catching up with family news. Ida had no children, so she was delighted to hold and amuse the baby. On the journey home, Helga slept soundly in her mother's arms, tired after all the attention she had received. It was already early evening when the bus weaved its way through the town along its route past the theatre. Josefa gazed out of the window and it was then that she witnessed a disturbing incident. A middle-aged couple, smartly dressed, were being pushed out so forcefully through the theatre doors, that they lost their balance and fell down two or three of the steps which led up to the main entrance. The woman's fox fur broke loose and slithered down more steps ahead of her, followed by one of her shoes. From the abusive tirade of their assailants, Josefa gathered that the couple were Jewish.

"Sit down and have a glass of wine, Jo," urged Johann later that evening when all the children were tucked up in bed. "I can see you're upset by what you saw today."

"Thanks," said Josefa as Johann placed a glass of red wine in front of her. "It did rather spoil my day." She took a few sips.

"What you saw today was probably caused by that Polish teenager shooting one of our diplomats in Paris. Remember? It has sparked off a lot of trouble for Jews. It's been in the news." Johann reached for the bottle and filled his glass again. "Thank God Jacob and Isaac got away when they did."

Josefa made no response. She just took a few more sips from her glass and stared at the table.

"By the way, Jo," continued Johann in an effort to change the subject, "we can expect more trade from the airfield.

140

Business is looking good." Josefa lifted her head, a weak smile on her lips.

"A new lot is arriving in a few days for a crash course."

In a flash, he realised he had chosen the wrong word. He paused and then, with a serious expression, looked into her eyes. "One, or our usual pilots won't be coming again. He misjudged his landing and clipped a tree." Johann dropped his gaze.

"Oh no! Which one? Not Werner?" Josefa asked with a look of anguish. Johann nodded.

"How will we tell them? He was their favourite. Hans and Erich loved kicking a ball around the yard with him."

"We'll just tell them that he had to go home," was the reply.

A few days later, a letter from David Kuhn in Berlin arrived. Johann opened it and read it out to Josefa. "My mother and I have experienced the most horrific time since the diplomat in Paris died of his wounds. Incited by the venomous propaganda on the radio and in the newspapers, excessive violence has broken out. It has escalated into an orgy of vandalism, looting and generally destroying anything belonging to someone with Jewish blood. In the city, the pavements are strewn with glass from shattered shop windows. Synagogues have been wrecked and cemeteries have had gravestones smashed and graves dug up. Jewish homes and businesses have been set ablaze."

"How terrible," said Josefa with her eyes fixed on Johann's agonised expression as he turned the page with a shaking hand and continued. "We are distraught with worry about my grandparents' safety. We would not trouble you otherwise, but we are desperate for news of them. We would come ourselves, but we have lost everything. Our apartment was set alight and when we called the fire brigade, we suffered the agony of seeing them parked outside our neighbour's house, doing nothing to help us. They were just watching that the fire did not spread to the Aryan family's home next door. We've had no assistance in clearing up the broken glass and charred remains of our furniture and there will be no insurance pay-out, we will just have to learn how to survive somehow. I often think of the happy time I spent at the Gasthof with your family."

Johann put the letter down on the table and they both sat in silence for several minutes.

"I'll call to see her later on today," said Josefa, her voice trembling with emotion. I'll take Helga in her pram. It's a good walk, but Emma can see to the boys' Brotzeit.

As she approached the sizeable detached house that afternoon, Josefa noticed that the curtains were drawn. She rang the doorbell twice before she heard a slight sound on the other side.

"Who's there?" whispered a husky voice.

"I'm a friend. We've had a letter from David."

"Please come to the back of the house."

The terrified elderly couple were cowering in a dark lobby surrounded by suit cases and boxes. They motioned to Josefa to enter with the pram, before quickly shutting the door.

"We've been preparing to go to America. They'll give us permission if we agree never to return here, but we've found out that our bank account has been frozen. We can't buy the tickets. We want to take our daughter and David as well."

In the dim light, Josefa could see two pairs of moistened eyes glistening. She stood motionless, feeling absolutely helpless. How could she possibly offer to pay for four passages to America? There was their own future to think about with six children.

Not giving them the full details of David and his mother's ordeal, Josefa left them, saying she would try to call again, although she realised she was taking an enormous risk of being seen helping Jews. She was so engrossed in thought on the way back that she was unaware of how close she had got to a man sweeping the street. Faintly surprised that the quality of his clothing did not match his occupation, she swerved the pram to avoid him. He threw her a sideways glance. At the sight of his face, her eyes opened wide in disbelief. It was Dr Rosenbaum. He put a finger to his lips and shook his head before turning his back and continuing to sweep.

"I wouldn't have known what to say anyway," she told Johann. "I was in a state of shock."

"Dora called in to see you and the baby this afternoon, she also has had a shock."

"What was that?"

"She saw a man collecting rubbish."

"Well?"

"He was the gynaecologist, Dr Goldberg!"

A few days later, Josefa hung up her apron, went into the Büro and, with a deep sigh, flopped into a chair. Emma was left to finish clearing up the kitchen and Johann was busy serving drinks in the Stube. This opportunity to sit alone quietly and reflect on the past year as it entered its last month was very welcome. Coping with six children and a busy kitchen trade invariably led to total exhaustion at the end of the day. Also, the scenes she had witnessed and the incidents she had experienced or heard about in recent months had disturbed her and, at times, deprived her of sleep. Although there was seldom open discussion about such occurrences, she sensed there was a general feeling of uneasiness everywhere. In spite of this, their business was thriving, for which she was very relieved and grateful.

Johann poked his head around the door. "Everything OK, Jo? The boys seemed noisier than usual at bedtime."

"Helga settled down quickly, but the boys were restless," she replied. "Nervous excitement about St Nikolaus' visit tomorrow, I expect. I hope Papa's got his costume ready. His mitre kept slipping off last year. Do you remember? He asked Hubert, Bertl's farm-hand, to be his Knecht Ruprecht. I hope—"

"It won't be too much trouble for that one to make himself look menacing," butted in Johann. "He's got a permanent scowl on his weather-beaten face. Still the beard will cover quite a bit of that. Oh God, there's a call for more drinks. Must go."

Johann turned and stumbled over little Rudi, who came wandering in at that moment, barefoot and half asleep. Johann ruffled his son's hair as he sped back to the bar.

"Hello. What are you doing here?" Josefa asked with a smile, holding out her arms for a cuddle.

"Will nasty Knecht Ruprecht really smack me if I'm naughty, Mama?"

"I don't think so," she replied stroking his forehead. He'll bring his birch broom with him to tap naughty children on their bottoms, but if you promise to try to be good next year, St Nikolaus will give you some goodies."

143

"What sort of goodies, Mama?"

"An orange or apple. Biscuits perhaps or sweeties. Come on back to bed now, it's time three-year-olds were asleep."

Having settled Rudi in his bed again, Josefa came downstairs. She was just about to pour out a glass of wine for herself when she heard a tapping on the window. It was pitch dark outside, apart from the street lamp and a light in the yard. She leant out of the window and could just make out a shadowy figure close to the Gasthof's wall.

"Who's there?" she enquired. Someone stepped forward.

"Frau Birk, it's David Kuhn's grandmother." Her voice was barely audible.

"Oh, please come in."

"Oh no, Frau Birk, I daren't for both our sakes," she whispered. "I just wanted to tell you that we've managed to raise enough money to buy two tickets to go to America. We wanted my daughter and David to use them, but they insist that we go. They feel, being younger, their chance of survival here is better than ours. They don't like the idea of never being allowed back into Germany and the consequences if they do. There's no time to argue with them. The ship sails tomorrow. I just wanted to say thank you."

Not waiting for a response, she dabbed her eyes with her handkerchief before disappearing into the darkness.

The following morning, Leonhard stood in front of a full-length mirror.

"I think I look all right, don't you, Aga?"

"Yes, dear, but I think you ought to go now. The boys will be excited and Hubert is waiting for you."

"Our first call will be at the Gasthof and then we'll go on from there."

Leonhard told his Knecht, who was dressed in his medieval outfit and carrying his broom. Leonhard strode ahead leaning on his staff. When they arrived at the kitchen door, Josefa led the way into the Büro. The boys had scrambled for cover when they heard the bells ringing on Hubert's costume.

"They've all been good boys, St Nikolaus," their mother said as she returned to the kitchen and noticed four faces apprehensively emerging from behind the chairs.

Having executed his first visit, their grandfather threw his sack over his shoulder and left the boys happily munching biscuits, relieved that Ruprecht had not used his broom.

"Bye, Jo. Those goodies will keep them quiet for a bit," Leonhard called out.

"Papa, can you spare a minute?"

"What's the matter?" he asked, slightly concerned by her clouded expression.

"There's just been an announcement on the radio. All Jews are prohibited from using sports halls and playing fields, in fact, banned from all public facilities, parks, gardens, beaches, cinemas, concerts, theatres and exhibitions." She gasped for breath. "I immediately thought of Dr Rosenbaum's grandson. He's such a wonderful athlete. He'll be absolutely devastated."

Leonhard raised his eyebrows, lowered his gaze and slowly shook his head. Without a word, he went to join Hubert, who was waiting outside.

As Christmas approached, Johann and Josefa learnt that they would have to employ another waitress in the new year. Lisa was leaving and was clearly very upset. She enjoyed life at the Gasthof. Her pretty face and ready smile made her very popular with the pilots and the regulars.

"My mother needs my help," she told them, her voice quavering with emotion. "Her brother married a Jewess, a musician who just cannot accept that she can no longer go to concerts or perform in them. Her nerves have gone to pieces. She says her life's not worth living anymore. She's lived alone since my uncle died, two years ago, and my mother's finding her difficult to cope with." Lisa turned her head to hide a tear.

"You'll have difficulty finding another like her," remarked Dieter when Johann broke the news at the regulars' table.

"You sure will," chimed in the others.

"Especially as the Messerschmitt factory has gobbled up most of the local workforce," concluded Dieter. "Not surprising really when you hear that Wilhelm Messerschmitt has been awarded the German prize for art and design in engineering and Ferdinand Porsche for car design."

"Yes, I heard about that," said Peter, who was on two days' leave from the army. "Talking of cars, there's couple of very nice ones parked outside. Looks like you've got some wealthy businessmen sitting over there, Hanni."

"Well, the booming industry has boosted the confidence to invest and that does us a bit of good, too, it trickles through," replied Johann.

Christmas passed in the traditional way. A visit to church, followed by a happy family meal and for the boys, the usual gifts from the Christkindl. These included some sort of clothing, socks, shirts or underwear, together with an orange, an apple and spicy homemade biscuits. Their greatest excitement, however, was when they each received one toy from their parents. Every year, Josefa and Johann would make a pre-Christmas visit to a large toy shop in the town centre. Understandably, the ones they chose were mechanical—a car, train, tractor or tank, which induced a variety of engine noises from the recipients.

The advent of 1939, which followed, was celebrated with much raising of glasses to toast a promising and prosperous new year as fireworks lit up the sky. The snowfall was heavy that winter and about a month later, the boys were snowballing outside whilst Josefa and Johann were inside drinking their after-lunch coffee.

"Did you hear that?" asked Josefa. "Sounds like fireworks. Someone must have found a few that he'd forgotten about."

"Sounds more like shooting rabbits. A bit difficult in all that snow," came a reply from behind a newspaper. Suddenly, the door burst open and four excited boys with bright red cheeks stormed in, their woollen hats heavily decorated with snowflakes.

"Mama, Papa, come quickly. There are lots of soldiers and shooting."

"Come on, come on," insisted Erich tugging at his father's arm. Grabbing the two younger boys' hands, Josefa joined the family exodus.

"What the hell is happening?" muttered Johann taking in the scene of armed soldiers crouching and darting from one house and street corner to another. At that moment, he noticed Heini hurrying towards them, coming from the direction of the mayor's office. Breathless, he blurted out the answer to their question,

"The mayor has just informed me that our village is to be used for military manoeuvres because it resembles a Russian village! Can you believe that? They'll take place every three or four weeks. He says he had no say in the matter. Orders from above."

Josefa and Johann looked at each other aghast. Before they could utter a word, Heini continued, "He said they'll last about two hours. Firing blanks of course."

"Papa, Papa, can we stay and watch?" pleaded the three older boys, jumping up and down gleefully as they started to imitate soldiers using machine guns.

"If you promise me you won't move from this spot."

"We won't, Papa, we promise."

Leonhard took purposeful strides towards the Gasthof. He could not contain his indignation at what was taking place in the village a moment longer. He just had to open the sluice gates of his mind, where a deluge of thoughts were bursting to be released. As he was approaching the main door, he was startled by shrieks of "Bang! Bang! Bang!" as his two elder grandsons sprang out from behind a tree, armed with pieces of wood held like rifles.

"Did we scare you, Opa?" they called out gleefully.

"You certainly did," replied their grandfather smiling as he feigned an act of taking cover by shielding his head with his arms. Safely inside, he sought his son-in-law. He found him in the Büro entertaining the regulars and a few close friends.

"You're just in time to sample this new wine I'm going to stock," said Johann about to open the third bottle. This gave Leonhard a few moments to realise what the occasion was and that it had slipped his memory.

"Happy birthday, Hanni," he said raising his glass to him. Having clinked glasses with everyone, he tasted the wine, moving his mouth to assess the bouquet, flavour and vintage.

"That's a good one, Hanni," he said taking a further sample. "I'm glad we've got something to celebrate. What are they doing to our village? Turning it into a war zone? Strikes me, it's been our leader's intention ever since he came to power." He reached for his glass and took a large gulp.

This statement was met with a few moments of thought-provoking silence. Volkmar was the first to break it.

"Well, I must say our lives have improved on the land over the last few years. We've had some bad spells and been short-handed, I know, but now help's on the way, or so we've been told. Let's hope… but there are restrictions," he added after a moment's thought. "We're not allowed to supply our milk direct to the public. In future, the whole output will be controlled and sent to central depots."

"Well, let's face it, since the Nazis came in, unemployment's plummeted," interjected Albert, another farmer. "And what's more, inflation is down." He leant forward and helped himself to a few nibbles.

"We've got some damn good roads, too, now," mumbled Heini, who was already munching some.

"You're doing OK, aren't you, Hanni?" asked Dieter. "The Stube seems to fill up nicely and sometimes it's difficult to find a table when the pilots are in for lunch."

"Yes, their trade's helped a lot, I must say."

"Do those trigger-happy fellas on manoeuvres come here, too?" Dieter ventured to ask as he reached for the bowl of nuts.

Johann shook his head. "No, they go back to the barracks in town." Leonhard was biding his time whilst they toasted Johann's health again.

"What about our youngsters? What about our freedom?" All eyes turned towards him. "I reckon you could be arrested if you openly complained about the manoeuvres here. Ask yourself, why is unemployment down? I'll tell you why, because there's a big armoured tank and aircraft building operation going on, not to mention the huge pilot training programme. It can only mean one thing. War!" He gritted his teeth. There was a silent pause whilst Johann topped up the glasses.

"I think we're all feeling apprehensive," resumed Leonhard, "living in fear of Gestapo. Not surprising when an unguarded comment could get you arrested and not only that, a misconstrued facial expression could, too. You'd soon find the Gestapo on your doorstep if someone reported it." He reached for his glass and took a large gulp.

Albert replaced his glass on the table and, casting his eyes downwards, said thoughtfully, "I personally feel very uncomfortable with this excessive hatred of the Jews. I know they've never been popular. Probably the result of envy, because they're clever and mostly very successful." At that moment, Josefa came through the door.

"Hello, Papa, I thought I heard your voice," she said brightly.

Her entry came at an opportune moment. The mood of the gathering had changed and it was Volkmar's suggestion that they give the family members some privacy and move into the Stube for a smoke. They all agreed.

Chapter 17

"Hanni, do you think I should sign this?" Josefa asked when they had left.

"What is it?"

"They want our permission for the children to receive ideological instead of religious instruction, and I've been told there are penalties if we don't agree. That's outrageous, isn't it?" A look of dismay spread across her face.

"Don't do anything at the moment, Jo," replied Johann cautiously.

"Most certainly NOT," said Leonhard clenching his fist and angrily thumping the table, causing spillage from his glass. "Our youngsters are indoctrinated with enough Nazi ideology at their Hitler Youth meetings." He emptied his glass. "Innocent minds are easy prey for political predators."

"You know why the kids put up with that, Papa, because of all the exciting activities on offer—sport, camping, climbing, shooting, etc.," reasoned Josefa. "Another thing, they have to swear allegiance to the Führer, so where does that leave the parents?"

Johann picked up the wine bottle and poured into Leonhard's glass, he was glad this conversation had taken place privately. He knew his father-in-law was right. Their freedom had been eroded. He was worried about Nazi infiltration into schools and the influence they had on the children. It was essential, he thought, that parents should not lose their grip on their offspring.

"Remind Mama that it's Hans' birthday tomorrow, Papa."

"Oh yes. How old is he?"

"He's reached double figures now. Well, I've got a lot to do. Must go. See you tomorrow." Josefa shut the door behind her. Now alone with Leonhard, Johann felt free to speak his mind.

"You know what happened, don't you?" he said.

"What are you talking about?" Leonhard asked as his eyes met Johann's.

"I voted in a democratic election, but then we were let down by Hindenburg." Johann hesitated a moment. "Life was pretty tough when Jo and I were first married, but somehow we managed to struggle through with Aga's help, for which we were very grateful." Leonhard just nodded and listened.

"Now we have six children and, at present, a flourishing business. What would you expect me to do? Throw it all overboard?" Leonhard, with his brow furrowed, shot a glance at his son-in-law.

"You know as well as I do what would happen if I took my Nazi membership plaque down from the Stube wall," Johann fidgeted nervously. "It would be the same as before I joined." Johann took a gulp from his glass, his hand trembling a little. "My milk churns would be turned upside down, the customers would have their tyres slashed and the Stube would be almost empty." He paused for breath. "The windows would all be broken and we'd have graffiti on the walls, but what's worse, Jo and I would lie awake at night worrying about the safety of the children." He took another deep breath. "Ours is a very strong marriage, but the strain, stress and anxiety Jo and I would suffer, could take its toll."

Leonhard nodded slowly in agreement but remained silent. He felt Johann had still more he needed to say.

"Only young men, without the burden of a family to support, can afford to protest in a dictatorship. They risk only their own lives. I have seven other lives to look after. There is one thing I do not want and that is war. I had my belly full of that when I was a teenager and saw mass slaughtering on the battlefields of France." Johann's hand was now shaking uncontrollably as he reached for his glass. Leonhard stood up, focused his eyes on Johann's and as a gesture of completely understanding his son-in-law's situation, he laid one hand on Johann's arm and patted him on the back with the other.

"Enjoy the rest of you birthday, Hanni," he said with a smile. "I must leave now."

Else was a tall, angular heavy-boned woman in her early twenties. She was a single mother who had left her small daughter in the care of her own mother. Not afraid of hard work and long working hours, the job as a waitress suited her. She was Lisa's replacement. Brought up in a rural community, she was a rough diamond type, who was more in tune with the farmers' earthy jokes and leg pulling banter than with the aristocratic, mainly Prussian pilots' conversation. She warned her new employers that she was prone to epilepsy but had not had an attack for a long time. In view of the shortage of applicants, they decided to take the risk. The boys got on well with her, especially as she plied them with long cool drinks when they came indoors, hot and dusty from kicking a football around with the pilots. This was only one of the pastimes they enjoyed in the company of the men in uniform, another being playing cards in the back parlour during the evenings. The boys had built up a firm friendship with a small group of them, with a bond so strong that they were extremely upset when there were fatal flying accidents. These occurred when exuberant young pilots took risks in their eagerness to perform aerobatics. Seeing a place setting removed at lunchtime provided the evidence, leaving a nervous and emotional tension among the trainees. It was never long before replacements arrived.

Although the villagers usually welcomed the arrival of snow each year like an old friend, this winter had been different. They had been impatient for its departure and the end of the manoeuvres. Else was carrying out her first duty of the day, sweeping the main entrance steps. She had chipped away the obstinate traces of ice, which the weak rays of spring sunshine had difficulty in melting. She looked up as a man passed by on his way to work.

"Morning, Sigi."

"Good morning, Else. Have you heard? Our troops have moved into Czechoslovakia."

He carried on walking, not waiting for reply. "I'm late this morning. I'll be in for a lager on the way back."

Else stopped and stared after him for a moment, absorbing the information. She hurried indoors just as Josefa was coming downstairs with Helga in her arms and Gerhard following. He was cuddling a fluffy toy which he had received on his second birthday, two weeks previously. Johann came in from the back yard and was hurrying towards the cellar steps as Else broke the news. Anxious glances were exchanged as they passed each other on their pressing missions, Johann to check beer delivery in the cellar and Josefa to feed the baby in the kitchen. Emma was having breakfast with the boys and Gerhard scrambled onto a chair to join them.

"There's a cold wind today. Make sure you have your hoods up," she told Hans and Erich as they prepared to go to school.

"I don't like Fräulein Gruber, Emma," said Hans looking downcast.

"Why not?" she asked, as she helped Rudi onto his chair.

"She frightens me. She's been horrible to Paul, cos his Papa won't let him come to the 'Jung Volk' meetings. She's nasty to him all day and she tells the other boys to be nasty to him as well in the playground. He's a few weeks younger than I am and she says when he's ten, like me, he'll have to go to the meetings cos it's law and his Papa will be in dead trouble if he doesn't let him go."

"I think you ought to be going now boys or you'll be late," Josefa called out from the other side of the kitchen. When they had left, she placed the baby in the pram and then asked Emma, "Did I hear Hans say he doesn't like Fräulein Gruber?" Emma nodded before replying.

"I don't blame him, she'd frighten anybody. I've seen children cringe with fear when she's around. She's very large and swaggers about with her Nazi badge always pinned to her lapel. If a parent complains about her, that child would be in for a bad time at school."

At that moment, Johann kicked open the kitchen door, his arms laden with provisions brought up from the cellar.

"We're getting low on butter and coffee, Jo," he called out breathlessly.

"Wasn't able to get any more. The wholesaler says they're in short supply. We'll have to use some from the pilots' quota for the time being."

"So it doesn't look as if I'll be baking myself a birthday cake then."

"Oh God, I'd forgotten, Jo," he said looking up at her. "I'll tell you what, you know you said you wanted to go on a cookery course to give the pilots more variety? Well, that can be your birthday treat."

"Oh, that'll be nice." Josefa smiled broadly at the prospect of several carefree hours. "Can you cope, Emma?" she asked. "It'll only be for a few hours in the day for a week."

"Of course, don't worry at all," was Emma's answer. "Relax and enjoy it. We'll look forward to sampling some new exciting dishes."

"My mouth's watering at the prospect already," chuckled Johann as he scurried off in the direction of the Stube.

"It's a bit early for you, isn't it?" remarked Johann as Dieter pulled out his chair at the regulars' table.

"Have you heard the news, Hanni?"

"About the Czechs?" Dieter nodded.

"Else told us earlier, but I just haven't had a second to take it in. Sounds serious, doesn't it?" Dieter's worried expression revealed his concern.

"I don't like it."

"What don't you like?" asked Heini, making a sudden appearance.

"The latest news? No, neither do I. There's a hell of a frenzy going on at the airfield. Those pilots are buzzing around all over the place."

"Talking of pilots," said Johann, "Jo's decided to go on a cookery course. She thinks they must be bored with the same old menus and could do with something a bit different."

"They won't do without her Spätzle though, that's for sure. There'd be a riot. It's the best in Bayern. How will you manage without her?" asked Dieter.

"Frau Burger's coming to do the cleaning and help generally."

"She's a great Führer fan," said Heini. "Thinks he is wonderful because he's given poor kids access to all sorts of sporting activities and camping. Her brood like the camp fires and sing songs, she told me. She likes it cos it gets them away from under her feet."

Heini reached for his krug of beer and then fumbled in his pocket for a Virginia and matches.

"I shouldn't think her kids have much excitement otherwise. They're quite hard up. Her old man left her." Dieter paused before adding thoughtfully, "We'll have to be careful what we say when she's about."

"The kids will have plenty of excitement now. All those rehearsals for the Führer's 50th next month," sniggered Heini.

It was Easter Sunday when Josefa broke the news to them that there would be no Easter egg hunt. There were tears and tantrums.

"But, Mama, why haven't you painted them and hidden them like you always do?" wailed Sepp.

"I couldn't because there aren't enough eggs to buy."

The boys looked puzzled. There was no point in trying to explain to them that there was a dire shortage of certain foods and a rumour of possible food rationing. It was also whispered that the government was stockpiling it.

"I'll tell you what though, it's Rudi's fourth birthday on Wednesday and I've saved three eggs to make a lovely chocolate torte," said their mother in an effort to appease them. "Would you like that?"

This suggestion was received with joyous cries of "Yes! Yes! Yes!".

There was no restraint in procuring ingredients to cater for pilots and the new culinary skills Josefa had learnt had come just in time. She was given instructions to provide an extra special menu for the pilots on the Führer's birthday, the following week. The preparations for the event were reaching fever pitch. Hans and Erich were always rushing off to practise marching, the rhythm of which had to be in perfect unison with their swinging arms.

"Is there no school again for you today?" asked Emma one morning. "You seem to be off an awful lot these days."

"We have a lot of rehearsing to do, Emma," replied Hans, about to eat another pretzel.

"Yes, we've got to have everything perfect for the Führer's birthday," said Erich spreading a roll thickly with mettwurst.

After they had left, dressed in Hitler Youth uniforms, Leonhard called in.

"Are the boys all at school?" he asked Josefa.

155

"No, they have yet another day off to make sure their display is flawless on April 20th," she answered with a shrug.

"Sounds like their schoolwork is getting neglected, Jo."

"It's what a lot of parents think, but our authority's being undermined, whilst our children are being influenced by the Party." Josefa's voice trailed off as she returned to the kitchen. Leonhard raised his eyebrows, pursed his lips and slowly shook his head. *I need a drink,* he thought and headed for the Stube.

Bunting decorated the village in the main street. The villagers gathered around the podium where the mayor, flanked by SA members, gave a speech. A large flag blazoned with the swastika swayed in the light breeze as he extolled the virtues of the Führer.

"He is a man who has given back to the Germans their pride and self-esteem", he said proudly, "and someone who has rescued them from the abyss of a dark, desperate past and brought them to the brink of a sound, thriving future."

There was no service. The church was not represented. A brass band struck up, the instruments shining like newly minted coins. The columns of Germany's young citizens, all dressed in HY or BDM uniforms, waited for a cue to start marching.

A comparatively quiet day followed the extremely long and busy one at the Gasthof. Totally exhausted, Johann and Josefa sat with the children at the breakfast table. Emma tapped on the door before opening.

"Here's the post, Herr Birk," she said brightly, smiling at the children. Johann sifted through the envelopes. One in particular took his attention.

"This' for you, Jo," he said handing it to her. Josefa looked surprised. With a mystified expression, she slit open the envelope and read the contents.

"Well, what d' yer know," she whooped. "I am to be decorated with a silver cross on Mother's Day."

"Why, Mama? What for?" asked Hans.

"For having all you lot. That's what!"

"I don't want a medal," shouted Josefa, in order to be heard above the noise her sons were making.

"The Führer is proud of you, Jo. Don't offend him. What I would like to know is why I don't get some recognition," Johann sniggered. "I must have had something to do with it."

The boys were becoming boisterous and their father suggested they go outside to play.

"We didn't have children just to please the Führer," protested Josefa with a hint of annoyance when they were alone. "We wanted a girl to replace the one we lost and three more little boys came along in the process." Her voice quavered a little and her eyes moistened as they rested on baby Helga, whose chubby little fist she held.

"Yes, I know, Jo," Johann said with a reassuring smile. "Strange, only yesterday Emma remarked about how different the characters of our boys are. Hans is shy and reserved. An engineer in the making, I would think. Just give him a tool and he's happy. Erich loves sport and the outdoors. He has a grin from ear to ear when it starts snowing and he can get on his skis."

"His teacher says his maths is good, too," said Josefa shifting the baby to a more comfortable position on her lap. "Sepp will take life at a slower pace, I think. He has such a caring nature. It's a pity he has to wear glasses so young."

"Number 4, Rudi is the dreamer," said Johann with a shrug. "He's quite happy with his own company, especially when he's got a mechanical object to take to pieces to find out how it works and then tries to put it together again. But doesn't always succeed."

"And the bits belonging to toy cars and other things I find lying about are evidence of that!" confirmed Josefa with pursed lips and a heavy sigh.

"But he's very determined, Jo. You must give him credit for that. Well, as for our toddler Gerhard, I think he'll be the happy-go-lucky one, don't you?" Josefa nodded.

"Let's have another look at your post, Jo. Have you read the small print?"

"No, not yet."

"That settles it!" exclaimed Johann after he had finished reading it through. "You've just got to accept. Look at these concessions you could have," he said excitedly. "You're one of three million mothers who've got an award. Why not take

157

advantage of being allowed to jump queues?" Josefa looked up at him curiously. "Our boys will love this bit," he giggled. "Hitler Youth members have been told to salute you."

This statement made Josefa smile. "Let me think about it," she said. "I've got till May 14th."

"Come in," Johann called out in answer to a knock on the door. Volkmar's head appeared.

"Good morning to you both. Just thought I'd find out if you were all right, Hanni, after last night's fracas."

"Err, yes, we're fine, thanks, Volkmar," replied Johann, his facial expression sending a message, 'don't say any more please'. "I'll be in the Stube in a few moments."

"OK. I'll go and join the others." Volkmar withdrew, shutting the door.

"What was that all about?" asked Josefa with a look that implied 'what haven't you told me?'.

"I was going to tell you, Jo, but I was waiting for the children to leave us and then your special post arrived." Josefa kept her eyes firmly fixed on his face.

"It happened after you'd gone to bed last night." He shifted in his seat. "Two SA thugs came into the Stube, well, the worst, for drink. Having been celebrating the Führer's birthday. They were abusive to other customers and spilt their beer all over the table." Josefa listened with bated breath. "They were vulgar and crude and when one was sick, they told Else to move her arse and clear it up. It got to the point when I couldn't tolerate it any longer."

A frown of anxiety clouded his face and he was silent for a few moments. Josefa stared at him awestruck in anticipation of what might have happened next.

"Well, I showed them the door," continued Johann. "They were almost legless, so it wasn't too difficult to shove them outside. Then I locked it. I heard their car engine start. There must have been a third one out there, because they weren't in a fit state to drive. Anyway, don't let's worry about it. I must go in the Stube now."

Johann could not wait to spread the news about Josefa's silver medal. His insistence that a joint effort should have a joint reward caused many a chuckle.

"You could have gone for gold, you know, Hanni. You could manage a couple more kids, couldn't you?" Gustav's suggestion caused more laughter.

"What's more, if you'd ten children and the last one happened to be a boy, he would be honoured by having Hitler as a godfather, but you'd 'ave to name 'im Adolf of course." This information was supplied by Bertl.

"Poor little sod," muttered Volkmar, but his comment was drowned in the guffaws of the others. As the merriment died down, Dieter raised his glass.

"Seriously," he said, "I'd like to propose a toast to a special mother of the Reich, our very own landlady." They all raised their glasses, expressing congratulations. Josefa was not present, but Johann assured them he would pass on their good wishes.

"I've got some good news as well," said Volkmar. "I've got a couple of farmhands to help me. They're Czechs. Damn good workers, too. They don't seem to mind coming here to work. They say their country's in turmoil and they thought they'd be better off 'ere."

"Seems like good news all 'round," chirped in Albert, "except some foods are getting scarce. My wife gets a bit het up about it. She says she hasn't been able to get any oranges or bananas anywhere."

"I'll tell you who's got the best bloody news, the amnesty prisoners being released for Adolf Hitler's birthday. It must have been the best public holiday they've ever had," said Dieter as he raised his arm to attract Else's attention to his empty beer mug.

Volkmar cast a furtive glance around the Stube. He was just about to mention the disturbing radio report slating Poland when the approaching rhythmic sound of marching feet brought all conversation with a political theme to a close. The pilots made their entrance just as the cuckoo was announcing 12 noon. Erich had forged a firm friendship with one pilot in particular and had given his father instructions to deliver a message to him.

"Herr Florian," said Johann as he placed two large baskets of bread on their table, "Erich has asked me to tell you that he won't be able to play cards this evening because he's attending a post-Führer's birthday gathering. I think they're having a campfire sing song or something. Erich said he'll see you tomorrow."

"Thank you, Herr Birk," replied the tall, blond, handsome officer. "We enjoy your sons' company. They provide light relief for us in the evenings, which is very welcome after the daily work pressure. We enjoy your wife's cooking as well of course. We've had some interesting dishes lately, but nothing matches her Spätzle."

"Thank you very much, Herr Leutnant. I'll convey your compliments to her. You'll be pleased to hear that Käsespätzle is on the menu today."

Chapter 18

Josefa had bought a new dress for the award ceremony. The direction of the venue had been sent to her. A reticent heroine, she felt rather apprehensive about the whole affair. Through careful economising, Emma had been able to bake two torten for a special treat to celebrate the occasion. For this reason, the boys were impatient for their mother's return. The lure of the torten far outweighed the interest in the Silver Honour Cross. They all took a brief look at it before scrambling to take their places at the table.

It was a couple of days later. Johann was snoozing in the Büro after a very busy lunchtime trade. He was roused by a tapping on the door and Else's voice. Slightly irritated by being disturbed, he shouted, "Come in, Else. What is it?" She came in.

"Herr Birk, there are two men here to see you."

"Is there no peace?" he sighed. "Tell them to wait in the Stube; I'll be about ten minutes."

"I think they want to see you now, Herr Birk. They're from the Gestapo!" Johann's pulse quickened. He gulped, swallowing an excess of saliva.

"I'll be straight out, Else," he said.

Johann led the two members of the secret police force to a small back room where privacy could be assured. Having loosened their coats and taken off their trilbies, they sat down and confronted him. The more senior one was the first to speak.

"Herr Birk, I'm sure you are aware of the reason for our presence here."

"Yes," replied Johann quietly, his hands clutched tightly beneath the table. "I believe so."

"In normal circumstances, you would be arrested for the action you took against the SA members. However, there are a few points, not so much in your defence, but in your favour."

He leant back in his chair and it was now time for the second one to take over.

"It's not the first time that the behaviour of those two has been brought to our notice and they have been subsequently cautioned. This, in itself, would not play any part in your defence, nor would it exonerate you." He paused for a moment or two, his penetrating eyes boring into Johann's face. "Your Bürgermeister, who is a faithful party member, speaks very highly of you. We have also located and interviewed one or two of your clientele, who have confirmed our suspicions of what exactly took place."

Johann sat rigid in his chair. His thoughts flashed back to that fateful evening and he tried to remember all those who had been present. His eyes moved to the more senior one again as he opened his mouth to speak.

"It's the location of your Gasthof near the airfield, Herr Birk, that has come to your aid. We are scouring the area for a suitable establishment for a top-ranking SS officer to take a break after landing here. He will be en route to the Ordensburg," the SS training centre at Sonthofen. He cleared his throat before adding, "I would like you to know that we have had a very good report of your kitchen and service from the commander at the airfield." He turned his head towards his colleague, inviting him to speak next.

"Of course, if there were another occurrence regarding your intolerance of SA members, Herr Birk, you would be most certainly apprehended. Finally, we understand that your wife has recently received a Mother of the Reich Honour Award, for which we would like to offer our congratulations."

"Thank you," said Johann meekly.

The two men stood up and prepared to leave. Johann was feeling physically weak from enormous relief.

"May I offer you some refreshment, a beer perhaps or wine?" he asked reticently. The negative reply was most welcome.

It was clear that news of the Gestapo's visit had reached Josefa. She did not look up from the stove as Johann

162

approached her. She bore the expression of someone anticipating the pain pending an injection, with pursed lips and furrowed brow. The fear that the Gestapo could, at any time, instigate the destruction of their lives was always present. Johann came up behind her and hugged her tightly, whispering in her ear, "They've gone. It's all right. Everything's all right," he emphasised. Josefa turned around, her anxious look was replaced by a questioning one.

"Oh God. Do you really mean it?"

"There's no need to worry, Jo. We'll talk later."

She replied with a half-hearted nod and made an effort to smile.

The boys had just returned home from school one day towards the end of the summer term.

"Mama, there's a funny noise coming from the barn, what is it?"

"Go and look."

"Will it hurt us?"

"No, of course not."

Hans, followed by Erich, Sepp and Rudi, crept cautiously towards the barn door. They opened it wide enough to peep in.

"Wow! Piglets! Six of them!" exclaimed Hans.

From the kitchen door, Josefa called out.

"Go around the back of the barn, but don't forget to shut the door first."

"This time, the boys raced along, with Erich in the lead. He opened the small shed door. The boys shrieked as they were swept backwards by the flapping of wings and the screeching of chicken. Their mother had followed them, with Gerhard toddling beside her.

"They arrived today," she told them. "They can stay out now, but we must put them in tonight. We don't want the foxes to get them, do we? Just think, boys, we'll have our own eggs. Perhaps I can bake Sepp's birthday cake with them next week."

"I'll be six," said Sepp puffing out his chest. "I'll be able to go to school then."

Johann was busy stocking up the bar.

"I nearly ran over a chicken in your yard, Hanni," said Gustav as he took a sip of his first beer of the day.

163

"Cor, you'd have to answer to Jo for that. She's just bought them. She likes baking and wants a reliable supply of eggs. We've got some piglets, too. It's a good outlet for any kitchen waste food and they love beer dregs. Gives Klaus some extra work, but he doesn't mind. He likes animals."

"D' yer ever hear from the one you had before Klaus?"

"David, you mean? Not a word. His grandparents went to America. We haven't heard any more from them since."

At that moment, Volkmar came in. "I'm gasping," he said, exposing a dry tongue. "Bring me an ice cold beer as quick as you like, please, Else." He emptied half a krug without taking a breath.

"How are things, Hanni?" he asked with a knowing look.

"OK. Thanks," Johann replied. Then suspecting Volkmar had heard about the Gestapo visit, he added with half a wink, "All is well."

Leonhard came from the direction of the kitchen just as Dieter arrived. They joined the others at the regulars' table.

"Aga's just popped in to see Jo," said Leonhard putting a glass of red wine to his lips. "They're up to their eyes in jam making. Jars everywhere. That's all in answer to the government's call to start preserving for the winter. Now they've started bottling plums and then it'll be pears and apples. I left them to it. Looks like hard work to me. Anyway, they've raked in Jo's sister Ida to help."

"Ida, is she the one who's secretary to the commander at the large Luftwaffe base at Kaufbeuren?" asked Dieter.

"Yes, that's the one," confirmed Leonhard taking hold of his glass.

"I was watching the gliders earlier," said Gustav, casually changing the subject. "They don't make so much noise as those planes darting about all over the place. All part of the training, I suppose."

"By the way, have you heard that Stefan's sons have been called up?" asked Dieter. "Gave Stefan a bit of a shock."

Not realising that they were already old enough, the regulars were all momentarily stunned by the news.

"Well, there's certainly a war of words against Poland at the moment. Have you heard the verbal onslaught on the radio? It's—" Volkmar was interrupted.

164

"And in the papers, too," Albert butted in. "They are full of it."

"That's all fabricated," retorted Leonhard. "All lies. And because the British stand up for the Poles, he's launched a verbal attack on them now."

"I don't think it will come to anything. After all, Adolf signed a peace treaty," Heini said optimistically, lighting up yet another cigarette.

Leonhard's lips tightened but said nothing until his second glass of wine arrived. He spoke quietly, although he knew all the other customers were out in the Biergarten, enjoying the sunshine.

"We all sighed with relief when he signed that. Now in less than a year, we're faced with the fear of being led into another war. Six years ago, let's face it, we were in a bad state. Now when we're just regaining our national pride and getting a taste of prosperity, it looks as if we're going to lose it again and be plunged back into the turmoil and violence we suffered then."

Johann was feeling uneasy about the way the conversation was going. He clamped down on it when a small party of customers entered the Stube.

"Perhaps we could have a pig roast one of these days," he said cheerfully.

Getting the message, they replied, "That sounds like a good idea. You have our full vote of approval."

As Johann approached the cowshed, he could hear snivelling.

"Whatever's the matter, Klaus?" he asked when he discovered the red-eyed youth crouched in a corner early one morning.

"I want to go with my brothers," he sniffed.

"Go where?"

"They're in the army. Gone to war."

"I am sorry to hear that, but you ought to be glad you haven't had your marching papers yet. You're younger than they are."

"That's the trouble. I want to go. I want to do what my brothers are doing—wearing a uniform and going to other countries."

165

"Oh, come on, Klaus, it's dangerous. Anyway, we need you here. There's plenty of work. I thought you enjoyed helping me in my workshop and you get on well with Felix too, don't you?" Klaus lowered his head and nodded.

"It's difficult to get help these days. All working in factories or being called up. That's why the orchards are full of unpicked apples. Come on now. Cheer Up. I think Felix could do with some help milking."

As Johann returned to the kitchen, he saw his three elder sons making their way across the meadow. Sepp turned around and waved to him. It was to be his first day at school. Johann waved back, silently offering a prayer of gratitude that his sons were too young for combat.

Bürgermeister Hermann walked at a quick pace through the village, smiling confidently at anyone he met.

"Good morning, Johann. Thought I'd just call in. I hear you've been asked to cater for the pilots. A good boost for the business, eh?"

"Yes, Hermann. Would you like a drink?"

"No thanks, I'm in a hurry. Just wondered how you and the family were."

"OK. Thank you." Johann looked at him expectantly. He sensed there was something more that Hermann wished to say.

"It didn't take long, Hanni, did it?"

"What didn't?"

"Poland," he replied with a faint smile.

Before Johann could comment, the arrival of some pilots looking totally exhausted cut the conversation short. They ordered beer, which they drank without a word as Hermann made his departure. Johann welcomed the silence to dwell on his thoughts. He had known Hermann since he was a boy, when they would often play together. Now it appeared that Hermann revelled in the news of their country's conquest, whilst his own reaction was one of apprehension and fear. Two years his junior, Hermann had escaped serving in WW1 and witnessing its horror. He had no children, having remained unmarried. Johann attributed Hermann's staunch support for the Führer to the hardship he had suffered as a child. His father remained unemployed for a very long period after his small business had collapsed and Johann felt sure that 'this had contributed to

Hermann being convinced that Hitler was Germany's saviour, who had rescued it from doom'.

Else jolted Johann from his reverie. "There's one place less for lunch," she whispered as she leant over the table. "Florian has been killed over Poland."

Visibly shaken by the news, Johann said without looking up, "Else, would you collect the rationing stamps from that couple in the corner please."

When she handed the stamps over to Johann, Else said, "They didn't seem very happy. He was looking very grave and she was tearful."

"I'm not surprised. When they came in, they told me that their son had been called up and they'd just seen him off at the station," replied Johann solemnly. "They found it very upsetting seeing all those young men with their luggage."

Rudi was waiting impatiently for his brothers to return home at lunch time. The five-year-old preferred the company of his older siblings to that of his younger ones. Schooling took place between 8 a.m. and 1 p.m., enabling him to enjoy their company in the afternoons. There were so many exciting things to do. About half a mile away, on the edge of the village, there was a lake where they would spend hours bathing in the summer heat. They played on the meadows, climbed trees in the wood, watched the aircraft take off and land. In winter, they would go tobogganing or skiing on the nursery slopes behind the Gasthof.

On that afternoon, they undertook another of their favourite pastimes in the transparent water of the boulder-strewn brook. Having made its way from the pine forest and moorland, it flowed through the village until it joined the River Iller.

"Mama, look what we've got," said Sepp excitedly as he placed two brown trout in the kitchen sink.

"Oh, they're good. They're quite big. Who caught these?"

"I did," said Rudi triumphantly.

"No, you didn't," shrieked Hans. "Erich did. You lost your balance on that boulder and nearly got a soaking."

"Well, I stroked one," retorted Rudi defiantly.

"But I grabbed them and yanked them out," shouted Erich, giving his little brother a shove. Josefa intervened.

167

"Stop that now, boys. Go and wash your hands, ready for Brotzeit. Spread the butter thinly because we haven't got much. Do you hear?"

As the boys left the table, Josefa collected the plates and said, "The pilots told me to tell you they won't be playing cards this evening." The reaction was as she expected.

"Why not?" moaned Hans, pulling a face.

"Florian promised," groaned Erich.

Josefa hurried to the kitchen carrying the plates, passing Johann as he went through to see the boys.

"Why can't the pilots play cards with us, Papa?"

"Because they're very tired and", Johann hesitated, "Florian has had to go away."

"Why, Papa?" asked a very disappointed Erich.

"I'm not sure. For some more training, I think. But I want you to do something for me. Sticking the ration stamps on the cards. Will you do that, Rudi?"

"OK."

Since war had been declared, trade had been quiet in the Stube. It was mainly farmers, who were also exempt from military service, who called in regularly. During the pleasant autumn evenings, they grumbled about the continual movement of troops in armoured vehicles through the village, which shattered its tranquillity and prevented them from sitting outside in the Biergarten. As the days shortened and there was a chill in the air, they played cards inside in the Stube. Else found that the time dragged with the reduction of trade. As midnight approached, she would open the windows in the hope that the cold night air might induce them to head for home. Stacking the chairs on the tables in order to sweep the floor was another ploy she used to get her message over. When the farmers stood up, she sighed relief and looked forward to the warmth of her bed. This dream was short lived. To her dismay, the farmers put on their overcoats, returned to the table and carried on playing.

The children were huddled around the Kachelofen, keeping warm with their mother. She was sewing a pillow, filled with the down feathers she had plucked from the ducks over the summer months. The winter evenings dragged for the boys as well, since there was no more card playing with the pilots.

"Where's Papa gone?" enquired Hans.

"He's just popped over to the station."

"What for, Mama?"

"I'm not quite sure."

Looking puzzled, Hans rushed to open the door when he heard footsteps outside crunching in the thick snow. Johann entered with three others, a man and two women. The children stood up and stared at the strangers.

"Here are Stanislav, Aniela and Sofie," said Johann.

Seven pairs of eyes focused on the man and two women who were in their twenties.

"They're going to work and live with us. They come from Poland," Johann informed his family.

Bewildered, travel-worn and with faces tinged with fear, they stood forlorn with their hands in the pockets of their ragged, dusty, stained garments. Clothes that were totally inadequate for the February temperatures. Josefa's eyes darted backwards and forwards across their faces, whilst the children just gaped. She stood up with Helga grasping her hand and partially hidden behind her skirt.

"Do they speak German?" she asked.

"Just a few words, I believe," answered Johann.

"Have they eaten?"

"I don't know?"

Looking at them and moving her hands up and down to her mouth to signify eating, Josefa said, "Essen?" Their eyes opened wider and they held out their hands.

"Well, they've got to wash their hands first. Erich, show them the sink and, Hans, put the kettle on whilst I get some bread and sausage."

Josefa went straight to the fridge, with Helga toddling close behind. The three other boys stood in a line like soldiers, trying to comprehend what was taking place. They then joined their brothers to witness a loaf of bread and a variety of cold meats being washed down with mugs of steaming coffee disappear at a fast rate.

"Have they any luggage?" asked Josefa quietly.

"No, not really. Just the very small bags they're holding."

"They couldn't have a change of clothing in those," said Josefa with a sigh. "I'll have to go and look out some of your old clothes, Hanni. Else, Emma and I will have to find some for the women. Emma said she'd got some clothes she won't need anymore after she's left here to work in the factory."

"Now what about the sleeping arrangements, Jo?"

Josefa raised her shoulders and took a deep breath. "We were given such little notice," she said putting her hand to her forehead. "We can put a camp bed in Klaus' room for the man. He'll have the room for himself when Klaus joins the army. He's bound to be called up soon. I've heard him counting the days already. The women can have the other attic room, there are two beds in there. When I've got the children to bed, we'll talk about what work they'll be doing."

Josefa sighed deeply. All of a sudden, there was a lot more to think about and arrange, added to her already heavy load. The language would certainly be a problem, but with Klaus and Emma about to leave, the situation without staff would have been far worse. Emma showed them where they could wash, handed out clothes and indicated what time they should appear the following morning by displaying fingers.

When the key was finally turned to lock the Stube door that evening, Josefa and Johann sat down to work out the division of labour. It was decided that Aniela and Sofie would take on the laundry, servicing guest rooms and general cleaning. In quiet periods, Aniela could help in the kitchen and Sofie could help with the milking. Stanislav would assist Felix with the livestock and general maintenance, which included making sure there was a good supply of logs for the winter. They would have to impress on Stanislav that it was essential to take the milk churns to the collection point at the Käserei on time. It was there that the churns were emptied into a large steel container and the weighing took place. The Nestlé lorry collected twice daily.

As they sat quietly reflecting on the events of the day, Josefa said,

"I'm so glad Hans is showing an interest in machinery," her voice revealing her exhaustion. "He could learn a lot by watching you doing repairs."

"Yes, I still get asked to do small jobs. Volkmar's tractor needs sorting out and Hubert's got trouble with his rotovator," said Johann wearily. "Let's go to bed now, Jo."

170

Chapter 19

Predictably, there was the inevitable frustration of trying to make the newcomers understand, but with a few words and a great deal of hand signalling and patience, a routine was established. At first, during meal times, when the Poles joined the family, the children were unusually quiet. They would glance furtively at the newcomers, whose eyes did not leave their plates until they were completely empty. Then, if they did look up, the boys dropped their eyes shyly. The Bavarian dialect was proving to be another hurdle for the Poles to overcome. The few words they did know were of the classical language and the dialect that the boys spoke was almost unrecognisable as German.

A few days later at breakfast, the boys completely forgot their inhibitions. Gustav, the butcher, was expected. He came every two months. Helga, who really didn't understand the significance of the visit, found her brothers' excitement infectious. The slaughter of a pig had appetising implications for the boys. It meant there would be black pudding, sauerkraut and potatoes for supper and a good supply of liver sausage. On his early arrival, Gustav, a short, jovial character, at first, made sure that he had sufficient hot water. He donned his long rubber apron and sharpened his knives before fetching the squealing pig. He put a stun gun to its head, stunning the unfortunate animal before plunging a knife into its jugular vein and collecting the pumped out blood in a bucket, which one of the boys kept stirring vigorously to prevent it from clotting. The government's wartime regulations stipulated that the hide of all slaughtered animals should be sent to the tannery for leather making. For Gustav, it meant extra work to skin it and for the family, it meant no crackling. The boys were not too squeamish about this gory spectacle. Their parents believed that they should not shield them from the realities of life on a farm and the process of food from its source to their plates. When an old boiler chicken was due for the pot, it was the older boys who were sent to deal with it and present it in the kitchen, already plucked.

Sofie had taken the sheets out of the old Miele washing machine. A large wooden tub with an open top and pulsating prongs. Having rinsed them well, she fed them through the mangle and carried the full laundry basket to the meadow which was behind the barn. The sheets billowed in the March wind and Sofie knew they would be ready for ironing by late afternoon. Josefa was in the kitchen preparing the evening meal. Suddenly, she heard what she had come to recognise as Polish expletives. She rushed outside, together with Aniela, to investigate the commotion. Stanislav was bringing the cows back to the stalls for milking. Both Josefa and Aniela gasped in horror like bulls charging at red cloaks, the cows charged at the white linen sheets. Ripped and muddy, with some trampled into the ground and chewed up, it was a pitiful sight and an exasperating end to Sofie's morning work. Like naughty children, the cows jumped about gleefully and revelled in the havoc they were causing. The boys found the spectacle very amusing.

By nature of it being a public meeting place, the Gasthof became the rendezvous for a band of Poles who had been allocated to farms surrounding the village. They gathered each evening in a small backroom, where they chatted, played cards and smoked a vile smelling tobacco substitute, a hybrid of plants. Its obnoxious odour wafted at times into the Stube and entrance hall. The local policeman, who carried out the curfew promptly at 10 p.m., would arrive holding a handkerchief to his nostrils. He was the father of one of Rudi's school friends and was known for his friendly disposition and good humour. He informed the Poles that they had the freedom to go into town when they were not required to work. As the summer progressed, rumours began to circulate that from the influx of foreign labour in the area, there was a small percentage who were not happy with their accommodation or the treatment they received. There was the case of one young male individual who, in the futile hope that he would be sent home, cut off two of his fingers.

The two local couples sitting at the far end of the Stube were not unduly surprised to see Vincent at work. It was not unusual for the village barber to make home visits, especially to those in business. As the plastic cape was removed from his shoulders, Johann stood up and brushed down his trousers. Vincent had collected the broom and swept thoroughly, leaving no trace of any hairs. The completion of the haircut was well timed. Volkmar, Dieter, Heini and Albert arrived at that moment on their return from the market. Their visits to the Gasthof were more frequent these days since the foreign workers had lightened their work load.

"Morning, Hanni," was their combined cheery greeting.

"You look well shorn," said Volkmar casting an eye over Johann's head.

"Yep, Vince's handiwork. You look very happy. Had a good day at market?"

"Not bad, not bad," was their typically understated reply as they sat down.

"No Else today?"

"No, I gave her the morning off," Johann told them. "She had an epileptic fit last night. She threw a tray of full beer mugs up in the air. Frightened the life out of me." He started to fill four tall beer glasses. "Someone with First Aid know-how rolled her on her side and pulled her tongue out. Stanislav helped me carry her into the Büro. I knew she'd had them when she was younger, but this was the first time here."

"Poor Else. Thought there was an extra strong smell of beer," said Heini.

"Well, I'd rather that than the stink of those Virginias you smoke," said Dieter screwing up his face and holding his nose with his finger and thumb. "Not to mention that filthy habit of dipping it into your beer." Heini just grinned.

"Let's drink to her speedy recovery," said Dieter reaching for his glass

"I'll drink to that," said Johann, "I'll need her next week when we're all hay-making."

"Yea, we'll all be busy, won't we?" said Volkmar having acquired a beer-froth moustache. "When Peter rang me, he said he wished he could be here to help. Funny, he used to make himself scarce this time in the year when he was at home."

"Because he didn't want to get up so early." Titters of laughter followed.

"How is Otto?" asked Johann as he took Dieter's glass for a refill.

"OK. He is in Poland. Doesn't talk much about it. A bit homesick, I think."

Eager to change the subject, about which he was also worried, Volkmar raised his glass. "Let's drink to sunshine for the harvest." Readily, they all joined him for the toast.

After an early breakfast, Klaus set off with Aniela, Sofie and Stanislav and the boys. He had at last received his summons to army service and his face bore a smile which disguised a slight feeling of apprehension. Helga and Gerhard stayed behind and were to join them later on with their mother. The band of harvesters was loaded with a good supply of drink for the day. The mowing was already completed when they arrived at the meadow. Gabi, the cart horse, Trudy's successor, was enjoying a well-deserved respite from pulling the grass cutter. It was now time for the newly mown hay to be shaken and dispersed with a rake for drying. Rudi was given the job to fan away the flies that pestered poor Gabi.

Before returning to the Gasthof that evening, the hay was rolled to prevent it from getting damp. After almost three days of shaking, tossing and rolling, it was dry and ready to be loaded onto the wagon and brought to the hay barn, where Gabi had to pull it up a ramp for unloading. In spite of their own exhaustion, the helpers assisted her with this final arduous task by a concerted effort to push the wagon up the ramp.

Looking weary, dusty and very bronzed, the boys' protests and complaining had been minimal, due to the reward which would follow. An annual fair was held in their meadow at the rear of the Gasthof, which caused a great deal of excitement. This was in spite of offering little more than a large boat-shaped swing and carousel. For two days, the boys, who were now known in the village as the 'Engel Buben', lived a dream, enjoying free rides given in exchange for the site being free of charge. They were allowed to go to bed later and stayed outside until dusk. Added to this was the opportunity to earn pocket money by selling homemade ice cream. The day the fair moved on coincided with Klaus' last day at the Gasthof. Before leaving, he told them that in spite of his obsession to follow his brothers, there would always be a place in his happy memories of his time at the Gasthof Engel.

With just two weeks before school was due to start again, the boys were looking for adventure. They did not have many toys. Only a few survived the treatment of five boys and remained intact. The village was their toy box. One morning, they set off with their swimming trunks to go to the lake, which was about half a mile away on the other side of the airfield. There were four of them and two bikes. Sepp and Rudi, being younger, had the passenger seat on the cross bars. Rudi could not swim, but with his three older brothers scoffing at his caution, he ventured further and further into the lake. Out of his depth, he splashed about with all four limbs to keep his head above water. His cries for help appeared to be ignored, but his brothers' eyes never left him. They were relieved when he returned to firm ground and their life-saving skills had not been called upon. This experience gave Rudi the determination to become a competent swimmer.

On the way home, the spluttering of an engine caused them all to look skywards. A light aircraft, obviously in trouble, was losing height rapidly and in danger of overshooting the runway. Frightened at first, but realising there was no danger to themselves, they started to run towards the village where the malfunctioning plane was heading. From a distance, they could see pilots at the airfield racing around in panic. They quickened their pace, the younger boys struggling to keep up on their tired legs. Just topping a hedge, the plane disappeared from view. The boys turned the corner of the street leading to the airfield. There was an ear-splitting crunching sound as the plane skidded across the road, narrowly missing a house which adjoined a waste piece of land, where it finally came to rest. The pilot climbed out, seemingly unharmed, just as a stream of breathless aircraft personnel arrived on the scene. The boys raced home to tell their parents. Only Erich remained. He was reliving the shock he had experienced when he had eventually learnt of Florian's death. For a moment, he imagined his friend, for whom he still grieved, would climb out of the cockpit, but, slowly, he returned home disappointed.

The training at the airfield had intensified so much that the pilots were too exhausted to socialise in the evenings these days and, in any case, the Poles now used the small room for their recreation. This left the boys seeking other company elsewhere.

"Let's go and see Oma and Opa," Hans said to Sepp. "Opa will play cards with us."

Agatha opened the door. "Hello," she said, a little surprised. "I expect you want to see Opa. He's in the living room."

They went in and startled Leonhard, who was listening to the radio. Looking alarmed, he got up from his chair and quickly turned it off.

"Hello, Opa. Will you play cards with us please?"

"Err, yes, be glad to, boys. Where is Erich?"

"He's gone to meet some people he met by the lake. Mama says they're very nice people and that he should go," said Sepp.

"Who are they?"

"What was the name, Hans? It was a funny foreign name, wasn't it?"

"Chandler," replied Hans. "They're American. They said they'll teach Erich some English."

It was the following evening after their meal. The Poles had left the table, eager to finish their duties and join their friends. Leonhard remained thoughtful and made no comments.

"I know what 'Guten Abend' is in English," said Erich proudly.

"How do you know?" asked his mother.

"Herr and Frau Chandler told me."

"What is it then?" asked Hans challengingly.

"Good evening."

"That's what I heard on Opa's radio!" exclaimed Hans.

Josefa and Johann both looked up. "When?" they asked incredulously.

"When we went to play cards."

Johann and Josefa just stared at each other for a few moments. There were so many unsaid and unanswered questions swirling around their heads. *Is it possible? Have we made a mistake? He couldn't be so careless, could he? Does he realise what would happen if he were caught? Surely, he wouldn't take such risks!*

"I think I'll go and see Oma and Opa this evening," said Josefa with as much calmness as she could muster.

Johann helped himself to another cup of coffee just as the postal van arrived delivering a large box. Josefa, who had just popped a spoonful of egg into Helga's mouth, got up quickly. She handed Johann the egg spoon and hurried to the back door.

"There's a box of trouble for you, Frau Birk," said the young driver cheekily. Josefa knew exactly what the box contained. Printed on it in large letters was 'LIVE CONTENTS'. She placed the box beside the warm stove and lifted the lid to reveal a host of chirpy, yellow one-day-old chicks. Her initiative to buy hens had proved to be so successful that she had decided to restock. It helped with the egg shortage and the old boilers had provided meat for soups and stews. Curiosity had got the better of the others present in the kitchen and soon, Johann, Aniela and Helga were peering into the box.

"Aren't they cute?" said Josefa excitedly, "The boys will love them."

"But Helga will hug them to death if we're not careful," warned Johann.

Josefa replaced the hole-punched lid and turned to Aniela. Speaking slowly whilst pointing to the box and then stretching the palms of her hands towards the stove, she said, "They are to stay here to keep warm." Aniela nodded.

As predicted, the boys were delighted to see the new arrivals, but after a while, their mother decided the chicks needed a break from all their attention. She suggested they go to see their grandparents for an hour before bedtime.

"No playing cards tonight," she called after them. "You've got school tomorrow."

As usual, Agatha and Leonhard were pleased to see them.

"We've got some different children at school, Opa," said Hans.

"What do you mean, different?"

"They don't speak German like us. They come from Berlin. They're staying with some of the other boys' families. It's cos of the war, they told us. There were bombs where they lived."

"They are silly, Opa" giggled Erich. "They asked us where the cheese mine was. They think we dig it out of the ground. Everyone laughed at them and told them it's made from cows' milk.

"Then we asked them if they knew what a cow was and if they'd ever seen one," the boys chuckled.

"That made them very cross," said Sepp. "Then they laughed at us because we've never been on an underground train like they've got in Berlin, but we—"

"Who's that, Oma, in that picture?" interrupted Rudi, who had been sitting quietly staring at a framed photograph on top of the dresser.

"He's Opa's grandfather. He was a soldier. Opa will tell you all about him."

Rudi went to sit on his grandfather's lap whilst Hans, Erich and Sepp sat on the floor, at his feet.

"There was a French emperor called Napoleon," Leonhard began.

"What's an emperor, Opa?" asked Rudi.

"Like a Kaiser or a king. He wanted to conquer Russia. He gathered a lot of soldiers from here in Bavaria to join his army, about 30,000 of them."

"Whew, that's a lot!" exclaimed Hans.

"Now Russia is a very, very large country. The soldiers were not given much food. Napoleon expected them to live off the land."

"What do you mean, Opa?" asked Sepp.

"Like catching fish in the rivers and shooting animals to eat. It took a long time to get to the big town of Moscow. When they did get there, they found it had been set on fire and all the people had gone." They boys listened attentively.

"The soldiers had orders to retreat. To turn 'round and go back, but by then, it was winter. They have much worse winters than ours, absolutely freezing." Leonhard paused for a minute.

The boys didn't move. They were spellbound by the story.

"There was so much snow, the horses had nothing to eat and were dying. Ten men had to share one loaf of bread. When they reached the river called Berezina, they found the bridge had been blown up. Some tried to swim across to escape the Russian soldiers, but they either drowned or froze to death."

Leonhard took a deep breath and his eyes scoured the fixed expression on his grandsons' faces.

"What happened to your Opa?" asked Hans. His eyes wide open in expectation.

"He couldn't swim. Guess what he did." They all shook their heads without a word.

"There was one horse. He led him into the water, held on his tail and the horse swam pulling him across. Then my grandfather hid in a church until it was safe to come out. It was May when he got home. It had taken him six months. He was one of the lucky ones. Only 2,000 Bavarian soldiers survived."

Hearing the end of the narrative, Agathe poked her head around the door and jolted the boys out of their reverie.

"I think that's enough family history this evening," she told them. "Your mother will want you home now."

An autumnal sunset had set the sky ablaze as the brothers sauntered home. In their thoughts, they were in Russia, trudging through thick snow.

With certain foods in short supply, Christmas passed modestly and there were neither lavish celebrations nor fireworks for the New Year 1941. Blackout rules were in place and the windows were covered in black paper. Josefa's sister Ida and her husband had joined the family over the festive period. At the first opportunity to be alone together, the two sisters sat and chatted incessantly. They had always been extremely close and had implicit trust in each other to keep secrets. They talked mainly about Josefa's children. Sadly, Ida was unable to have children of her own, but she took a great deal of interest in her sister's family. She was a personal assistant to the commander of a military airbase, which limited any conversation about her job to a minimum. It was when they decided that they were getting very tired and it was time for bed, that Ida leant over and whispered in her sister's ear. Josefa's reaction was one of shock and incredulity. Her eyes opened wide, her eyebrows reached their maximum height and her mouth dropped open.

"Please don't tell father, Jo," pleaded Ida. "It's not certain yet and you know what he's like."

"Of course I won't. You know me. Come on, let's get some sleep."

It was a few weeks later that Johann received a telephone call.

"Who was it?" asked Josefa noticing Johann's puzzled expression.

"It was the standards control office at Nestlé."

"What do they want?"

"They want me to call at their office at my earliest convenience."

"Can't think why, but there is only one way of finding out. I think I'll go now. Shouldn't be too long, Jo."

Josefa dismissed Nestlé's request as a minor accounts query and was not unduly concerned, but when Johann returned looking worried, she sensed it was something serious.

"What's happened, Hanni? What's wrong?" she asked anxiously.

"They said our milk is not up to standard."

"How can that be?"

"They say it's been watered down."

"What! It can't be!" shrieked Josefa.

Johann put his finger to his closed lips. "Not so loud, Jo. They said they'll give us another week to solve the problem. Don't mention it to anyone at this stage. We've got to find out about this ourselves."

They carried out some unobtrusive detective work and were dismayed to discover that Sofie was the culprit. She was privately selling milk and making up the shortfall in the churn with water. Johann could not risk jeopardising his income from Nestlé and in spite of assuring them it would not happen again, they said they had no alternative but to report it. Sofie was sent to prison, where she existed on a diet of mainly bread and water for two months. She had learnt a hard lesson and paid the price.

She was able to breathe the fresh alpine air again when she returned on a beautiful spring day, just after Gerhard's fifth birthday. Shortly afterwards, it was Easter and she revelled in her freedom to join the children in the egg hunt, the eggs that their mother had decorated in bright colours.

Chapter 20

"I didn't sleep too well, it was such a warm night," said Johann making his first appearance of the day a bit later than usual.

"What do you expect this time of the year," was Josefa's reply.

"It seems exceptionally quiet down here this morning," he remarked as he helped himself to a cup of coffee.

"Perhaps it's got something to do with the fact that four of our boys have not long gone off to school. Make the most of it; they break up for the summer hols next month."

"Oh, that's the reason, is it? Rudi's settled in quite well, hasn't he?" remarked Johann.

Their peace was short lived. At that moment, a very agitated Leonhard stormed into the Büro, shutting the door firmly behind him.

"He's an imbecile, I tell you. Have you heard the news?" he roared, his face bright red.

"Keep your voice down, Papa, please," Josefa pleaded.

"He's marched into Russia. He's mad. Hasn't he learnt any history?"

Johann looked a little stunned. Josefa remained silent. She had kept her word and had been preparing to brace herself for her father's outburst when the news was officially announced. Hearing Helga calling for her, she left the two men and smiled, when she thought of Hanni's 'exceptionally quiet morning'.

Volkmar looked sombre as he joined the others at the regulars' table the following week-end.

"You look glum" remarked Dieter.

Volkmar just sat staring downwards for a few moments, then looking up, he replied dolefully, "Peter's been sent to Russia."

They all lowered their eyes. Heini was the first to break the silence.

"I don't think there'll be much trouble. There wasn't in Czechoslovakia, Austria and Poland. From all accounts, our Panzers managed to cover 50 miles on the first day."

"But Russia is different, Heini. It's so vast," protested Volkmar.

"They say it won't take long. He'll be OK. They took the Russians by surprise and they hadn't got their act together," said Gustav reassuringly.

"Anyway, Hitler says it'll be over by the autumn. Some of the top brass expect to celebrate Christmas in Red Square," said Heini encouragingly.

"Let's hope so," said Volkmar with a sigh. "Peter says they've only been kitted out with summer gear."

There followed a moment of silence as thoughts of being inadequately clad in a Russian winter and the consequences flashed through their minds.

"Well, the top brass are obviously very optimistic," said Dieter, who was becoming increasingly worried about his son Otto's deployment to Russia.

"Let's hope Hitler 'as got it right, cos that kit'll be no bloody good in a Russian winter," grunted Gustav as he filled his pipe.

"Don't worry, Volkmar, it won't be long before a young female Muscovite offers to keep him warm," said big Bertl light heartedly in an effort to lift spirits.

Volkmar shrugged off this remark. He wasn't in the mood. The others just forced a smile concealing their genuine concern.

"There's someone wanting your attention, Hanni," Gustav called out. Johann turned around and saw Sepp standing in the doorway.

"What do you want, Sepp?"

"When will Rudi be back from Austria, Papa?"

"Not till later this afternoon."

"I wish I could have gone."

"The driver only had room for one on his big lorry. He had so many beer barrels to deliver. You'll get your turn one day."

Sepp sauntered through the kitchen on his way to the yard to await the lorry's return. His mother was stirring the contents of a large saucepan.

"Mama, everyone's talking about Russia. That's where Opa's grandfather went with Napoleon, isn't it?"

"Yes, that's right," she replied watching him go outside, deep in thought. It was obvious that he was suffering from a touch of boredom. Hans was at the Hitler Youth meeting and Erich was immobile. He injured his foot when he jumped down from the hay wagon in the barn and landed on the pitch fork.

At last, the sound of an engine pulling into the yard sent Sepp scuttling to greet his brother. Rudi looked a weary little figure as he dragged his feet across the yard to the kitchen entrance. Powdery dry earth rising from the alpine paths, combined with the occasional shower, had stiffened his hair so that it stood up in peaks.

"I'm starving," he moaned as he slumped onto a kitchen chair, ignoring his mother's enquiry about his trip.

"The bockwurst is already in the water, heating up. They won't be long," she called out as she left the kitchen to thank the driver.

"He was very good," he told her. "No trouble, but I think he's very tired and hungry." He looked around and lowered his voice. "We came back a slightly different route. There's a camp been set up about five kilometres from here. Looked like foreign workers behind the wire fencing. Probably troublemakers taken off the farms and those foreigners working at the Messerschmitt factory."

Lifting his shoulders and slowly shaking his head, he climbed back in his cab and glancing in Jo's direction, he drove away.

A piercing scream brought Josefa racing back to the kitchen. She was confronted with a toppled saucepan and Rudi holding a scalded arm.

"Couldn't you have waited?" she yelled, grabbing a towel to wrap over the bright red skin. She clutched his other arm and pulling him along, deaf to his protests, she ran with him to her mother. Agatha had a proven reputation to have the power to heal burns. She was a deeply religious woman. The proof was there again when Rudi returned home without any pain or discomfort. He was in good spirits now. Having satisfied his ravenous appetite with potato salad and a bockwurst dipped frequently into mustard, he told them about his day in Tirol, where they had driven along hair-raising high altitude roads to deliver beer to remote alpine inns.

"How's your arm, son?" asked Johann as he got up to go back to the bar.

"Not so bad, Papa."

"That's good because I want you to take Gabi to graze in the far field at the weekend. Sepp, I want you to take the harness to the saddler. It needs stitching."

Sepp accepted his task without complaint. He had a happy-go-lucky reliable character and since he had worn glasses from an early age, he had not got involved in sport.

"I've got some other jobs lined up, too," Johann added, turning his head towards Hans and Erich who had not been quick enough to disappear. "Mama says your foot is much better, Erich. You two can give me a hand."

"Oh no, Papa, we want to go to watch planes," they wailed, but Johann, anticipating protests, had made sure he was out of earshot.

"Mama, what's vermin?" Rudi asked suddenly.

Looking surprised, she asked, "What do you want to know for?"

"Well, when we drove past that place where they're all dressed in stripes, Max's mate, who came with us, said he'd heard on the radio, that's where they put the vermin."

"I don't know," said Josefa hurriedly. "Come on, it's time for bed. You should sleep well tonight."

Rudi awoke shading his eyes from the low rays of the rising sun. He scoured the attic bedroom he shared with his brothers. Their beds were all empty. He lifted his legs in the air, swivelled around and, with the accuracy of a crane driver, dropped his feet into his lederhosen whilst pulling the floral-patterned braces over his shoulders. The short calf leather trousers, worn throughout the summer and never washed, had become so stiff, it enabled them to be free standing beside the bed. The ideal garment for boys' activities, it withstood wading in streams, climbing trees or fences, mucking out pig sties and rolling in mud when settling a dispute with a brother or school peer. The task he was assigned today was one Rudi quite enjoyed. It suited his character. He was a dreamer and to sit astride Gabi, bare back, holding the reins in one hand and a salami-filled bread roll in the other whilst she plodded along, just suited him.

It was one day during the autumn term that the boys found their mother with red eyes and tear-stained cheeks when they came home from school. They all stared at her.

"Are you all right, Mama?" enquired Hans.

"Yes, I'm OK. Now, boys, sit down. Your lunch is ready."

With their healthy appetites, they needed no prompting as they tucked into a plate of sauerkraut, potatoes and bratwurst. They were unaware that their mother's gaze did not leave their faces. Unknown to them, she had just received news that young Klaus had been killed. Ironically, not on the fighting line, but on a street in Berlin where a bomb fell close to his training barracks. Josefa's mind kept flashing back to his rosy smiling face and shuddered at the thought that he was only four years older than her eldest son.

"Sepp had a couple of whacks on his behind today, Mama," said Erich as he stuffed another spoonful into his mouth. "He had squabble with one of the Berliners."

"So Fräulein Gruber pulled down his pants in front of the class. She was smiling, Mama. I don't like her," said Hans scraping his plate. "Then she made us all stand up to do the Nazi salute. She didn't punish the Berliner, because he told her his auntie had been killed by a bomb in Essen."

Before Josefa could comment, she heard Johann's breathless voice behind her.

"Here's an order for Dieter and Volkmar. Hermann's just come in. Must go." He disappeared.

"Hello, Hermann. Is this a social call or are you on mayoral duties?"

"No, no, Hanni. Just wondered if you'd heard the news. Our men are just 40 miles from Moscow. Temperature is dropping like a stone and it's snowing, which will slow down the advance of course, but they'll make it. The siege of Leningrad is ongoing. I don't think the Russkis can hold out much longer."

Volkmar became very tense and Dieter shifted uncomfortably in his chair. He set his eyes on Hermann's flushed face, eager for any more information. He knew better than to make any critical comment. Hermann was an ardent Party member. Johann, well aware of the situation, was quick to offer Hermann a drink and was relieved to hear his decline.

"No thank you, Hanni. Duty calls. I must go. Greetings to your dear wife. Trust all the family is well."

Johann's affirmative nod sufficed and Hermann took his leave as Johann went into the kitchen to collect the order.

"Greetings from Hermann, Jo." He glanced at the children still sitting at the table and lowered his voice to a whisper, "I've got something to tell you later on."

The children left the room and Josefa embarked on a solitary reflection about what the lorry driver had told her, the anxiety she had experienced lately with Erich's foot and Rudi's arm, Klaus' death, the escalation of bombing raids in the north and the continual worry about her father's carelessness, both in speech and listening to the BBC. She just hoped Johann had good news to tell her.

When the last customer had left, the door was locked and the children were asleep, Johann poured out two glasses of wine.

"Well, what was it you wanted to tell me?" asked Josefa struggling to keep an urgent need for sleep at bay.

"I had a call from the SS headquarters in Berlin."

This information induced Josefa's heart to race, her eyes opened wide and she became very alert. Seeing the fear in her eyes, Johann was quick to allay it.

"Don't worry, Jo. It's about the VIP coming here on his way to Sonthofen. Remember?"

"He wants to have a break here and have something to eat. Right." Josefa nodded. "They want accommodation for two drivers and two SS officers as well, but there's no date fixed yet. I think it will be at very short notice."

Josefa took a deep sigh. "I think I'd like to go to bed now. I feel very tired."

It was not surprising that the visit did not take place until the new year. At the beginning of December 1941, they learnt that the Russians were retaliating. The German army was

187

suffering colossal casualties, both on the battlefield and through the cruel Russian winter. A month later, whilst they were still reeling from the bad Russian news, America had entered the war.

When Johann and Josefa learnt the identity of the VIP and the date of his arrival, they made arrangements for the two young children to spend the day with their grandparents and the four boys were given money to go and amuse themselves in the town after school. The boys were delighted with these arrangements, although they were all very curious about this unexpected treat. Josefa was given an official reminder to provide homemade Spätzle. Whilst the boys were in town, they were unaware that their father was serving the most hated man in Europe, Heinrich Himmler.

The snow ploughs had already cleared the roads of the night's heavy fall, but as the children made their way across the fields, their skis left an intricate pattern in their wake. Arriving at school, they stacked their skis neatly outside on the last day of autumn term. The four brothers were very excited about the forthcoming Christmas holidays, in spite of knowing that their father would be compiling a long list of jobs to occupy them. Josefa was finding it difficult to muster her usual enthusiasm for the festive period. The interminable daily dose of propaganda on the radio was in complete contrast to the disturbing news of Russia, which filtered through the net of secrecy.

Aniela was busy in the kitchen when the boys emerged from their slumber the following morning.

"There are fresh pretzels on the table," she called out to them. They put their fingers to their lips, hoping they would get out to play in the snow before their father detected them. Too late, Johann was already standing behind them.

"Hans, I want you to take Gabi to the farrier this morning. She needs winter shoes. Erich, it's your turn to collect the whey from the Käserei. Sepp and Rudi, get the big sleighs ready. After lunch, you'll go to the lake with Stanislav to get the ice."

These instructions were met with a chorus of moans. The ice box, insulated with peat, was the size of a small room. It had been erected in the barn over an area where steps led down to the store of beer barrels. In winter, it was filled with big chunks of ice sawn out of the lake. The melting ice dripped through between the floor boards and kept the beer cool in the summer.

The snow had muffled the familiar sound of Gabi's hooves, so Johann was not aware of Hans' return until he saw him lead her into the stable. With his eyes fixed to the ground, Hans walked back across the yard.

"Everything OK, Hans?" There was no reply. "What's the matter?"

"Günther has been killed."

"Oh, no! Where?"

"In Russia. Herr Neumann is so upset. His apprentice was there coping on his own."

Johann sat down on the wooden bench without a word. He was visibly shaken by the news. Günther had always been a good friend. He was a kind, caring man with a passion for horses. He had told Johann, when he was called up, that as the army still used horses, he hoped he would be assigned to smithy duties. Hans broke the silence.

"Papa, a siege is when you stop food and supplies getting through to somewhere, isn't it?"

Johann lifted his head looking puzzled. "Yes. Why?"

"I heard someone whispering about Leningrad and a siege. It can get very cold in Russia, can't it, Papa?"

"Yes, son, as low as 30–40 degrees minus."

A sudden thud made them both spin around towards the window, where a flattened snowball was sliding down the pane. They looked out and saw Erich returning with the sleigh carrying two churns of whey. He was being bombarded with snowballs by his younger brothers. He called out to Hans.

"We've got to attend a gathering of remembrance for Günther on Saturday. All Hitler Youth members have to be in uniform." Hans just nodded.

That evening, the mood was subdued on the regulars' table following the news of Günther's death. He had been popular and much respected in the village. Volkmar was becoming increasingly worried about Peter. Just two weeks previously, they had been discussing the Japanese attack on America and what it could lead to. Now they knew. America had entered the war and was supporting Britain. They wondered whether it was this news or because of Christmas that the Poles, gathered in the little room, were more excitable and louder than usual. The farmers were quite relieved when the local Bobby arrived to impose the Poles' curfew. Whilst Johann served the policeman a nightcap, Volkmar's attention was taken by his farm labourer Georg, a Polish shoemaker. He was so engrossed chatting to Aniela, that he was the last to leave.

Tante Ida and her husband, together with grandparents Leonhard and Agathe, joined the family to celebrate Christmas. The Gasthof was closed for the day, allowing them all to enjoy a festive meal uninterrupted. Having eaten, the six very much exited children received their gifts and the adults left them to play in the Stube whilst they retired to the Büro for coffee and schnapps.

"What's the news in Russia, Ida?" Leonhard asked his daughter.

"Not good," she replied lowering her eyes. "They're having a very tough time and morale is low."

"I saw pictures of Russian POWs. They looked better kitted out compared with our men. Really thick boots and quilted winter coats," continued Leonhard before emptying his glass in one.

"The instruction from above is to stick it out! The Führer insists there'll be no withdrawal." Ida's voice was barely audible now. "He won't listen to advice."

The conversation came to an abrupt end as the door opened and little Helga appeared.

"I'm tired, Mama," she said sleepily. Josefa took her hand and led her upstairs to bed. Later, the rest of the family attended midnight mass, leaving Helga in Sofie's care.

There had been the minimum of celebration to greet 1942. It was three weeks into the new year when Johann noticed his neighbour vigorously digging.

"What's that for?" he enquired.

"A shelter, Hanni. We've got to have some protection if they start bombing us here in the south. I'm making some steps down to the cellar to have access from the outside." Johann looked pensive for a few moments.

"Do you need any help?"

"No thank you, I can manage, but if your two older boys could give me a hand at the weekend, it'll be very useful. You've got enough to do. I shall make the concrete steps next week."

This piece of information triggered off a plan and Johann hastened to share it with Josefa.

"We've got two birthdays to celebrate, Jo, don't forget. I've got some logs for Stanislav to saw up. We've just got to synchronise it all with the concrete mixer. I know it's a risk, but it'll be OK."

The plan they had just hatched was the clandestine slaughter of a piglet. They had to create as much noise as possible to drown the squealing. Each farmer had a limited quota for his own consumption and if it exceeded this, there were severe penalties. Gustav, the butcher, knew that Johann had already had his quota and declined to help. He was not willing to take the risk. One morning, directly, they heard the concrete mixer, Stanislav started sawing, the car motor was running and Johann did the deed. Simultaneously, Josefa turned on the noisy high-pitched machine which separated the cream from the milk. The centrifuge was in the cellar and this was also illegal. The accomplices were well rewarded. They all enjoyed a good joint of roast pork on Johann's birthday.

The joviality of the celebrations was short lived. From the snippets of hushed information that they heard, they realised what excessive hardship their troops in Russia were suffering. They also learnt the tragic news that Klaus' elder brother had been killed in Stalingrad.

Chapter 21

Rudi pulled up his thick woollen socks to reach his breeches just below the knees. He mourned the freedom of going barefoot as he did in the summer and hated the restriction of winter clothing. Looking out of the window, he knew the sunshine and blue sky this morning gave a false impression of the temperature outside. He was always the last to get up. Anyway, there was no immediate rush to meet his brothers.

Hans and Erich had been instructed, with other Hitler Youth members, to collect bone, metal and rags. It was their duty to help the Führer and Vaterland, they have been told. The arrangement was that Sepp and Rudi would take the sleigh to the top of the hill to help bring the sacks down to the village collection depot. Sepp was already waiting by the sleigh by the time Rudi had finished his breakfast. Together they dragged it up the steep incline, their warm breath creating puffs of vapour. Hans and Erich and their two friends piled the sacks on the sleigh before clambering on-board. The two younger ones took a back seat, allowing the older ones to steer. There were shrieks of laughter as they careered down the hill, narrowly missing vehicles and pedestrians. After they had unloaded, the six pairs of eyes made a unanimous decision. That the experience was too exciting not to do it again!

"Is lunch ready, Mama?" the four hungry boys asked at the kitchen door as they took off their boots. Josefa cast a disapproving glance at the clumps of ice and snow rapidly melting on her kitchen floor.

"Your lunch is ready, but first, your father wants to have a word with you," she answered sternly.

"We're hungry, Mama," they wailed.

"That may be, but there have been complaints and Papa's not too happy, I can tell you. He's in the Büro."

The boys were too amazed to offer any defence against their father's reprimand for reckless behaviour on the sleigh. They just stared at him without a word. They had never seen their father in uniform before.

"As you can see, boys," said Johann having regained his composure, "I've joined the Volksturm and have been supplied with a pistol and a pickup truck. Did you notice it outside? It's got bench seating so that I can provide the transport for other members."

The brothers still silent, stood absorbing the information, but when Johann suggested it was time for lunch, there was a rush to the door. He followed them calling out.

"You're to stay in doors for the rest of the day. I don't want any more complaints from the villagers, d' yer hear?"

Their response was drowned in the noise of their scramble to the kitchen table.

"Jo, one of Gabi's shoes is a bit loose, I'll have to take her myself," said Johann as he stepped out of the door leading to the yard. "Hello, what's Aniela doing over there at Friedrich's? Who's she talking to?"

"That's George, the Pole from Volkmar's. I think he's been sent to give Friedrich a hand," replied Josefa peering out of the window. "Tell Aniela I need some help here when you go past, will you?" she added with a harassed sigh.

It had begun to snow again as Gabi was led to the blacksmith, Herr Neumann, Günther's father was stoking up the furnace. He turned his sad, drawn face towards Johann.

"I'm finding it difficult to carry on, Hanni," he said quietly. He fumbled in his pocket and handed Johann a crumpled envelope, smudged with soot. "Günther asked his friend to send this to me if anything happened to him. When Günther fell, the friend found this in his pocket. He kept it safely until he was airlifted out when his leg was blown off."

Whilst Herr Neumann attended to Gabi, Johann took the piece of paper out of the envelope. As his eyes skimmed over the spindly erratic handwriting and read about the suffering his friend had endured, he blinked away the moisture in his eyes. Frost bites had robbed Günther of three fingers on his right hand, but even worse for him was the sight of severely injured and starving horses. He pleaded with his father, if he did not

193

return, to keep the forge going. A hissing sound of liquid on hot metal caused Johann to look up. Tears were streaming down Herr Neumann's face and dripping on the tongs he had just taken out of the furnace.

About a month later, during the Easter holidays, Hans and Erich went with their father to check the growth of the saplings they had planted the previous autumn. Their top shoots had been painted with blood from a slaughtered pig to prevent the deer from eating them. In winter, at designated sites, the forest ranger would provide hay and horse chestnuts for the deer. Today, it was Rudi's task to cycle to the woods to take his father and brothers their packed lunches, which were carried in a basket over the front wheel. The winding path was steep in places and Rudi's legs ached terribly. He was relieved when he had delivered the goods and could lie flat on the grass to recover, knowing the return journey would all be downhill.

Reaching the village, he rode down the main street. As he approached the Gasthof, he was aware of something unusual taking place in the yard. There were men in uniform wearing jack boots, who were in the process of cleaning two cars. They were the sort of cars he had never seen before. He decided to go in the front entrance and make for the kitchen.

"Mama, who are those soldiers? Why are they cleaning their cars in our yard?"

Josefa, who was making pasta dough, looked up at him.

"How are they getting on in the woods? Have they much more to do?" she asked ignoring his question.

"Nooo," was the impatient reply. "Who are those outside? What cars are they? Where are they going?" Rudi's frustration was very apparent.

"They've got to collect a special person from the airfield tomorrow and they're making sure the cars are nice and clean. Now, no more questions. Take this cheese over to Oma, please. She's waiting for it."

Looking disgruntled, Rudi took the cheese. He was determined to find out more when his brothers returned.

That evening, the SS bodyguards, with three accompanying officers, were in the Stube, fully occupied, consuming large quantities of beer. Josefa was putting Helga to bed. This provided an ideal opportunity for the four brothers to take a good look at the strange cars in the yard. They were surprised to find that there were two open-topped Mercedes, both shining beautifully.

"Cor!" exclaimed Hans, leaning over the passenger door. "Look at those machine pistols clamped inside each door. They must be guarding someone very important. Wonder who it is."

At that moment, they heard the creak of the barn door being opened. It was dusk now and difficult to identify the two shadowy figures that ran across the yard. When they opened the kitchen door, the shaft of light revealed Georg and Aniela. By the time the boys went inside, the two had already joined the other Poles at their meeting place in the small back room.

The following morning, Aniela was stirring a large saucepan of soup whilst the children were having breakfast. The boys began to tease her about her friendship with Georg.

"We saw you, Aniela. We saw you," they chanted.

"Stop it! Stop it!" she hissed.

They wouldn't until a soup ladle hurtled through the air, narrowly missing Rudi's head. Aniela's face turned ashen when the possible consequences of her action flashed through her mind. Hearing the commotion, Johann, followed by Josefa, rushed into the kitchen.

"What's happened?" he demanded. He listened to the explanation and then calmly asked Rudi if he were hurt in any way.

"No, Papa. It just missed me."

"In that case, we shan't say anymore about it."

Shooting a stern glance in Aniela's direction, he added, "But it must never happen again." Aniela's face expressed a concoction of anxiety and relief.

'CLOSED TILL 4 P.M.' Johann felt his hand trembling as he hung the notice on the Gasthof's main door. He had had a restless night and felt a wave of nausea as he thought of the day ahead. The chief of the secret police, one of the most powerful men in the country, close to Führer Hitler, would be here, under his roof, having lunch cooked by Jo! Added to this was the worry of keeping it quiet, which he had been instructed to do. It would necessitate a very good explanation for the closure when he faced regulars later on. Stanislav had been sent to the woods to do logging. Jo had made sure Aniela and Sofie would be fully occupied servicing the guest rooms upstairs and the children were either with the grandparents or at school. Fortunately, it just happened to be Else's day off. As he busied himself stocking up the bar and preparing the table, he was thinking how surprised he was at Josefa's calmness. *Probably due to the fact that she makes Spätzle so often and could cook it with her eyes shut,* he thought.

Punctually, at the estimated time of arrival, Johann saw the two large Mercedes staff cars come to a halt just outside. He opened the door wide to the sound of Jack boot heels clicking as the VIP stepped down from his vehicle. He walked past his uniformed and armed personnel, who stood erect and were saluting. Johann nodded humbly and straightaway led the high-ranking officer and his entourage into the Stube, pausing for Himmler's braided cap to be hung up on the stand. There was very little conversation as they satisfied their thirst with Bavarian beer, whilst Johann made sure the main door was securely locked. Himmler's eyes widened at the sight of the large tureen brought to their table, containing veal and liver dumplings in a clear consommé, known as 'Knődel Suppe'. This was followed by the officially requested Bavarian speciality 'Käsespätzle', homemade pasta topped with grated Emmentaler cheese and crispy fried onions. A portion of Josefa's 'Apfelstrudel' concluded the meal.

It was difficult to imagine that this inconspicuous man could command such allegiance. Was it through fear that his staff was so obsequious? His squinting eyes cast a piercing gaze through his small-rimmed spectacles. In plain clothes, one could mistake him for a benign, avuncular individual. Instead, he wielded enormous power and had earned himself the reputation of being the most feared and hated man in Europe. Johann was well aware that a slip of the tongue or a misconstrued statement could have extremely dire consequences.

When the last spoon was laid to rest, Johann approached the table in trepidation.

"Was the meal to your liking, Herr Reichsführer?"

"Excellent, Herr Wirt," Himmler remarked as he stood up to leave. "Compliments to your wife. She runs a good kitchen," he added with a faint smile.

"Thank you, Herr Reichsführer," Johann replied meekly.

The escort was in place for the departure and once again was accompanied by the clicking of heels. As the two vehicles drove away, Johann took down the 'closed' notice and scurried back inside. Josefa was sitting down in the kitchen, recovering from nervous exhaustion. She had been so relieved to see the empty dishes and plates.

"Jo, Herr Himmler sends his compliments to you. He was very happy with his meal," Johann said with a huge sigh of relief, followed by a broad grin.

"I should jolly well think so," was the reply. "Let's sit down now and have our lunch and a stiff drink in peace before the children get back."

The regulars turned up not long afterwards.

"Someone told me you were closed this morning, Hanni," said Gustav inquisitively.

"Yes, we had trouble with the boiler. Had no hot water. I just had to work on it, and there was no Else today," replied Johann, not lifting his eyes as he filled their beer krugs. Nervously, he reminded himself to be careful and to steer them away from their curiosity. He could tell they found his explanation unsatisfactory.

"Any news of Peter?" he enquired. Volkmar just shook his head.

"Did you hear about Ernst Zurschmide?" asked Dieter.

"I heard that his son was in Russia, that's all," replied Johann, eager to pursue another subject.

"He's been taken away. To Dachau, most likely."

"Why's that?" Johann's eyes anxiously scoured the faces around the table.

"His daughter is a nurse at the military hospital where they've brought back some of the wounded from Russia. She must have told her father something that made him imagine the hell his son is going through. So Ernst went around ranting and raving about the agony our men are suffering. He was cursing those responsible, so they picked him up." With a helpless

197

shrug of his shoulders, Dieter picked up his glass and took several gulps.

The sound of children returning gave Johann the opportunity to move away without further comment.

"Are the soldiers with the big car still here, Papa?" Sepp asked.

"No, they've gone," replied Johann, ushering them into the Büro and out of earshot.

"Oh, we wanted to see them," the older boys whined.

"I expect they'll come again. Now tell me what you've been doing," Johann asked turning to the younger ones.

"We went to the woods and collected hazel wood sticks," they replied excitedly.

"Opa had some string and helped us to make bows and arrows."

"We saw Stanislav. He was cutting up logs from old trees."

"What did you do, Helga?" Johann asked as he helped her take off her coat.

"Oma and I baked a cake for tea. It was yummy."

When Johann returned to the Stube, he was glad to see the regulars were absorbed in playing cards. He collected their beer glasses, which were in need of a refill. The card playing continued to the early hours. In contrast to the previous day, Johann slept very soundly that night.

Gerhard looked longingly at his four brothers as they set off for school. He was due to start next term and was eager to go. It wasn't so much fun attending kindergarten with a younger sister. They came home earlier than their four brothers for lunch and he knew the time would drag until they all sat down for a good portion of smoked pork, which had been illicitly stored in Bertl's chimney. Afterwards, he and his brothers charged over to the airfield. He was not allowed to go there by himself. The airfield was much busier these days and there had been lots of crashes, Johann had told Hans. This was usually when the pilots qualified to fly solo. They took risks and showed off.

Until now, the boys had not been aware of the implications of all this uniformed activity, but, recently, Hans and Erich had begun to absorb the snippets of hushed conversation they overheard when they mingled with the customers in the Stube and Biergarten. They could read on their faces that all was not well and going to plan. The two boys became quite competent at interpreting the opinions of the customers by their hand signals, lipreading and eye contact.

By autumn, they had gathered that the situation in Russia was horrendous. One day, at the end of September, they called to see their Opa. He was listening to a broadcast by the Führer, who was saying that Germany would never surrender to Russia. It was then that they experienced an outburst from their grandfather. In the privacy of his own home, Leonhard let his anger overflow.

"He's demented. He'll bring us all down. They won't be able to take another Russian winter. How can the Luftwaffe keep up with the supplies? They'll need everything— ammunition, rations, medicines and winter clothing. It's madness!"

Seeing their grandfather so stressed, the boys decided this was not the ideal moment for a social call and it was not long before they slipped out of the house to return home. Ahead of them, as they drew nearer the Gasthof, they could see a young man on crutches being supported by an older man.

Hearing them approaching, the older man turned around. It was Volkmar. The younger man, who they could barely recognise, was his son Peter. He was about half his usual weight. His face was blanched and his eyes sunken. The sleeves of his jacket fell loose as did his trouser legs, so thin were his limbs. Both his feet were heavily bandaged.

"I've got him back," whispered Volkmar with a forced smile. The boys just stared, not knowing what to say.

The following day, they learnt from their father that Peter was convalescing at home.

"He considers himself as one of the lucky ones," they heard him tell their mother. "He was airlifted out of Stalingrad just in time. He's unable to stand unaided because he's suffered severe frostbites and lost some toes and a heel."

Two months later, Johann was informed that Heinrich Himmler would be visiting Sonthofen again and would be taking a late lunch at the Gasthof.

"A morale boasting trip, I expect," Johann muttered to himself.

"The news is bad enough," said Josefa overhearing him. "There are the Americans to worry about, too. We've been warned!" After a long pause, whilst they both sat deep in thought, she asked. "Shall I make Käsespätzle like last time?"

"Of course, that's what he comes here for. It's his favourite," was the reply.

"The children can stay here this time. Anyway, there's a HY meeting that afternoon," said Josefa resignedly.

The visit followed the same procedure and Reichsführer was once again delighted with his meal and sent his compliments to the kitchen. The noticeable difference this time was the extreme sombre atmosphere at their table, which was momentarily lifted as they were departing. They came across Hans and Erich returning from the HY meeting.

"You must be the Wirt's sons," said Reichsführer, his penetrating gaze burying into their faces with the obvious approval of the uniform that they were wearing.

They both stood to attention, totally in awe of this high-ranking officer, their chests swelled with pride. Sepp watched from a distance. He had trouble mastering the coordination of arms and legs when marching and had not taken part in the parade. Wasting no more time, Himmler climbed into his vehicle and, with a signal to his driver, was driven away.

Christmas approached and the enthusiasm for the festive season was lacking. The cessation of radio reports about the Russian offensive led the people to believe the news was getting worse. Then a frightening incident occurred one afternoon when the boys were building a snowman. Suddenly, the sound of a loud siren sent them racing to the kitchen, where their mother was anxiously looking out for them.

"Mama! Papa! Did you hear them? They weren't Messerschmitts. They were different planes!"

Chapter 22

No fireworks lit up the sky to hail the arrival of 1943. If there were any celebrations, they were behind closed doors and blackened windows. One morning, two weeks after the children had gone back to school, Johann went into the Büro, where he found Josefa sitting with clutched hands and a frown of anguish etched on her face.

"What's the matter, Jo? What did the doctor say?" he asked anxiously, searching her eyes.

"I've got to go to München for some tests."

Trying to disguise the shock he felt, Johann asked, "Do you know when?"

"Next week, but I shall have to stay a couple of nights at the hospital. How will you cope?" Her brow was now deeply furrowed as she pondered. "My mother will be more than willing to help with the children."

"Don't worry, Jo. We'll manage somehow. Sofie can be in the kitchen; Daniela will do the guest rooms, the cleaning and be on hand to assist your mother with the children if needed. I will take and collect you. Else won't mind shifting her day off. She'll be OK in the Stube whilst I'm not here."

These arrangements seemed to ease the turmoil in Josefa's mind and she endeavoured to smile.

"How's the pain?" Johann asked as he took hold of her hand.

"Not bad at the moment. I've taken one of my tablets. If they diagnose cancer, I shall have to have radiotherapy."

"Let's hope it won't come to that," Johann replied optimistically, gently squeezing her hand.

As they approached the industrial suburbs of München, on their way to the hospital, they saw the evidence of the American bombing raids. There were heaps of rubble and half-standing buildings. Neither of them spoke very much, their minds being full of worrying thoughts. Johann left Josefa in the care of the nursing staff, promising to come promptly when she was due to be fetched. The following day, he received a telephone call to say it would be necessary to keep his wife in hospital for a further three weeks for radiation treatment. His worst fears had been confirmed. He sat still for a few moments contemplating how he could tell the children, in particular, Helga, who had been crying for her mother.

The air raids and gloomy news from Russia, circulating in whispers, contributed to a light downturn in trade, for which, at this time, Johann was slightly relieved. It was the last day of January, the day after his 44th birthday, when, with a cup of coffee in his hand, he sat down in the kitchen and switched on the radio. The music was very sombre and Johann was just about to turn it off when an announcement was made.

"Our Führer, Adolf Hitler, wishes to deliver a statement to the German people." Johann turned the sound up and listened intently to the devastating report that the German army had been defeated at Stalingrad and was in retreat. He was in deep thought imagining the suffering such as Peter had endured when Aniela startled him.

"Here' the post, Herr Birk," she said handing him a bundle of letters. Among the recognisable bills were two official-looking envelopes addressed to him personally. His hands trembled as he opened one of them.

"Good God," he uttered under his breath. His heart was racing and his muscles tightened. "What am I going to do now?"

The envelope contained army call-up papers and a date for him to report for training in München. So engrossed was he, thinking Josefa would not have the strength to cope with the business and look after the children, that he overlooked the other letter, until it fell at his feet. He picked it up and, with his mind still occupied, he opened it and pulled out the enclosure. He found he was holding a signed photograph of Heinrich Himmler. His thoughts immediately turned to Josefa again.

Won't she enjoy believing he sent it in appreciation of her cooking? After all, he is a Swabian and I bet he doesn't get his native dishes in Berlin. Or was it because he was so pleased to see the boys in uniform? he mused. Then his thoughts reverted to the first letter. He sat for a while deciding what course of action he should take before reaching for a piece of writing paper and a pen. He resolved, he was not going to cause Josefa any more anxiety by telling her about his summon to army service until he had received a reply to his letter.

The children were very excited when they set off for school that morning. Mama was coming home. Johann's face bore a smile as he gave instruction to the staff before setting off to München. In contrast to the journey to the hospital, he and Josefa had a great deal more to talk about on the way back. One piece of news took priority.

"Jo, I didn't tell you before because I didn't want to worry you. I received call-up papers whilst you were in hospital." Not stopping for breath he added, "But I've been made exempt."

The emotions of shock and relief overcame Josefa in quick succession. Before she could utter a word, he continued. "On account of my age, having a sick wife and six children to care for, together with running a business which caters for trainee pilots and includes a small dairy herd, I've had a reprieve!"

He gasped for breath and almost took a wrong turning on the road through lack of concentration. When they reached the Gasthof, Josefa felt emotionally and physically exhausted. She spent a little time with the children, who had stayed up later for her return, before Aniela helped her upstairs to bed.

Later that evening, after Aniela had checked that the children were asleep, she asked Johann if she could have a few words with him. He led the way into the privacy of the Büro.

"Herr Birk, there's something I should like you to know. Today, whilst you were away, two SS trainees stopped here on their way to Sonthofen. They came to the back door and asked Sofie for water for their car's radiator." Aniela shifted uneasily from one foot to the other. "They were very fresh and familiar with her. She was very upset." Aniela spoke in a strong Polish accent and, at times, struggled to find the appropriate German word as she carried on. "Stanislav moved forward to protect her and they threatened him with arrest."

Johann dropped his eyes and his lips tightened as he tried to suppress his anger. After a few moments, he looked up at her.

"Thank you for telling me, Aniela. I'll speak to Sofie tomorrow. I do appreciate what you two have done whilst my wife was in hospital. I feel very tired now and must get some rest. Good night."

As he climbed the stairs to bed, Johann knew he dare not risk the consequences of a formal complaint to the SS.

The following day, Leonhard called at the Stube.

"Good morning, Hanni. Just popped in to see how my daughter is."

"She's doing fine but is very tired and has just dozed off. Could you manage a beer?"

"I certainly could," Leonhard replied as his eyes scoured the wall in the Stube.

"I'll bring it through to the Büro. It's not busy here at present."

There were a few moments of silence whilst they quenched their thirst. Then Leonhard put down his beer mug, wiped the froth from his mouth and engaged in a face-to-face stare with Johann.

"Why have you got that odious man's photo on the wall in the Stube, Hanni?" he asked sternly. "You know what I think about that bunch of thugs. They abuse their power and they'll bring disaster on this country. The catastrophe in Russia is just the beginning, you'll see."

"I'll tell you why if you give me a moment," replied Johann irritably. He then proceeded to relate the incident of the SS trainees. "It occurred to me when I received the photograph that this was one way of protecting my family and staff from the actions of jumped-up trainee SS hooligans! They're not likely to try anything on if there's a signed picture of their bloody boss on the wall. They're just as scared of him as we are." Johann thumped his fist on the table to emphasise his point as his face took on a shade of pink.

Leonhard remained silent for a few moments as he thought this through. There was a small chance that his son-in-law could be right. Through the window, he saw customers arriving and decided it was time to bring this animated conversation to a close.

"I'll just go and see if Jo's awake now," he said as he stood up and patted Johann's shoulder. I've got to tell her that her mother is coming this afternoon."

The weeks passed by and by as Easter had approached, Josefa regained most of her strength. The bombing continued but was mainly aimed at München. The American raids took place in daylight and the sight of the squadrons flying over provided entertainment for the boys, much to their mother's concern.

"Don't worry, Jo, the boys know the drill," Johann assured her. "They've got to run like hell back here when they hear the siren. The school packs them off home pretty nippy when there's an air raid warning. They're used to it now. Anyway, at the moment, they're happily playing football in the field with their friends."

Rudi left the others playing. His throat was parched and he was in desperate need of something to drink. As he approached the Gasthof, he could hear great hilarity coming from the direction of the Stube. Curious, he poked his head around the door. About six men were sitting at a table. One looked up and spotted him standing there, his cheeks bright red, his hair very windswept and his knees muddy.

"Hello, young man, what are you looking for?"

"I just came to get something to drink," he answered shyly. By now, all six heads had turned towards him.

"Come and join us," they called out smiling.

"I think you are just what we are looking for," said the first man.

"Don't be frightened. Come over here a minute," said one of them encouragingly.

Rudi still hesitated until he saw his father appear from the direction of the kitchen. Apprehension changed to relief and he took a few steps forward.

"What do you want, Rudi?" Johann asked as he cleared the plates.

"I am thirsty, Papa."

"Get the boy a drink and put it on our bill," the first man said. "Then perhaps the young fella will come and join us."

Johann looked pleased with this suggestion and beckoned Rudi whilst telling him to pull up another chair.

"This gentleman is making a film in the village," he told his son as he placed a long cool drink in front of him. "And this is Herr Rühmann, the famous film star."

Rudi shyly lifted his head a little and shifted uneasily in his seat.

"Don't be nervous," the film director said. "We're just looking for a few local youngsters to be extras in the film. Would you like to come for an audition at the airfield tomorrow?"

Rudi nearly choked on a mouthful of apple juice which he was just about to swallow. Without waiting for a reply, the film director continued, "The film is called *Quax der Bruch Pilot*. It's all about this crash pilot. 3 p.m. tomorrow at the airfield. All right?" Rudi just nodded timidly as the men stood up to leave.

That evening at the supper table, Rudi was subjected to an interrogation.

"What's the film about? Who else is in it? Why you? Will you go up in a plane? What's Herr Rühmann like? Will you get lots of money?"

Even the Poles were curious about it and sent Aniela from their meeting room to get more information.

Late afternoon the following day, the aspiring film extra returned home disappointed. He had not met with the criteria for the part. He was supposed to be fitted with a flying suit and to follow, with some other boys, Herr Rühmann and his bride to the church. Unfortunately, it was decided that he was just too tall.

"Never mind," said his mother. "You'll be able to go to watch them filming. But it's back to school tomorrow. You'll just have to go over there in the afternoons."

"OK," said a dejected Rudi as he slouched away out of the kitchen. Moments later, Johann rushed in with an order.

"All the actors and film crew are in. The locals have heard about the audition and everyone's talking about the film," he called out. Then seeing they were alone, he moved nearer to Josefa.

"There's some sad news. Ernst Zurschmide has been released from prison, but they say he's a broken man. His son's been taken prisoner in Russia."

"Oh no!" exclaimed Josefa.

"Ernst was knocked about badly in prison, but he's worried sick about his boy. He's seen some of them who've come back, half-starved and frostbitten. Poor blighters." He sighed heavily. Then hearing someone call from the Stube, he was gone in an instant.

During the following term, the siren sounded more frequently and the boys became used to running home at full speed. Sometimes they watched the dogfights up above when the Messerschmitts tried to intercept the American planes heading for München. Sepp's tenth birthday fell just before they were due to break up for the summer holidays. Josefa wanted to make a fruit loaf and sent Rudi to buy the dried fruit at a small shop on the other side of the road from the Gasthof. He was returning with the paper cone full of sultanas when he suddenly stood rigid, transfixed by the sight of a cart being pushed along by two men escorted by two SS guards. Slowly, they passed him by. His eyes continued to follow them for a while before he shot across the road, arriving breathless in the kitchen.

"I wasn't in that much of a hurry for them," said his mother as he handed the cone over to her.

"Mama, Mama. I've just seen some of those men I saw when we went to Austria in the beer lorry. The ones in striped clothes. Two of them were pushing a cart."

"Well, what was in the cart?" she asked as she began to weigh the ingredients for the tea bread.

"Bodies," whispered Rudi clasping his hands tightly and looking at the floor. Josefa turned around sharply to face him, catching the scales with her elbow and upsetting the flour over the work surface and floor.

"The dead ones were in striped clothes as well. The soldiers behind kept shouting at the two men to walk quicker."

Lost for words, Josefa put her arm around him and pulled him closer to her. Sepp saved the awkward situation by rushing into the kitchen, full of excitement.

"It's my birthday tomorrow. Yippee! Have you started baking yet, Mama? Wow, who did that? Look at all the flour on the floor."

Later that evening, when they were alone, Johann told Josefa that he had heard the parish council had put aside a piece of land to bury prisoners from the camp, where forced labourers who worked at the Messerschmitt factory were held.

"I just hope they keep a record of those they bury, poor souls," commented Josefa.

The sky was deep blue and the heat blistering as the four brothers sauntered home from school. It was Erich's last day at the primary. He would be attending the grammar school next term and Gerhard would be starting at the primary.

"I expect Papa's got some jobs lined up for us during the hols," moaned Hans.

"You bet," said Erich kicking a small stone away from the path. "It'll be haymaking for sure." He pulled a face.

A few days later, as predicted, they were following Stanislav to the meadow, armed with pitchforks to toss the hay. The three younger siblings remained at home, on call to do errands for their mother. Suddenly, they heard tapping on the kitchen window and they all looked towards the door, where a woman stood carrying a basket filled with loaves of bread.

"Rosa!" Josefa exclaimed in surprise. "I didn't recognise you at first. Come in. How are you?"

"I'm OK, Jo, but I'm having a difficult time. I've come to ask a favour."

"Sit down, Rosa. Hanni's just gone to check up on the haymakers. Would you like something to drink?"

"No thanks. I can't stay long. It's just that I need a bit of help delivering the bread this week. The two young lads who worked for me were called up when the war started. One's been killed." Her lips began to quiver and her eyes welled up.

"Horst and I have struggled to keep going, but now he's been called up. Could one of your boys possibly help me? I've got a bike he could use and he could earn some money."

"I'll go. I'll go. Mama, please let me," Rudi pleaded.

She looked at him.

"Perhaps if Sepp goes with you." Then turning to her sister-in-law, she said, "I'll just have to ask Hanni first. We'll let you know, Rosa." Just as she finished speaking, the siren sounded.

"I must get back now," said Rosa anxiously. "I brought this bread for you." She unloaded the loaves onto the table before making for the door.

"Good bye. Thanks, Jo. I'm still sad about Hanni and me," she called out as she ran to her transport.

Chapter 23

By now, Josefa was worriedly looking out of the window in the direction of the meadow. The deafening noise of low aircraft and the sound of their mother screaming sent the children to cower in a corner of the kitchen. The haymakers were running back home. About a kilometre ahead of them, in the direction of the railway, the ground was being strafed by enemy planes.

"Whew! That was close. They must be after ammunition trucks," gasped Johann. Terrified and breathless, they all collapsed on chairs in the kitchen. It was about an hour later when the 'All Clear' siren sounded and they were able to return to the meadow. During the alert, Josefa told Johann about Rosa's visit.

"So it's all right if Sepp and Rudi go to help her tomorrow?"

He shrugged. "Of course, if they want to," was his response as he cut a slice of Rosa's bread for himself. Josefa knew her husband's indifference was caused by his stubborn pride. It prevented him from healing the rift between him and his sister, which he so badly wanted.

The two boys arrived at the bakery the following morning. They loaded the large bicycle basket with the orders for the more isolated farms and set off. Sepp suggested a race on a stretch of path. This resulted in a collision and a spillage of loaves in a ditch. Satisfying themselves that there were no witnesses, they quickly gathered them up and carried on.

They helped Tante Rosa throughout the summer, taking it in turns to either deliver or serve in the shop. Assisting their father, working at the bakery and attending Hitler Youth activities eroded their leisure time and the holidays slipped by very quickly. It was not quick enough for Gerhard, who was longing to start school.

Helga held her mother's hand as they watched the brothers leave for school on the first day of the autumn term.

"Come on, Helga, it's just the two of us now. Let's go and finish our breakfast. First, I must get Aniela to start making the soup."

"She's not here, Mama."

"I'll expect she'll be here in a minute." It was ten minutes later when Aniela appeared. Her face looked blanched.

"What's the matter, Aniela?"

"I'm sorry, Frau Birk. I've just been sick."

Josefa shot a questioning glance in Aniela's direction. Their eyes locked together in a stare for a moment. Aniela stood awkwardly, shifting her weight form one foot to the other.

"Is there something you wish to tell me?" Josefa asked, with thoughts flooding her mind about Aniela's recent emotional behaviour and gossip about her friendship with Georg.

Aniela looked down at her feet. She swayed to and fro with folded arms as if cradling a baby, then patted her stomach. Her face bore a faint smile when she lifted her head. A natural impulse prompted Josefa to put her arm around the expectant mother's shoulder, although she was unable to disguise her worried expression. What would happen now? She knew that Aniela and the father would never be allowed to cohabit.

"Sit down and have your breakfast, Aniela," said Josefa, deciding to ascertain the father's identity later on. "I'll get Sofie to do the rooms upstairs today. You can give me a hand down here. We'll have to sort out a new routine."

At lunchtime, like a hurricane blasting its way through the kitchen, the boys arrived back from school. School bags were slung down on the Büro floor before they all scrambled to be first at the dining table. Once their appetites were satisfied, they raced across to the airfield, where there was always an abundance of activity in the sky to keep the brothers entertained in the afternoons. They were becoming quite adept at recognising different aircraft and recently a Stuka had taken up residence for training. However, the damaged American bombers with smoke trailing, heading for the safety of Switzerland, provided the most excitement.

The evenings were drawing in and it was almost time for the cattle to be housed in the stall for the winter. The four older boys had a rota to bring in the cows for milking before dusk. One day, when it was Rudi's turn, there was a particularly exciting spectacle. A Messerschmitt 109 was engaged in a dogfight with an American plane and was forced to make a belly landing at the airfield. Five pairs of eyes were glued to the lop-sided plane, waiting to see the pilot stagger out of the cockpit. So engrossed were they in the drama, that thoughts of cows, already assembled to be brought in for milking, were furthermost from Rudi's mind. It was post-dusk by the time he had collected them from the meadow and escorted them back to the stalls. The forgetful herdsman received a spanking from his irate father and was sent straight to bed. From then on, during the long dark evenings, they pursued their passion of playing cards with their grandparents.

Once again, Christmas 1943 was celebrated modestly and an air of apprehension and demoralisation greeted the new year. Nowadays, the mood in the Stube was sombre. Laughter lines had been replaced with furrows of anxiety. There was no more gossip and speculation since Georg had been established as the father-to-be, Aniela's pregnancy passed without problems and attracted little attention from the boys. They had seen their mother several times with a bulge. Only Helga was curious.

"Why does Aniela have a big tummy, Mama? Does she eat a lot?"

Unlike her disinterested brothers, she was delighted when a baby boy arrived just before Easter 1944.

There was an escalation in the air raids and the children were finding it difficult to concentrate in school. The fanatical Nazi teacher was becoming even more bossy and keener to hand out punishment for minor misdemeanours. The children's favourite teacher was, on occasion, reduced to tears by her Nazi colleague's bullying. The interruption of lessons and the impending danger was causing frayed nerves.

Then one very hot day in June, the siren sounded and the school was quickly vacated. Josefa was looking out for her sons at the kitchen door. To her horror, she saw a fleet of enemy aircraft approaching, the drone of the engines increasing in volume to a deafening pitch.

"The Amis! The Amis!" she yelled out to Johann. She grabbed Helga's hand and beckoned to the boys frantically, who were now only yards away.

"Quickly, follow me NOW!" They knew from the tone and urgency of their mother's voice, it meant instant obedience. The all ran to the neighbour's house, flew down the steps and into the shelter. Shortly afterwards, there was an enormous explosion, followed by screams, terrorised shrieks and panic-stricken yells. Commanding the children not to move an inch, Josefa ventured to poke her head out of the door. An incendiary bomb had landed beside the barn and set it alight. Mercifully, Gabi, the cart horse and the cattle were out in the meadow. Moments later, the sight of Else rushing out to scrape off the blazing phosphorous momentarily paralysed Josefa and she could neither move nor speak. Suddenly, she was blasted backwards into the shelter by a series of explosions. Landing at the feet of her stunned and petrified children, she got up and made for the door again. Like a glorious sunset, the sky was lit up with leaping flames from the neighbouring village, where the planes, aiming at the Messerschmitt factory, had shed 150 incendiary bombs. It was nothing less than a miracle that no one was injured at the Gasthof. When the family eventually emerged from the shelter, they saw the yard strewn with glass from the kitchen's shattered windows.

A baby crying divulged the whereabouts of the Poles, who had taken refuge in the cellar. The sirens of ambulances and fire engines were constant for the rest of the day and all night. Slowly, the news trickled through about casualties and damage. The mayor's family home, the bakery at the neighbouring village, had received a direct hit and there were no survivors of his family. Hermann had been in mayoral office at the time. Johann immediately sent his condolences to his former school friend and offered him accommodation at the Gasthof, a gesture which Hermann greatly appreciated. It was not until Sepp returned to school that he learnt his best friend had also been killed.

A month later, it was reported that there had been another attempt to assassinate the Führer. Hitler had survived unharmed, but there had been casualties. The perpetrators were being sought. Count von Stauffenberg was suspected of being the leader of the conspirators.

Shortly after the beginning of the autumn term, Josefa joined Johann for a cup of coffee at the kitchen table.

"Well, they're all at school now, Hanni. I just can't believe Helga is six already."

Johann remained silent, his eyes fixed on the table top, his expression very grave.

"What's the matter, don't you feel well?"

"I've just been listening to the radio."

"Well, what did you hear?" Josefa's voice was filled with fearful anticipation.

"Hitler's issued a decree, mobilising all men born between 1884 to 1928."

"Oh no! That means you, Hanni, at 45." A look of anguish crossed her face. "That includes 16-year-olds as well! Thank God Hans is only 15."

"But not for long, Jo, only for another four months!"

At that moment, the kitchen door opened. Josefa looked up forcing a slight smile. "Hello, Papa. Like a cup of coffee?"

"No thanks," replied Leonhard. "Just had a cup of revolting ersatz coffee. Tasted nothing like the real thing."

Leonhard pulled up a chair and joined them at the table.

"I'm longing for the day when I can enjoy a decent cup of coffee again, but by the way things are going, that's a long way off." There was no response. His eyes darted from one face to the other.

"You two are looking very glum," he continued. "I expect it's because your last baby's started school, eh?" As there was no response, he carried on. "Well there's still a boy in the house, Aniela's. What's his name by the way?"

"Josef," replied Johann with his eyes still lowered.

"Did you listen to the radio this morning, Papa?" asked Josefa.

"Yes, I did. The world service." Instinctively, Johann looked around anxiously and Josefa jumped up to make sure both kitchen doors were shut.

"I've just met Hermann. He told me how good you've been to him. Dreadful tragedy. He lost absolutely everything." Leonhard hesitated for a few seconds before adding, "I know

Hermann and I always had our political differences, but I couldn't help feeling terribly sorry for him."

"Hanni's going to be called up, Papa," said Josefa quietly. Leonhard's eyes and lips narrowed as he took a deep breath.

"That bloody lunatic Hitler," he uttered through clenched teeth. "What did I keep telling you? He's put us in a tight corner and it's getting tighter. East Prussia's been cut off by the Russkis, the Brits and the Amis are making their way through France and Italy, and all that idiot can do is get rid of our best generals." He brought his hand down onto the table so forcefully that it caused a coffee spillage.

"I'm sorry, Jo. It's just one piece of bad news after another. Have you heard about Dieter?"

"No." They both looked up.

"Haven't seen him lately," said Johann.

"His son's plane was shot down. He's alive, but", he paused a moment, "he's lost a leg."

"Oh no!" gasped Josefa. "Not Otto. The family must be devastated. We must call to see them."

Chapter 24

In December, Johann received the summons to report in München for active service, just prior to his 46th birthday in January 1945. Having made a concerted effort to make Christmas as happy a family occasion as possible, Johann's departure provoked a very emotional farewell from the children. Josefa sought to retain her composure, but as she watched Johann walk away towards village railway station, her tears flowed freely.

When he had disappeared from sight, she dabbed her eyes and went indoors. The burden of running the business, coping with the children, the staff and the livestock was now totally on her shoulders. Added to this was the situation outside of her domain, which was becoming increasingly frenetic. The snow ploughs were in full throttle clearing the roads for the constant stream of military vehicles. She made a silent resolve not to buckle under the weight. On two counts, she had to be very grateful, that her feared cancer had been diagnosed as being benign and that she had teenage boys to assist her.

It was only three weeks later that she heard a tap on the kitchen window. Opening the door, she gasped with delight when she saw Johann, still in uniform, standing before her. They hugged each other for a few moments and then the questions poured forth.

"What's happened? Have you got to go back? How long can you stay?"

"Just get me a beer, Jo, and I'll tell you. I'm absolutely parched."

He offloaded the heavy rucksack from his back before collapsing in the nearest chair. Josefa watched him as he emptied the tankard and, with an exhausted smile, handed it back to her for a refill.

"No, I don't have to go back." His voice was almost a whisper lost in a huge sigh.

Josefa's hands were shaking and splashes of beer fell to the floor. As he took the tankard from her, their smiling eyes locked for a moment. Then after a few more gulps, he began to answer her questions.

"When they told me they were dismissing me, I was so relieved, it was difficult to focus on the reasons they gave."

He paused, swallowed hard and shrugged. "But I gathered it was due to my service in the Volksturm. There's an urgent recruitment drive for home defence and they want me to organise enlistment in this area. The situation's getting desperate, Jo." He let out a deep breath between pursed lips before adding, "The Amis are advancing."

Josefa's smile faded and they both remained solemn and pensive for a few moments.

"Now tell me what's happening here. Have you managed to cope?" he asked.

"Not too badly. We've been OK. Sadly, we've lost some of the pilots, but they've been sending young replacements. The boys have been good, but I feel so tired. It's almost impossible to get any sleep. The rumbling of army traffic charging through the village is incessant."

"I know what you mean, Jo. That's the trouble of being on the main route to Austria and Italy," he murmured, struggling to keep his eyes open.

"And there's the constant noise of activity in the sky as well," Josefa added with a sigh.

"Go upstairs and have a rest, Hanni," she urged him, "before the children get home."

"I think I will," he said with a yawn. "We'll catch up with the news later."

The family's joy at Johann's return was short lived. The day arrived which Josefa had been dreading. Hans received his mobilisation papers. His mother gazed at him across the table, battling to keep her emotions under control as she thought how young and immature he looked. Johann went outside to cope with his feelings. He was horrified at the thought of his eldest son, who had just turned 16, going into combat. Gabi was fidgety in her stable. He walked over to her and stroked her nose.

"No, I can't let you go out, girl! You'd be too scared. We'll have to wait for a quiet spell." Gabi responded with a short neigh as if in protest.

Rumours of horrific injuries and severe frostbite suffered by troops in Russia spread through the village, causing Hans to have nervous restless nights. Also, several of their customers had been killed or had lost relatives on the battlefields. When the morning of his departure dawned, the family, with tear-stained faces, assembled on the kitchen steps to wave goodbye. Wondering whether he would see them again, he turned to face them once more and almost collided with someone.

"Hello, young Hans. Where are you off to so early?"

"Reporting for military service, Herr Bürgermeister," was the reply.

Hermann paused for a brief moment, looking downwards, before moving on at a quick pace. "I didn't know Hanni had a son old enough," he muttered to himself.

Easter was approaching. Patches of green were appearing in the meadows and the melting snow had swollen the flow in the brook. The cattle in the stalls were getting restless. They sensed that there were blossom buds on the trees and they could hear the birds singing in the spring sunshine. Instinct told them that it was time to be released from their winter housing.

"I'll have to risk taking the cattle to the field soon," Johann said one morning as he drank his mug of coffee at breakfast. Erich and Sepp can give me a hand. We'll have to go down the back lane."

"Take care. Those army trucks could cause a stampede," Josefa warned. "How about cutting the grass and bringing it back here?"

"They'll be all right. I bet you they'll head straight for the meadow." Johann replied, his voice rising in desperation.

Chapter 25

The Easter church service was well attended. Many prayers were offered for the return of loved ones from the battlefields and for the safety of families and homes. There were no painted eggs for children this year. They did not moan. They understood from whispers behind cupped hands that there was a dangerous time ahead. Everywhere, the mood was tense. Everyone became jittery as the news spread that enemy soldiers were getting nearer.

Very early one morning, not long after Easter, there was a violent thump on the Gasthof's main door.

"Papa, it's me!"

The sound of his son's voice made Johann's heart jump. Hans pushed the door open wide, staggered inside and threw himself into the nearest chair.

"What's happened, Hans? What's happened?" It took a few moments for him to get his breath to reply.

"They told me I could go. There's panic and chaos everywhere. Some of the rail tracks have been bombed. I had to walk the last three kilometres and my kit is bloody heavy!"

His head dropped in total exhaustion.

Alarmed by the commotion, Josefa had just appeared. She let out a gasp and flung her arms around her son.

"He's all right, Jo. He's not hurt. Let's help him to bed."

"Do you want anything to eat or drink, Hans?" his mother asked anxiously.

"Just a drink, Mama. I'm far too tired to eat."

Having regained his strength and caught up with sleep, Hans had an agreement with Erich to do alternate shifts, taking the cattle to the field in the mornings and collecting them before dusk, thus alleviating their father's workload. With the warning that the Americans were getting closer, the uncertainty of every aspect of the family's life was allowing Johann very little sleep. When it became no longer safe to take the cows out of their stalls, Johann succumbed to the idea of cutting the grass and bringing it back to them.

On the morning of April the 26th, 1945, it was Erich's turn to help his father. He heaved himself into the hay cart next to the scythes and rakes, whilst Johann took hold of Gabi's reins. Arriving at the field, they secured Gabi with a rope to a sturdy tree and left her to graze whilst father and son worked feverishly. So intent were they to harvest as much of the verdant pasture as possible, that they tended to ignore the sound of gunfire in the distance.

That was until the bullets started to whiz past them. The realisation that they were caught in the cross fire of the invading Americans and the remnants of the defending German Army terrified them. If they had not had the foresight to tether Gabi to a tree, the frantic animal would have bolted. Suddenly, a dogfight took place above them, resulting in the Me 109 bringing down the enemy plane in a trail of smoke and flames a few miles away.

"We've got to get back, Erich. Come on!" Johann called out, his voice carrying a tone of terrified urgency.

"We're almost finished, Papa."

"Now, I said NOW!"

Erich needed no more persuasion when an American plane swooped low, strafing the railway line. He clambered on-board the cart quickly and Gabi required no encouragement to speed up her pace homewards to the sound of fire and ambulance sirens.

"Bloody hell! What's that doing here?" yelled Johann breathlessly as he jumped down from the cart and raced to the Biergarten. He directed the question to a soldier as he pointed to an 88mm anti-aircraft gun with its barrel aimed down the road.

"We've had orders. The Amis are not very far away."

"But you can't leave that here! They'll blow us up sky high. Get it away from here," Johann bellowed.

"Sorry, sir. Orders."

Johann's face took on a deep shade of red and his whole body shook through a cocktail of rage and fear.

"Then where's your superior officer?" he yelled, his exasperation reaching its limit.

"He's in the mayor's office, sir."

"I see, so in the meantime, our home could end up as a heap of rubble!" Johann turned on his heel and rushed indoors to the kitchen to find Josefa.

"Take the children to the woods, Jo. Don't ask any questions," Johann said firmly as she opened her mouth to speak.

"Just go NOW! All of you."

Frightened by his urgent command, Josefa tore upstairs to round up the children, making sure they were suitably clad.

A white flag was just being handed over to Hermann as Johann stormed into the mayor's office.

"I have a wife and six children in that building and I want that anti-aircraft gun removed from our premises at once!" Johann blurted out breathlessly.

The army officer, still holding the flag, looked startled, obviously unaccustomed to being spoken to in this manner. Hermann quickly summed up the situation of which he had been unaware and took control. After a few moments of explanation and reasoning with the officer, he agreed to have the gun resited as soon as possible. Johann went home. He set off to the woods with a bag filled with food and drink for his bewildered family. After a while, he left them with the assurance that he would let them know when it was safe for them to return.

He fed the cattle as soon as he returned to the Gasthof and began to store the rest of the grass in the barn. He thought he could hear rustling in a corner at the back and he went to investigate. He was startled to find six German soldiers huddled together behind a bale of hay.

"What the hell are you doing here? Do you want us all to be shot?" he asked, fully aware that he must keep his voice down.

"It's finished. It's all over. We want to get home," replied one of them despairingly as the others drew back further into a dark corner.

"If we could just get out of this uniform, we'd leave. Got any civilian clothes we could have?"

221

Johann thought for a few seconds. "I'll see what I can find, but just stay put and lie low. You can throw your weapons down the slurry pit," he said with a frustrated shake of his head. He went indoors and gathered an assortment of his old clothes and some of which he had provided for Stanislav. As he was returning to the barn, he noticed that the anti-aircraft gun was being removed.

"Put these on and get lost," he said as forcefully as a whisper would allow.

"Hide your uniforms under the straw bales and don't forget to shut the barn door."

Once the gun was well away from the Gasthof, Johann collected the family from the woods. Josefa busied herself in the kitchen and fed her famished family. There was no necessity to coax the children to bed, they were all very tired. With the Gasthof's door firmly shut, they sat totally exhausted in the Büro, where Johann related the events of the day.

"You'll be short of clothes now," she grumbled.

"I just wanted to get them out of the way, Jo. I checked the barn. They've gone and there's no visible evidence."

"But I don't want the boys going further than the yard, Hanni."

"I've told them that," he replied.

"What's the matter, Hanni?" Josefa asked noticing he was frowning and cocking his ear.

"Did you hear that, Jo?"

"No, what was it?" she peered out of the window. "It's quite dark now. I can't see anything. I thought I could hear the sound of hooves. There's a horse in the yard. I think Gabi's got out. If Erich didn't bolt the stable door properly, I'll—"

He jumped up and rushed through the kitchen to the yard. Gabi was still safely installed behind a bolted stable door. She neighed. Hearing another horse neigh in reply, Johann turned around to face a rider in cavalry uniform approaching him.

"Can you help me," the soldier whispered. "Do you have push bike I could have?" he asked in perfect crisp German. "I can't pay for it, but you can have this horse in exchange."

Johann gulped. He stood and just gasped for a few moments, wondering if he was dreaming.

"Are you OK, Hanni? What's happening?"

"It's all right, Jo. Go back in." Turning to the rider, he said, "Wait here a minute.

He walked over to the barn and from underneath a pile of children's bikes, he pulled out an adult one. "It's not in best condition, but you're welcome to it. The tyres may be flat, but here's a pump you can have."

The soldier's face lit up. He dismounted, grasped Johann's hand in appreciation and handed over the reins. After pumping up the tyres, he sat on the bike's saddle and wrenched off his cap.

"Would you mind disposing of this for me?" he asked politely. Johann nodded.

"Wait a moment. I've got an old raincoat you can have." Johann disappeared into the kitchen. When he returned the, soldier had already discarded his jacket. He put on the raincoat, grinned in gratitude and cycled away at speed. Johann led the fine thoroughbred to the stable next to Gabi's. He put down some straw, filled the water bucket and left her a good helping of cut grass. As he walked back across the yard, he was serenaded by neighbourly neighing. *Gabi likes company,* he thought.

The following morning, Johann and Josefa felt very tired, having spent half the night discussing the events of the day. The children were already having their breakfast when they went down to the kitchen.

"Can we go out in the field, Papa?" asked the boys.

"No, not yet. I've got to find out what's happening first, to make sure it's safe." This reply was met with a cacophony of whining and moaning.

"Now stop that and let me drink my coffee in peace," snapped Johann, suffering from a surfeit of tension. He also wanted to think of a suitable explanation for the thoroughbred's presence before he was bombarded with questions. Josefa came to the rescue. "Someone asked us to look after his horse whilst he's away in the army. If you promise NOT to open its stable door and just play in the yard, I think you can go outside, but no further. Do you hear?"

Their answer was lost in the sound of a stampede towards the door.

Shortly afterwards, Josefa could hear Erich shouting, "Papa, Papa, Papa, come and see this. Quickly!"

Johann was down in the cellar. Josefa called to him.

"What do you want?" he asked crossly.

"The children want to show you something."

Muttering under his breath, Johann climbed up the cellar stairs and went out into the yard.

"Come and have a look," said Sepp excitedly. Johann followed them to the rear side of the barn. Beside a neatly stacked wood pile was an abandoned 500 BMW camouflaged motorbike with side car. Sepp and Rudi were just about to clamber onto it.

"Get off! Keep away!" Johann yelled. "Do you want us to be shot?" Shocked, the children pulled back. Josefa was peering out of the kitchen door.

"Our yard's being turned into a scrap yard and a dangerous one at that!" Johann told her angrily. "Keep the children in until I get back. Hans is coming with me to get some more grass. The others can help me feed the livestock afterwards. They're fed up being stall bound and they're getting very fidgety."

Later that morning, when Josefa was clearing away the well-scraped lunch plates, Johann heard the sound of a vehicle pull into the yard. Nervously, he looked out of the window just as the driver jumped down from the cab. It was a German army lorry. He rushed outside, startling the rest of the family.

"What have you got there?" he enquired gruffly. Not answering his question directly, the driver replied,

"Is there somewhere I can leave this for a while? It'll be too dangerous on the road. We're being strafed by enemy fighter planes."

"What's in it?" repeated Johann menacingly.

"Ammunition and land mines," the driver replied quietly.

"Are you mad?" bellowed Johann. "I have a wife and six children in there. The Amis are on their way here and if they hit that, the whole village will be blown up! Get away from here. Dump it in the woods somewhere."

Without a word, but with fear in his eyes, the driver clambered back into the cab and accelerated up the village's main road in the direction of open country. Johann went inside, his whole body shaking.

"We all stay inside today. Understand?" The children nodded silently. There was no protest. They knew by their father's tone of voice, he meant it seriously.

As the clock struck 2 that afternoon, they heard the sound of the siren giving warning that enemy forces were in close proximity. The family gathered in the Büro. Suddenly, Johann left the room and could be heard going down the cellar.

"Hanni, what are you doing down there? Stay with us," Josefa called out sharply. When Johann reappeared, his face was blanched, his hands blackened and trembling. He leant over and whispered in Josefa's ear. "I just remembered Himmler's photo. I had to burn it."

"What happened to those soldiers' uniforms?" the pitch of Josefa's voice revealed her terror.

"They all went down into the slurry pit, together with the rifles."

There was no activity in the village. There was no one to be seen. The siren's deafening message continued for two hours. When it stopped, the family gathered at the window, looking out to the road. They watched in silence as Hermann walked down the main street waving the white flag at the oncoming procession. The first tank rumbled along very slowly with a German POW perched on the front of it. A whole convoy of tanks followed. One of the jeeps, bringing up the rear, peeled off and came to a halt before the Gasthof's entrance. The three younger children clung tightly to their mother whilst the three older boys stood close together, their bodies taut with apprehension. Johann went to the door. As he opened it, an American soldier brushed past him and looked around the Stube whilst his companion stood guard. Ten agonising minutes later, a lorry of American troops pulled into the yard. Some of the soldiers had Red Cross bands on their arms. They started to stack up the Stube furniture and to carry in large boxes. One officer approached Johann.

"You speak English?" Not understanding, Johann shrugged and shook his head.

"Raus, raus," yelled the officer, utilising 50% of his German vocabulary. "Twenty minutes raus," he went on, putting up two hands with fingers stretched twice. "Versteh?" Johann nodded nervously and went over to Josefa.

"We've got to get out," he whispered. "We'll have to go to your parents. Just put a few things in a case. I'll stay here with the children. We only have 20 minutes."

Josefa hurried upstairs. Whilst they were waiting, Johann saw the American officer say a few words to one of the sergeants, who then walked over to Johann and the children. He spoke to them in German, saying they could return in a couple of days. These premises were needed for the wounded, he told them.

"You speak good German," Johann commented.

"My father was born in Germany," he replied. "My grandparents emigrated to the States."

Looking flushed, Josefa returned with a bulging suitcase and the family set off to the grandparents, a short walking distance. Along the way, they saw a column of prisoners straggling along from the south, escorted by armed guards. They were bedraggled, ragged and, in contrast to their American captors, very under nourished.

"Look, Mama," said Rudi. "There's Fräulein Schmitt coming along." The unpopular school teacher, with her eyes fixed to the ground, rushed past them with just a quick nod of acknowledgement.

"Did you see, Mama?" Rudi whispered. "She's taken off her Nazi badge."

Josefa helped her mother to push furniture aside to make enough floor space and raided her store of bedding to provide as comfortable a night as possible. The sheer relief that the fighting had stopped contributed to a fairly restful night in spite of sleeping on the floor. Satisfying the appetites of eight extra left Aga's food cupboard very much diminished and Johann decided to return to the Gasthof the following morning to fetch the contents of the larder. Josefa went with him, leaving the children with their grandparents. Arriving at the Gasthof, they entered the kitchen to find Aniela with the baby, Sofie and Stanislav having breakfast. They were chatting in Polish to an American soldier. Without interrupting the conversation, they opened the fridge and were surprised to find it stuffed full of unfamiliar food packets. They looked in the larder and salvaged what remained of their own provisions. Noticing there was very little milk, Johann asked Stanislav if the cows had been milked.

The reply was a very slow shake of the head. Then they caught sight of the dirty dishes piled high at the sink, which brought them to the realisation of the new order.

Chapter 26

They peeped through the door to the Stube as they were leaving and were surprised that it had been transformed into a hospital ward. It was full of bunk beds occupied by the victims of battle. Outside, they met the German-speaking sergeant again, who appeared to give his mouth no respite from chewing gum. He confirmed that they could return to the Gasthof in two days' time.

"We shall have moved on by then," he told them, "but there'll be new arrivals. It will be OK for you to tend to your livestock," he answered in reply to Johann's request.

Josefa returned to the children, whilst Johann went to muck out the cattle stalls and stables. He was about to replenish the water containers when he heard a voice behind him. He turned around to see an American Private standing there.

"I help you," he said pointing to himself and then to Johann before going through the motions of shovelling manure. Johann looked surprised until the sergeant appeared. "He was brought up on a farm and is feeling a bit homesick," he explained in German. "He'll help you feed and milk them." Johann smiled. "Danke," he said.

The following morning, the children rose early and looked towards the airfield from the second floor window of their grandparents' house. Since the curfew had robbed them of their freedom, the young ones were confused, as they were not used to being so confined. Suddenly, a drama was played out before them. American jeeps were speeding towards the runway at full throttle. A Messerschmitt 109 was preparing to land. Armed American personnel were in place and as the plane taxied to a halt, the jeeps surrounded it. A solitary pilot alighted from the cockpit, who was immediately arrested and handcuffed.

Excitedly, they related what they had witnessed to their parents and grandparents, who, later that day, learnt that the pilot was known to them. His family lived in the village. He had been stationed in Czechoslovakia and had become frantic with worry about his family's safety to such an extent that he made a spontaneous decision to take to the air and return home. It was a daring feat considering the fuel in the tank was dangerously low.

The following day, Erich returned to the Gasthof with his father. They found that Georg had joined Aniela and the baby. Several other Poles from outlying farms had assembled in the village and there were tales of reprisal where Polish workers had been badly treated. Johann was given confirmation that the family would be permitted to return to the Gasthof the following day. On their way back, Erich suddenly clutched his father's arm. "Papa, look," he whispered, pointing a few yards ahead on the other side of the road. "It's Mr and Mrs Chandler who helped me with my English. They're being taken away! Why, Papa?"

"I don't know, son, but I'm sure we'll find out soon."

Like refugees, the family trailed back to the Gasthof the next morning. The bunks still remained, but the wounded had been evacuated. The frontline professional soldiers were preparing to leave. Johann was surprised to see Herr Borst with a bottle. He handed it to the American officer in charge, who just grinned before stepping into his jeep and being driven away. Borst walked over to Johann.

"I gave him a bottle of schnapps. I'm just so relieved it's all over and we're unharmed," he said overcome with emotion.

Two days later, the church was packed to capacity with villagers eager to express their gratitude that the war was coming to a close. As the congregation assembled in the church yard, there was a roar as two fighter aircraft flew low overhead. They all craned their necks and were surprised to see swastikas on their tail fins. They were two Me 109 and seconds later, they attacked the military convoy snaking its way through the village. There was a lot of heavy machine gun firing and soon after, a petrol tanker burst into flames. Screaming in panic, the villagers stampeded back into the church. Those who were already making for home witnessed a huge fireball just outside the village. It was the final attempt by the Luftwaffe to impede the American advance.

Josefa started to feel very uneasy about the children's safety. Firing bullets in conflict was one thing, but indoors was quite another. Naturally, she was very upset that a sideboard, a wedding gift from her parents, had been being used as a shooting target, but she was far more worried about her family. *I'll get Hanni to have a word with the officer in charge,* she thought, *or rather the soldier who speaks German.*

"We're not allowed to come back yet," he said grimacing. "From what I understood, it will be a couple more days. The officer was tugging at his jacket and talking with his hands. Johann paused for a moment. I think he meant we can take more clothes, food and other essentials with us, if necessary." He took a deep breath. "I'll go and get the farm cart to load up, whilst you go and get the clothes and things we need."

As Johann pulled the cart along in the yard, he looked around for the children. He saw two of them peer out from the side of the barn. He beckoned and asked them to help him push the cart.

"Papa, look what we've found," Erich said excitedly. He was holding an army rucksack.

"Put it down. Leave it there," Johann said brusquely. "You heard what your mother told you. Don't touch anything."

"But, Papa, there looks as if there are tins of food in it."

Johann hesitated, "All right," he conceded. "They certainly won't be coming back for it. That's for sure!"

The cart was piled high with large suitcases of clothes, the remains of their food stock in the larder and some extra bedding. As they trundled along back to the grandparents', they were overtaken by an American soldier riding a bike. He was a few yards ahead of them when a minor explosive sound sent him springing into a ditch, covering his head with his hands. When the family drew level with the bike, they saw one of the tyres had burst. Seeing the children's amusement, the embarrassed soldier got up, gave the bike a good kick and pushed off, which made the children snigger all the more.

"What's this called?" asked Leonhard. "It tastes good. Got lots of nuts on the top."

"Dundee cake," replied Hans, reading from the tin. "It must be English."

"What else is in the sack?"

"Condensed milk. I've tried it. It's thick and sweet. Yummy," chirped in Sepp.

"Before you lot make yourself sick, how about a game of cards, or we could make something out of those pieces of wood that I've got?" Leonhard's suggestions were readily accepted. He was a master at keeping his grandsons occupied.

One morning, when they were down in their Opa's garage, the boys put their noses in the air and sniffed.

"I can smell smoke, Opa," said Rudi.

"So can I," the others chimed in.

They all looked out of the garage window and gasped in amazement. The view was one of leaping bright orange flames and clouds of black smoke forming a curtain over their view of a blue sky.

"What on earth!" exclaimed Leonhard fearing a horrific accident. Johann came rushing down the stairs to join them.

"Quite a bonfire, isn't it? The Amis have set fire to the remaining aircraft on the airfield including the Me 109," he told them breathlessly.

"Just when I've got to go and feed the cattle," he sighed. "I'm not going to go to the meadow in that smoke now. I've got enough feed to keep them going till later on. I'll try and find out if we can move back tomorrow." After a few seconds of thought, he added, "Keep inside children and don't open any windows. That smoke won't do you any good."

"Thanks for everything," said Jo to her parents as they set off the following morning, having been given permission to move back. They pushed the heavily laden cart back to the Gasthof, where the Americans were still in the process of moving out. The Stube was cleared of bunk beds, but a few remained stacked up in the yard, ready to be loaded onto one of the several trucks lined up. Josefa was dismayed to see some of her possessions on-board, including her large aluminium sauce pan. She just sighed deeply and concentrated on counting the minutes before they could settle in their own home again.

"Mama, we're ever so hungry," wailed the three younger ones who had stayed in the kitchen with her whilst the others had gone outside to play.

"You'll just have to wait for a while until I know what I can rustle up," she replied looking harassed.

At that moment, the three older boys rushed in carrying boxes, all the size of a brick. They were covered in a layer of wax and were labelled 'Breakfast/Lunch/Dinner'.

"What have you got there?" their mother asked with a worried frown. They stood grinning for a few moments.

"We found a way into the Amis' store cupboard. Several trailers full of food rations were parked in the skittle alley. Got in through that small door at the back of it. They've got so much food, they won't miss a box or two, Mama. Anyway, we're jolly hungry," said Hans as he opened one of the boxes. The others followed suit. Inside of them, they found quantities of tinned meat, cheese, instant coffee sachets and all manner of survival rations. Included in each box were six cigarettes.

"We'll try some of this for supper when your father comes in," Josefa said looking at the contents with interest. "He won't be much longer. He's seeing to the cattle. Sepp, go and ask Opa and Oma to join us."

Johann was busy milking when he could hear the sound of heavy boots being dragged along in the yard.

"Anyone about?" The voice was deep and gruff.

"I'm in here," Johann called out.

A tall burly figure with broad shoulders, dressed in German battle gear, filled the door frame. The stripes on his uniform revealed his rank as Sgt Major.

"My name's Stutzkowski, Hans Stutzkowski! Do you have a job for me? I'm not afraid of hard work. I've just come from Pfronten, where a few of us on the Breitenberg made a last stand against the Amis. Kept the buggers at bay for a while, but then they lobbed shells at us and we had to make ourselves scarce."

Johann almost tipped over the milk pail as he lost his concentration and stared at the stranger.

"Well, I could certainly do with an extra pair of hands. We're in a hell of a mess."

"Before anything else, I must get out of this gear before the buggers spot me," Stutzkowski said looking over his shoulder.

"Hang on a minute," said Johann. "I'm nearly done here."

Having introduced the stranger to the family and explained his predicament, Johann supplied him with a change of clothing and showed him where he could sleep. Afterwards, he was made welcome at the table for a meal, which was partially provided by courtesy of the American army. The obnoxious smell of the newcomer's breath was familiar to Johann. It reminded him of the homegrown tobacco smoked by the Poles, who, that evening, had congregated elsewhere, excited at the prospect of returning to their homeland.

"I'm glad to rest my feet, you can call me Stuzko, I walked a very long way today. Still, I'm used to walking. In Russia, when my boots were wearing out and I tried to find a dead Russian's boots to fit me, I stuffed them with several layers of newspaper. That was better than socks. When it got wet, I just replaced it. Russian newspaper is so thin, the Russkis used to roll their own cigarettes with Machorka. It stunk!"

The children had left the table, but Stuzko's story held the adults' interest, especially Leonhard's. Johann offered him one of the American cigarettes. He took it and said he would keep it for the next day. With heavy eyelids and a voice that was beginning to slur, he muttered, "Been in the army all my life." Nervous and physical exhaustion were taking their toll. Getting up from the table, he said quietly, "I think it's time for me to shut my eyes. I shall report for duty tomorrow morning. Thank you. Good night."

"Would you like a cup of American coffee, Papa?" Josefa asked opening a sachet. Leonhard readily accepted.

"That's the best cup of coffee I've had for a long time," he remarked putting down his cup.

"It certainly tastes better than the tea we've been having," said Josefa lifting her eyebrows. "We used tea bags that the Amis had already used."

Having regained some of their former freedom, the boys were eager to acquaint themselves with the damage that the village had suffered.

"Let's go over to the airfield," suggested Erich, a few days later. His four brothers agreed unanimously.

"Cor, look at that!" exclaimed Hans. "All those burnt out fuselages."

"The grass looks black with all that oil over it," said Gerhard. "What a mess."

"We'll get a better view at the top of this ladder," said Sepp, looking at one attached to the side of the hangar. His observation triggered a scramble to be first on the bottom rung.

That evening at supper, when they related their adventure, their mother was shocked to hear that they had played on a roof 30 feet high. Stutzkowski listened with interest.

"Any wheels about?" he asked.

"Plenty," answered Hans.

"I'll come over there with you tomorrow," he said.

The boys took turns to push the handcart to the airfield the following day.

"I've got something in mind, if we can get one of those wheels back here," said Stuzko, in a hushed tone.

"Tell us for what?" they asked with inquisitive excitement.

"You'll see," was the tantalising reply.

It did not take them long to select the least damaged front wheel of the Me 109. They removed the wheel and hauled it onto the cart and, with a seemingly team effort, pushed it back to the Gasthof's yard.

"Well, what now?" they asked Stuzko.

"We're going to make a wheelbarrow for your father. One that can run up a ramp easily," he replied grinning.

It was not long until their project was accomplished. Johann was delighted with the finished product and so were the boys. This was adventure and their quest for it was insatiable. They wanted more!

A notice was received, stating that the school would be reopening the following week. This would be the day after the occupying forces' special convoy had passed through the village. It was advised that all the children should be kept indoors at that time, because of the intense security.

Two days before the American convoy was due, the boys went out looking for adventure again. They were wandering along the bank of the clear, fast flowing mountain brook when Hans tripped over a large sack. He picked himself up and gingerly took hold of the sack and opened it. When he saw the contents, his eyes and mouth opened widely.

"Wow!" he exclaimed.

"What is it?" the others asked in unison.

"Hand grenades."

"They're dangerous," said Sepp instinctively drawing away.

"Only when the pin's pulled out," advised Erich.

"Let's throw one in the river, then see the splash," suggested Gerhard innocently.

"Could do," replied the two older boys thoughtfully. "Now, who's going to throw first?"

"I am," volunteered Erich, getting hold of the grenade's handle. Stand back!"

The explosion left them all lying on their backs, unharmed, but with wet clothes. Rudi felt something cold and slimy on his leg. He sat up.

"Look! A trout," he shouted gleefully.

This experience was worth another try. Completely ignoring the danger involved, they had two more attempts. Their mother had to steady herself, suffering from shock, when she learnt how half a dozen trout came to be lying on her draining board!

Chapter 27

Gradually, their lives began to take on a familiar pattern again. Johann was very pleased when Dieter and Volkmar called at the Gasthof one morning, albeit briefly. Johann was updated on the condition of both their sons' health. Peter was slowly putting on weight but was finding it difficult coping with the loss of fingers through frostbites. Otto was still on crutches and prone to bouts of mild depression, knowing he would not be able to fly again.

"I expect you've heard that Hitler's dead, Hanni?" said Dieter.

"No, I hadn't. I knew there were rumours flying about, but I've just had so much to do."

"Don't know any details yet though." Volkmar took a very deep sigh. "All I can say is good riddance. God only knows what our future holds now." Overcome with emotion by thoughts of his son, he averted his eyes and nervously fingered his beer glass.

"I have a lot to be grateful for," said Johann quietly. They looked up at him. "I have five sons who were too young to be involved in that bloodbath of a war."

"I've got two more bits of news," Dieter said before emptying his glass. "They got those two propagandists, the American Chandlers. If you believe the gossip, they've been strung up, but I've also heard they've been taken back to the States." This was received with shrugs of indifference.

"And the other bit of news?" asked Volkmar expectantly.

"Hermann has been sent away for the de-Nazification. But he'll be back." They all managed a suggestion of a grin. It was difficult not to like Hermann.

"We must go now, Hanni. Got things to do. Greetings to Jo, kids, OK?"

"Yes thanks, Dieter. It's good to see you both again."

Volkmar cupped his hand over his mouth and got closer to Johann. "That convoy tomorrow. I think it's General Patten."

The following morning, the children were sent to their grandparents'. The village was eerily quiet. The main street was closed to local traffic and most of the villagers decided to stay indoors. There were small gatherings of spectators, mostly teenagers, and such a group was visible from the grandparents' window. Leonhard noticed one boy had brought binoculars with him. At the sound of the military cavalcade, the children edged nearer to the window, concealing themselves partially behind the curtains. Although they were not aware of the importance of General Patten, they sensed this convoy was different from the others. Leonhard had a clearer view standing at the centre of the window. He watched intensively as the convoy came to a halt, a few moments after the general's jeep had passed by. An officer in a following jeep stood up and craned his neck to identify the problem. Spotting the binoculars, he spoke to the boy with the binoculars and obviously asked him if he could borrow them. A sparse knowledge of school English led the boy to nervously hand them over. As the officer put them to his eyes, the command "Forward" rang out. The cavalcade went into immediate motion and it was plain by the boy's expression that he would never see his binoculars again. The halt had been caused by a school girl, with a better understanding of the English language, being asked to translate an enquiry from an American in the first jeep.

The following day, Stanislav, Sofie, Aniela and the baby left to return to Poland. The children always had a good relationship with them and they had become part of their lives. Promises were made to keep in touch. Georg, the baby's father, travelled with another group of foreign workers, but Aniela hinted that once they were repatriated, there were plans for them to get married.

The mood in the village since the Americans had arrived was generally one of relief, although there was an underlying nervous tension of what the occupation might hold. For the five 'Engel Buben', each morning ushered in a day of excitement, without a hint of boredom. This was largely due to Rolf, who called at the Gasthof seeking a job, shortly after the Poles' departure. He was a brilliant engineer and had been employed by Messerschmitt. Unlike Stuzko, he was better spoken and more polished and instead of livestock, his interest lay in machinery. At the time, though, he was prepared to do any type of labour. One day, he was searching in the barn for mechanical objects to repair when he discovered 15 rusty motorbikes, evidence of Johann's business collapse in the '30s. The boys were now at an age when they also took an interest in them. With his employer's permission, Rolf salvaged the parts he thought would be useful and left the carcasses to the mercy of the boys' destructive streak. There was one bike the boys persuaded their father to let them ride; having assured him they would only take it up the lane which led to the wood. Unfortunately, with no cooling system, the engine tended to overheat. There was a simple solution to overcome this problem in the privacy of the woods. To relieve themselves on it.

Rolf managed to acquire a powerful drill on loan from one of the bombed-out factories in the neighbourhood. These factories contained, what was for Rolf, an Aladdin's cave full of machinery waiting to be repaired. He was dispirited to learn that the tools to do this were destined to go to Russia by order of the occupying forces. It was at this time that Rolf conceived the idea of constructing a short single rail track. With his enthusiasm and knowledge, it did not take him long to persuade Johann that it would facilitate the transport of the peat bricks on his moor. Once they were cut, they could stack them up in neat rows to let them dry out. They relied on this fuel in the winter months. Thinking that his boys would benefit from watching and assisting Rolf, who was clearly an expert in his field of engineering, Johann readily gave his support to the project. Once he had been given the green light, Rolf set about constructing a small gauge track and a flatbed cart in the old workshop. After its completion a few weeks later, the boys helped to load the track onto the cart and set off with Gabi to the moor in the forest. During the next few weeks, the boys travelled to the moor on the local and got off at the next halt, from where they would walk across the field to the peat moor. Once dried, the peat bricks would be brought back to the Gasthof to be stored in the barn.

Josefa was delighted by the unexpected arrival of her sister Ida one morning. "Just called to see how you all are. I've been thinking about you, but have managed to get here. It's been a difficult time."

"It's good to see you, Ida. Mother told me you were both OK."

"Mother kept me informed about you lot, too. I hear you had to move in with her three times when the Amis requisitioned the Gasthof."

"Yes, I don't know what we would have done without Mama's and Papa's help. Eight of us. Can you imagine?" Ida smiled. Josefa looked pensive for a few moments.

"I think the worst time for us was when Hans was called up," she said.

"I saw him just now. What happened exactly?" Ida asked.

"He reported in München, but there was such chaos, he was sent back. It was the journey home that was such a nightmare. The rail tracks had been blown up."

"I can imagine how you must have felt," said Ida sympathetically. "Jo, I've heard from our brother Josef. His son Wolfgang has disappeared."

"What do you mean, disappeared?"

"He'd been home on a short leave and left to join his unit, but never arrived. They searched everywhere, but there was no trace or sighting of him. They're ever so upset."

"How awful for them," said Josefa quietly. Then in an effort to brighten up the conversation, she continued, "Rudi's been accepted at the grammar school, but he has to go for an interview first."

"Oh, that's good, Jo. He'll be able to go with Erich."

Josefa took a deep sigh and shivered slightly. "He nearly lost his sight the other day."

"What!" Ida looked horrified.

"There's so much ammunition lying about, Ida, and you know what boys are like. He found a jerry can and opened it. It was empty, but he struck a match."

"Good God!" exclaimed Ida.

After several moments and a large intake of breath, Josefa carried on. "He lost his eyebrows and all the hair of his forehead! I just can't keep them indoors all the time. It's going to be a nightmare until the village has been cleared up."

At that moment, the door opened. "How are my girls?"

The two sisters turned their heads when they heard their father's voice.

"Hello, Papa. We're just chatting. Catching up with news," said Ida.

"I've just seen, Hanni," he replied. "He's taking his old tractor to the field, which he's had converted to wood gas because diesel's so scarce. The boys have gone with him."

"I'm glad about that," muttered Josefa to herself.

"Jo's just been telling me how close Hans came to be mobilised," said Ida.

"I don't think so," Leonhard said enigmatically. The two sisters cast questioning glances in his direction.

"I've just met Hermann, back from his de-Nazification session. He hinted that he made a good case for Hans's release and that he also backed Hanni's plea for exemption."

The two sisters just stared at their father.

"I didn't delve too much. I don't think he wants it to be generally known." Leonhard pursed his lips and raised his shoulders. "Hermann mumbled something about Hanni being so good to him when his family was wiped out." Before the two women could comment, Johann appeared.

"You all look dazed. What's the matter?" he asked.

"I'm so grateful that we're all still together," said Josefa quietly.

Still looking puzzled, he carried on. "Volkmar and Peter have just called in. Peter looks much better. They told me the airfield's being used for grazing at the far end of the runway. Can you believe that? Cattle on it!"

"I never thought I'd live to see that," said Leonhard preparing to leave.

"And what's more, Else's doing a roaring trade in cigs which she wangled out of the Amis," chuckled Johann. This piece of information brought a broad smile to all their faces.

Just prior to the autumn term, Rudi reported to the grammar school for his interview. His mother had asked him to take a parcel to the post office on his way there. The parcel contained old shoes, needles, strong cotton strings and other paraphernalia. The shoes were the ones that the children had grown out of or those that the family seldom wore. These were being sent to Poland in answer to a request from Aniela. She had written to Josefa, telling her that they were finding life very hard in their country. Georg, now her husband, was a cobbler by trade, but he had difficulty in making a living as leather was in short supply and almost unobtainable. Josefa also sent some boys' clothing, of which her brood had long since outgrown.

Rudi's interview went well in spite of his nervousness. When he left the school building, he was feeling much more at ease. A member of staff had told him that the Americans were organising a fair and were handing out bars of chocolate to children in the playing field across the river. He ran out of the school gates, down the cobbled street of the old town to the narrow bridge which spanned the fast flowing waters of the Iller. He came across a stampede of children, many young enough never to have seen chocolate. Babies and toddlers, being pushed in chairs by their mothers, were swept along in the tide of excited youngsters.

Rudi was jostled all the way to the bridge until he joined one of the long queues, which moved quite quickly. When at last he received his bar, he tore off the wrapping paper in the haste to savour the taste of chocolate once more, after so long. Satisfying himself that there was no chance of a second bar, he turned around and found himself crushed in the horde returning home. He shuffled along at the pace of the crowd heading for the bridge. When he was about halfway over, there was an almighty cracking sound as it collapsed and opened up beneath his feet. The weight of so many proved too much for the old wooden bridge. To the sound of piercing screams, Rudi found himself dropping down into the transparent water, with its thick white crust evidence of its velocity and volume. There was the sound of children gurgling, choking, gasping and the desperate cries of mothers seeing empty pushchairs bobbing about or being carried at speed downstream. Rudi struggled to keep his head above water. The smart jacket, trousers and new shoes, which his mother had bought for his interview, were now saturated and pulling him downwards. Panic was setting in when suddenly he felt a strong arm across his chest and beneath his arms. He felt himself being dragged to the river bank and being hauled out. When he was laid down on dry land, he looked up into the eyes of his rescuer. It was a type of face he had never seen before. It was very black. Water dripped from the American's uniform as he bent over Rudi to make sure he was all right. Satisfied that he was, he then went to rescue more victims.

Rudi just lay there for a short while before going to collect his bike, which he had left at the school. His cycle ride home was laborious due to the extra weight of his clothes. Josefa's mouth dropped open in horror when she saw him and listened to his gabbled account of what had happened. A hot bath, dry clothing and an early night was her prescription for him. Later that evening, when Johann and Josefa sat quietly together, they drank a toast to the unknown hero who had rescued their son.

The following day, they learnt more about the tragedy and the number of lives lost, mostly children.

"How tragic. They survived the war and died for the sake of a bar of chocolate," said Johann. He swallowed hard and sighed.

"Life is strange, isn't it, Hanni?" replied Josefa dabbing her eyes. "One of our sons could have been killed or injured in active service but was saved by a staunch Nazi. Another of our sons had his life saved by the enemy and I have been sending parcels to those in another country who were uprooted from their families and forced to work for us." She paused for a few moments. "Surely, that must give hope that human goodness will always rise to the surface."

End

Epilogue

Soon after the war, life at the Gasthof returned to normal. The Poles left for home and were soon replaced with refugees from the Sudetenland. With the introduction of the Deutsche Mark in 1948, there was a tremendous upsurge in business. Being on the main route to Italy through Austria and the Brenner Pass, coach parties and tourists started to arrive in droves. Business was booming. The regulars felt they were not getting the attention they deserved anymore. An extension was built on, which almost doubled the seating and sleeping capacity. It became a favourite venue for carnival balls and meetings. Rudi left in 1959 for England, married and settled there. Josefa died in 1962, after which, Sepp took over the running of the business. Daniela paid a visit to the Gasthof from Poland, accompanied by her son, who was born there 40 years before. Sepp retired in 1996. His son, a very good chef, declined to carry on. Gasthof Engel was sold and later purchased by the local Parish. Soon afterwards, the bulldozers moved in to demolish the Gasthof and sadly, the neighbouring historic house fell victim to a fire which destroyed it. The sole evidence of its existence is a bus stop called ENGEL.

Standing on the site now is a modern construction, green in colour, which serves the local community as a supermarket and a small housing estate.

Translation of German Words
Used in the Novel

German	English
Gasthof Engel	Angel Inn
Stube	Bar and Dining Area
Käserei	Where Cheese is made
Spätzle	Homemade Pasta. Bavarian Speciality
Rathaus	The Mayors offices
Knecht	Farm labourer
Zopf	Type of Brioche
Stammtisch	The regulars' table
Wechsel	Hire Purchase
Bürgermeister	Mayor
Luftwaffe	German Air Force
BDM (Bund Deutscher Maedchen)	League of German Girls
Arbeitsdienst	Work Conscription
Volksturm	Dads Army
Krug	Beer-mug
Brotzeit	Snack time
Wirt	Inn-keeper
SS (Schutzstaffel)	Fuehrer's Protection Squadron
SA (Sturmabteilung)	Storm Troopers

Gasthof Engel anno 1905

Johann Birk age 17, 1916 WW1